Oxford Japanese
Grammar and Verbs

T0041802

Oxford Japanese
Grammar and Verbs

Jonathan Bunt

OXFORD
UNIVERSITY PRESS

OXFORD
UNIVERSITY PRESS

Great Clarendon Street, Oxford OX2 6DP
Oxford University Press is a department of the University of Oxford
it furthers the University's objective of excellence in research, scholarship
and education by publishing worldwide.

Oxford is a registered trademark of Oxford University Press
in the UK and in certain other countries

Published in the United States
by Oxford University Press Inc., New York

© Oxford University Press 2003
First published 2003

British Library Cataloguing in Publication Data
Data available

Library of Congress Cataloging in Publication Data
Data available
ISBN 978-0-19-860382-5

Typeset by Graphicraft Limited, Hong Kong
Printed in Great Britain by
Clays Ltd, Elcograf S.p.A.

Contents

Preface

The *Oxford Japanese Grammar and Verbs* is part of a series of
Oxford grammars of modern languages. It includes information on
a wide number of structures likely to be encountered in the first
few years of studying Japanese at school or college and contains
everything that is essential up to A level. For those living and
working in Japan, it presents commonly seen and heard material.
It is designed to serve both as a source of information in itself, and
as a supplementary reference for users of textbooks which may not
cover grammar topics adequately.

The book is largely organized according to parts of speech.
This is not an approach often taken in textbooks and it has been
adopted here to try to present a picture of Japanese grammar
overall. Japanese parts of speech are discussed in their own
chapter (*see pp. 1–4*).

About the example sentences

The issue of style in Japanese grammar is crucial. In this book the
examples are presented in a mixture of styles to reflect formal and
informal spoken and written usage. If you are uncertain about the
styles of Japanese you should look at the chapter on style (*p. 10*).

To allow the book to be as widely usable as possible, a
romanized form of Japanese example sentences has been given.
As learning the kana scripts as quickly as possible will aid the
learner's pronunciation (and because the rows and lines of the
kana chart are important in making/explaining certain 'forms'),
there are kana charts as appendices.

The example sentences are given in two Japanese versions.
The first version presents a normal, Japanese version without
spaces, in a mixture of kanji (Chinese characters) and kana.
Numerals are not given in kanji as this is unnatural in horizontal

text. Whether or not kanji should be used to write a particular word is sometimes a matter of personal choice or of a sense of 'balance' between kanji and kana in a sentence, but the examples try to reflect current usage. Some words are mostly in kana although the kanji forms may also be common, e.g. くる and とき. Learners need to grow used to varied orthography at an early stage.

The second Japanese version is a romanized one with spaces between 'words' although this should not be taken to imply that the Japanese can or should be separated in this way. The romanization is given simply as an aid to learners and is very much secondary to the 'real' Japanese version. The system used for romanization is modified Hepburn. The Japanese examples have been kept as natural as possible while the English translations, while trying to sound natural, have sometimes been made slightly literal where this may help the user understand a structure in use.

Jonathan Bunt

Acknowledgements

Many people have contributed to the writing of this book. The Series Adviser (Dr Richard Ingham) and Academic Adviser (Dr Phillip Harries) made helpful and constructive comments and suggestions. Lynne Strugnell was heroic, cheerful, and clear-sighted in editing the text into its final form and getting this project to completion. The author would like to especially thank the Trustees of The Great Britain Sasakawa Foundation and Mike Barrett, the Chief Executive, whose support enabled him to take leave from teaching in order to complete this book.

The author would also like to thank: Suzuko Anai at the University of Essex; my friend and colleague Yukiko Shaw; Noriko Kajihara, Atsumi Griffiths, Minako Oshima, and Motoi Kitamura at the Japan Centre North West; and friends and colleagues in the British Association for Teaching Japanese as a Foreign Language (BATJ). Special thanks are due to the author's wife Atsuko (敦子), and sons George (穣治), and Harry (治輝). Thanks are also due to those students at the University of Salford, Manchester Metropolitan University, and Manchester University who tried out sections of the book.

The editors at OUP were extremely helpful and thanks go to Della Thompson and Vivian Marr for their support.

The author's sincere hope is that users of this book will sometimes say (sincerely) なるほど as well as まじ？

Proprietary terms

Parts of speech

Japanese and English are considerably different in structure as well as vocabulary. For example, meanings expressed with verbs in English may use adjectives in Japanese, and words that do not change form in English may do so in Japanese (and vice versa). The English sentence 'I want a car' features a pronoun ('I'), a verb ('want'), and a direct object noun ('car') with an indefinite article ('a'), but the Japanese translation 車が欲しい has no pronoun, no article, and 'car' is the subject of an adjective.

The grammatical terms for Japanese parts of speech vary a great deal in textbooks, dictionaries, grammars, and more scholarly works. The system for parts of speech used in this book is basically that taught in Japanese schools (sometimes called Hashimoto grammar, or Kokugo grammar) but with modifications to include terminology widely used in teaching Japanese as a foreign language (see, for example, the discussion of stems in the chapter on verbs, *pp. 21–24*).

Japanese classification recognizes as parts of speech certain dependent words such as ～ます and ～ない which cannot appear in sentences as words in their own right, but only when they are attached to other 'words'.

Japanese classification also makes a distinction between words that change their forms (to indicate, for example, past tense or negation) and those that do not. The term 'conjugate' is used to describe changes in the form of verbs and adjectives.

Information about the part of speech of a Japanese word can usually be found in a Japanese dictionary designed for native speakers of Japanese (こくごじてん・国語辞典). Textbooks and dictionaries for non-Japanese learners do not usually use the Kokugo categories for parts of speech. The English names given here are for guidance only.

A list of Japanese parts of speech

Independent words

part of speech	examples	characteristics
どうし・動詞 (verb)*	たべる よむ はなす あう	dictionary forms* end with a sound from the う line of the kana chart (see p. 255); conjugate
けいようし・形容詞 or イ けいようし・イ形容詞 (-i adjective)	あたらしい おおきい たかい	end with a sound from the い line of the kana chart; conjugate
けいようどうし・形容動詞 or ナ けいようし・ナ形容詞 (-na adjective)	きれい（だ） きれい（な） げんき（だ） げんき（だ） しずか（だ） しずか（な）	end with だ or related form (including な in front of a following noun); viewed as conjugating part of speech, as だ conjugate
めいし・名詞 (noun)	さかな ほん せんせい	can be joined to other nouns with particle の; do not conjugate
すうし・数詞 (counter)	ひとつ ひとり ふたり さんぼん ろっかい	expressions for counting; do not conjugate
ふくし・副詞 (adverb)	ちょっと よく なかなか もし	used in front of verbs or adjectives, or to introduce certain phrases; do not conjugate

part of speech	examples	characteristics
れんたいし・連体詞 (no English equivalent) most words classified as 連体詞 are dealt with in the chapters on こ・そ・あ・ど and adjectives; others (apart from the last three listed) are relatively uncommon	この・こんな その・そんな あの・あんな いろんな various … おおきな big … ちいさな small … わが our … いわゆる what's known as … あらゆる every kind of …	only used in front of nouns; do not conjugate
せつぞくし・ 接続詞 (conjunction**)	けれど（も） し 〜ば 〜たら なら	link sentences; do not conjugate
かんどうし・感動詞 (exclamation) かんとうし・間投詞 (interjection)	はい いいえ あのう … あら	sometimes express emotion; do not conjugate

* The dictionary form of the verb is taken to be the basic 'word'.
** There are some 'conjunctions' which are considered noun and particle combinations in Japanese grammar (e.g. あとで, それでは), and others which are usually taught to foreign learners as 'forms' of the verb or adjective, or as particles (〜たら, 〜ば).

Dependent words

These cannot appear on their own, but are used as endings or attachments to other words.

じょどうし・助動詞 (auxiliary***)	〜ます 〜ない 〜（ら）れる 〜（さ）せる 〜だ・です 〜らしい	conjugating suffixes (note that there are one or two which do not conjugate, such as 〜まい)
じょし・助詞 (particle)	は が を に で	added to nouns etc. to show grammatical roles and relationships within sentences; do not conjugate

*** Sometimes called auxiliary verbs. Many じょどうし are dealt with as 'forms' of the verb or adjective (see the section Suffixes and forms below). In this book, the term 'auxiliary' is used in certain explanations, and where possible だ・です is referred to without defining its part of speech.

Suffixes and forms

In this book, dependent, conjugating auxiliaries such as 〜ます, 〜ない, and 〜させる are mostly dealt with as if they were 'forms' of verbs (and/or adjectives) in accordance with the way that they are treated in most textbooks for foreign learners. だ (and related forms including です) is dealt with in a separate chapter (see だ・です) because of its importance, and is referred to throughout as だ・です. Conjunctive particles such as 〜たら and 〜ば are described in the chapters on verbs (*p. 20*) and conjunctive particles (*p. 129*).

For descriptions of parts of speech in English, see the glossary (*pp. 243–53*).

Topic, comment, and predicate

The terms 'topic' and 'comment' are common in the teaching of Japanese grammar. The topic is what is being spoken or written about. Japanese sentences often begin by stating a topic, about which a comment is then made. The comment can be information or a question. The most common topic marker is the particle は (pronounced **wa**):

topic	comment	meaning
あつみさんは	がくせいです	Atsumi is a student
えきは	どこですか	Where is the station?
にほんごは	むずかしいですか	Is Japanese difficult?

The topic and the grammatical subject may be identical. In the sentence 'Atsumi is a student' above, 'Atsumi' is the grammatical subject in terms of the sentence structure, but it is marked as a topic with the particle は in the context of focussing the conversation on 'Atsumi' and giving information about her. Topic is about focussing attention, and subject more a matter of structural relationships between elements of a single sentence. The particle は 'hides' the subject particle が when a subject is highlighted as a topic (see **particles**).

The predicate is the part of a sentence that gives information about the grammatical subject. It should be remembered that the subject is sometimes also a topic, in which case the subject marker が is hidden. Verbs, adjectives, and nouns followed by だ・です can form predicates in Japanese:

subject	predicate	
あつみさんは	がくせいです	Atsumi is a student
あめが	ふっています	It is raining
すしは	おいしいです	Sushi is delicious
にほんごが	むずかしい	Japanese is difficult

The difference between a word or phrase marked with は (topic)
and one marked with が (subject) can sometimes be a subtle
or contextual one. The first sentence below is a topic with a
comment, and the second is a general statement:

- 寿司はおいしい
  Sushi wa oishii   Sushi: it's delicious

- 寿司がおいしい
  Sushi ga oishii   Sushi is delicious

In these sentences, the topic particle は directs attention forward
to the predicate ('it's delicious'), and the subject particle が
emphasizes what precedes it ('sushi'). This distinction is not
always easy (nor indeed necessary) to convey in an English
translation.

    は is often used when introducing a topic which the listener
is assumed to know about in some way, and points forward
to new information being offered or asked about that topic:

- 田中さんは学生です
  Tanaka san wa gakusei desu
  You know Tanaka – well, he's a student

- 田中さんは学生ですか
  Tanaka san wa gakusei desu ka
  That guy Tanaka: is he a student?

Other ways of marking the topic include なら and って
(see **particles**). For further information and other uses of は,
refer to the sections on は and が in the chapter on particles.

In-group and out-group

In Japanese society, groups of people such as families or workplace colleagues form clear communities, and this is reflected in the language used to refer to people inside and outside the group. There is often a degree of mutual identification with other members of the group relative to outsiders. In formal situations, for example, a member of a group may refer to those outside the group using more polite language, and humble language may be used about one's own family or group relative to those outside it (see **keigo** *p. 213*, **verbs of giving and receiving** *p. 94*, **~て form + verbs of giving and receiving** *p. 47*).

Family members

The concept of in-group and out-group has a marked effect on terms describing family relationships. Words used to refer to the speaker's family are different from those used to refer to the listener's family (when the listener is not another member of the same family) and the families of third parties. The alternatives are given in the chart below:

English	own family ('my . . .')	other person's family ('your . . .')
mother	はは・母	おかあさん・お母さん
father	ちち・父	おとうさん・お父さん
mum	おふくろ	–
dad	おやじ	–
parents	おや or りょうしん	（ご）りょうしん・（ご）両親
wife	つま・妻 or かない・家内	おくさん・奥さん

English	own family ('my . . .')	other person's family ('your . . .')
husband	おっと・夫 or しゅじん・主人	ごしゅじん・ご主人
son	むすこ・息子	(お) むすこさん
daughter	むすめ・娘	(お) むすめさん
sister (older)	あね・姉	おねえさん・お姉さん
sister (younger)	いもうと・妹	いもうとさん・妹さん
brother (older)	あに・兄	おにいさん・お兄さん
brother (younger)	おとうと・弟	おとうとさん・弟さん
uncle	おじ (さん)	おじさん
aunt	おば (さん)	おばさん
grandfather	(お) じいさん	おじいさん・お祖父さん
grandmother	(お) ばあさん	おばあさん・お祖母さん
family	(うちの) かぞく・(家の) 家族	ごかぞく・ご家族

The informal (and distinctly male) words おやじ and おふくろ
for one's own parents might be translated with the colloquial
'my old man' and 'my old dear'.

The use of in-group and out-group words makes clear
whose family is being referred to without the need for possessive
markers such as the English 'my', 'your', etc. Note, however,
that relatives and older siblings (but not younger ones) are
usually addressed directly with the words for other people's
family members, as these are more polite. Older family members
also refer to themselves with the polite words when speaking
directly to younger members. (In English, a comparable usage
tends to be restricted to situations dealing with very small
children, e.g. 'Let Mummy kiss it better.') Natural English
translations of these terms are likely to be 'you', 'I', etc.,
or the person's name:

- お父さんはどう思いますか
  Otōsan wa dō omoimasu ka   What do you think, **Dad?**

- お姉さんと話したいんですが
  Onēsan to hanashitai n desu ga
  I'd like to talk to **you** (= older sister)

- お父さん買ってやるよ
  Otōsan katte yaru yo   I (= **Daddy**) will buy it for you

- お母さんはお兄さんに大丈夫だといったのに
  Okāsan wa **oniisan** ni daijōbu da to itta noni
  You (Mum) told **him** (= older brother) it was OK

- 安部さんこんにちは。お母さんはお元気でしょうか
  Abe san, konnichiwa. **Okāsan** wa o-genki deshō ka
  Hello, Mrs Abe. Is **your mother** well?

Note that some of the words in the chart can be used in a general
sense, and not only for family members, e.g. おじさん can mean
'man', and おくさん can mean 'lady':

- 奥さん！小包です。印鑑お願いします
  Okusan! Kotsuzumi desu. Inkan onegai shimasu
  I have a package for you, **madam**. Please sign for it.

- お姉さん！お水ください
  Onēsan! O-mizu kudasai   **Waitress!** Some water please

- あの小父さんに聞いてみましょうか
  Ano **ojisan** ni kite mimashō ka
  Let's ask that **man** over there

Style

Issues of style affect the form of Japanese verbs, adjectives, and だ・です. Most of the comments here are concerned with verbs. More details can be found in the chapters on adjectives (*p. 96*) and だ・です (*p. 15*).

Japanese has a range of polite, humble, and respectful ways of speaking which are collectively called **keigo** (敬語), sometimes referred to in English as 'respect language' or 'honorifics'. The polite style with 〜ます is a part of keigo. Learners usually begin to study verbs with the 〜ます form, and its usage is covered in the chapter on verbs (*p. 20*). The issue of keigo as a system is discussed separately (*p. 213*).

To understand how Japanese verbs work, it is essential to know the plain style forms as well as the polite style forms. Plain forms can be made regularly from the dictionary form, which is so called as it is the form under which verbs are listed in most Japanese dictionaries. For example, the verb 'to go' is probably most familiar to learners as いきます, but this form is not usually found in dictionaries, as it is derived from the dictionary form いく. Both いく and いきます mean 'to go', and they are to some extent interchangeable, but いく is in the plain style and いきます is in the polite style.

To help learners still unfamiliar with the dictionary form, there is a chart of endings of verbs as an appendix, with suggestions for changing them to find the dictionary form (*p. 258*).

Within the plain style, or **futsūtai** (普通体), and the polite style, or **keitai** (敬体), there are a range of 'forms'. The polite style forms are collectively called **desu-masu-kei** (デス・マス形), and the plain style forms are collectively called **futsūkei** (普通形). The following chart shows the plain and polite style forms of the verb いきます 'to go':

	polite style	*plain style*
non-past	いきます	いく
past	いきました	いった
negative	いきません	いかない
past negative	いきませんでした	いかなかった

In the following examples, the first Japanese sentence in each pair is in the polite style and the second is in the plain style:

あした　えいがを　みます
あした　えいがを　みる
I will see a film tomorrow

きのう　えいがを　みました
きのう　えいがを　みた
I saw a film yesterday

ドイツごが　はなせません
ドイツごが　はなせない
I can't speak German

あさごはんを　たべませんでした
あさごはんを　たべなかった
I didn't eat breakfast

きょうはあついです
きょうはあつい
It's hot today

げんきです
げんき（だ）
I'm fine

Only the ending of a sentence needs to be in the polite form to give the whole sentence the tone of the polite style. Any verbs or adjectives used within a complex sentence are in plain forms, regardless of the context and choice of style at the end (**modifiers**). If there seem to be two polite forms of a verb in a single sentence, it is probable that there are two sentences joined with a conjunction (*p. 129*). In the following sentence there are four verbs, and although the overall style of speech is polite, note that it is only the final verb which has a ～ます ending:

- 夏休みに毎年ヨーロッパへ行く人が年々増えているそうで
  すが、オーストラリアへ行くひとの方が多いと旅行会社の
  情報で分かりました
  Natsu-yasumi ni maitoshi Yōroppa e **iku** hito ga nennen **fuete iru**
  sō desu ga Ōsutoraria e **iku** hito no hō ga ōi to ryokōgaisha no
  jōhō de **wakarimashita**
  We **know** from information from travel firms that the number of
  people who **go** to Europe every year for their summer holidays **is**
  increasing year by year, although greater numbers **are** still **going**
  to Australia

Uses of the polite style and the plain style

The choice of polite style or plain style depends on the situation.
The polite style is used primarily in the spoken language, and the
plain style is used in informal spoken language, in most books and
magazines, and in newspaper articles.

Although the polite style is primarily found in spoken
language, it also carries over into writing where the writer is
'speaking' to the reader (e.g. emails, letters, postcards, lectures,
radio and TV news, etc.) or quoting someone's words. The use of
the polite style in writing is also widespread for stylistic reasons.

The polite style features the auxiliary 〜ます on sentence-
final verbs, together with adjectives and nouns marked with です
when used as predicates (*p. 5*). In the plain style, だ is used instead
of です (だ・です), and い adjectives do not need だ・です.
(For adjectives with です, see the chapter on adjectives,
pp. 96–111.) It is usual to keep a conversation or piece of
writing consistently in one style.

Polite, plain, and written styles of Japanese

In addition to the plain and polite styles discussed above, there is
also a written style which has a small but consistent variation in
the forms of だ・です. Each of the styles is briefly described and
illustrated with examples below.

'desu-masu' style (デス・マス調)

This style is used mostly in spoken language or in letters, and features polite style verb forms and です (including です following い adjectives). Keigo, or respect language, comes within this category (*see p. 213*):

- ロンドンは首都ですからさすがに美しいです
  Rondon wa shuto desu kara sasuga ni **utsukushii desu**
  *You would expect London **to be beautiful** as it is a capital city*

- 前略。母さんの誕生日に、帰れなくて申しわけありません
  でした。仕事が忙しくて、どうしても都合がつかなかった
  のです
  Zenryaku. Okāsan no tanjōbi ni kaerenakute **mōshiwake
  arimasen deshita**. Shigoto ga isogashikute dōshite mo **tsugō
  ga tsukanakatta no desu**
  *In haste! Mum, **I'm sorry** that I couldn't come home for your
  birthday. I was under pressure at work and just **couldn't
  manage it***

'da' style (ダ調)

This style is used in informal style, spoken or written, and features plain forms of verbs, だ, and い adjectives without です:

- 今日も暑いね
  Kyō wa **atsui ne**   *It's hot* today, eh?

- 僕は来週また中国へ行く。最近出張が多い。お前はどう？
  Boku wa raishū mata Chūgoku e **iku**. Saikin shutchō ga **ōi**. O-mae
  wa dō?
  *I'm **going** to China again next week. I've **had lots of** business trips
  recently! How about you?*

'de-aru' style (デアル調)

This style is used for writing in factual, newspaper style, and features plain forms of verbs, and である in place of だ or です:

- 東京は４年連続高物価世界一位である
  Tōkyō wa yo-nen renzoku kōbukka sekkai-ichi-i **de aru**
  Tokyo **has been** the world's most expensive city for four years
  running

- この点について現段階では詳しいことは分からないが、そ
  れぞれの地点で、音声的な事情が複雑である。また、年齢
  などによる差もあろう。さらに多くの情報を集める必要が
  ある
  Kono ten ni tsuite gendankai de wa kuwashii koto wa wakaranai
  ga sorezore no jiten de onseiteki-na jijō ga fukuzatsu **de aru**. Mata
  nenrei nado ni yoru sa mo **arō**. Sara ni ōku no jōhō o atsumeru
  hitsuyō ga **aru**
  At this stage, the point is not clearly understood. The phonetic
  data in each location **is** complicated. **There is** also a probable
  difference according to age. **It is** necessary to gather further
  data

だ・です

だ・です is often treated as an equivalent of the English verb 'to be', and it is usually translated as 'is/are', but this important element is not a verb at all. It functions principally as the ending required by な adjectives and nouns forming predicates (see p. 5). だ is one of a class of words called **jodōshi** (助動詞) in Japanese, sometimes referred to as 'auxiliaries' in English (see **auxiliary suffixes**). For the use of だ・です with adjectives, see the chapter on adjectives (p. 96).

Conjugation of だ・です

Like most other auxiliaries, だ・です conjugates (changes the ending to show, for example, negation or past tense). The plain and polite forms of だ・です are shown in the chart below. Because of issues of style (see p. 10 and p. 213), there are numerous possible forms:

form	plain style	polite style	literary style
positive	だ	です	である
negative	ではない or じゃない	ではないです or じゃないです or ではありません or じゃありません	ではない
past	だった	でした	であった
past negative	ではなかった or じゃなかった	ではなかったです or じゃなかったです or ではありませんでした or じゃありませんでした	
tentative	だろう	でしょう	であろう

There is also the very polite version でございます. For ございます, see **keigo** (*p. 213*).

だ produces the following forms when nouns, clauses, or conjunctive particles are added (see **conjunctive particles**). Some examples are given below:

form	plain style	polite style	literary style
〜て	で	で	であって
〜たら	だったら	でしたら	であったら
〜なら 〜ば	なら（ば）	なら（ば）	であるなら or であれば
attributive	な	な	な

For more on な, see below and the section on adjectives (*p. 96*):

- このシャツは長袖でおしゃれなカフスがついています
  Kono shatsu wa **nagasode de** o-share-na kafusu ga tsuite imasu
  This shirt **is long-sleeved and** has stylish cuffs

- 日本語は特有な言語であって、近隣諸国の言語とあまり似ていません
  Nihongo wa tokuyū na gengo **de atte** kinrinshokoku no gengo to amari nite imasen
  Japanese **is** a very distinctive language, and does not much resemble the languages of neighbouring countries

- 来週の土曜日が暇だったら一緒に映画を見に行こうよ
  Raishū no doyōbi ga hima **dattara** issho ni eiga o mi ni ikō yo
  If you are free next Saturday, let's go and see a film together

- 来週の土曜日お暇でしたら、一緒にお食事でもどうですか
  Raishū no doyōbi o-hima **deshitara** issho ni o-shokuji demo dō desu ka
  If you are free next Saturday, would you like to have dinner or something?

- 好きなら好きとはっきり言って
  Suki nara suki to hakkiri itte   **If you like it,** say so clearly

The classical form なり is sometimes found as a predicate:

- 時は金なり
  Toki wa **kane nari**   Time **is money**

Uses of だ・です

After nouns and な adjectives, だ is used to mark the ending of a sentence or clause. It can be in the plain form or polite form, and shows tense and negation:

- 試験は明日です
  Shiken wa ashita **desu**   The exam **is** tomorrow

- 幸子は先生だ
  Yukiko wa sensei **da**   Yukiko **is** a teacher

- これは僕のくつじゃない
  Kore wa boku no kutsu **ja nai**   These **aren't** my shoes

- 1980年の夏でした
  Sen kyū-hyaku hachi-jū-nen no natsu **deshita**
  It was the summer of 1980

Sometimes だ is omitted if the sentence can stand alone, as in a newspaper headline:

- 緊迫化で自治停止（だ）
  Kinpakuka de jichiteishi (da)
  Self-rule (is) suspended as tension grows

だ is sometimes omitted in conversation, especially in questions and answers:

- 土曜日暇？
  Doyōbi hima?   Are you free on Saturday?

- うん。暇よ
  Un. Hima yo   Yes, I'm free

- 明日雨
  Ashita ame   Rain tomorrow!

- 私は日本人。あなたはイギリス人
  Watashi wa Nihonjin. Anata wa Igirisujin
  I am Japanese. You are English

な is the form of だ・です used to join a noun to the nominalizer の, or compound particles with の (*see p. 206 and pp. 166–167*):

- 僕が書いた本なのにお金はもらえなかった
  Boku ga kaita hon **na no ni** o-kane wa moraenakatta
  Although I wrote the book, I couldn't receive (any) money for it

な must be used when a noun follows a な adjective (hence the name). For examples and discussion, see the chapter on adjectives (*p. 96*).

じゃ and では with negatives

じゃ is the contracted form of では, and is used in the various negative forms of だ・です. じゃ is found more often in spoken language, and では is more common in the written form, although it is also encountered in speech:

- 私は学生じゃない
  Watashi wa gakusei **ja nai**   I **am not** a student

- 彼らは警察じゃなかった
  Karera wa keisatsu **ja nakatta**   They **were not** policemen

- 反対ではありませんが疑問があります
  Hantai **dewa arimasen** ga, gimon ga arimasu
  I **am not** against it, but I still have reservations

Uses of だろう・でしょう

This tentative form of だ is used to indicate conjecture, although it is not always necessary or appropriate to translate it into English with 'probably'. It follows the plain forms of verbs, adjectives, and nouns:

- 真弓ちゃんは小学生でしょう
  Mayumi chan wa shōgakusei **deshō**
  Mayumi is an elementary student, **isn't she?**

- 明日雨が降るだろう
  Ashita ame ga furu **darō**   It will **probably** rain tomorrow

- **イギリスで外食するのは高いでしょう**
  Igirisu de gaishoku suru no wa takai **deshō**
  *Eating out in England is expensive, **isn't it?***

An adverb of conjecture, such as たぶん 'maybe', 'perhaps',
is sometimes used with だろう・でしょう (see **adverbs**):

- **田村先生は多分来ないでしょう**
  Tamura sensei wa **tabun** konai **deshō**
  *Ms Tamura **probably** isn't coming*

だろう・でしょう can be used in questions as a polite equivalent
of だ・です:

- **ホールさんでしょうか**
  Hōru-san **deshō ka**   *Are you Ms Hall?*

- **日本人は土曜日も学校へ行くのでしょうか**
  Nihonjin wa doyōbi mo gakkō e **iku no deshō** ka
  *In Japan, **do they go** to school on Saturdays too?*

だろう・でしょう is commonly used to seek agreement with a
statement. This is similar in function to the tag question in English:

- **お母さんは日本人でしょう**
  Okāsan wa Nihonjin **deshō**   *Your mum's Japanese, **isn't she?***

- **雨だったら試合がないでしょう**
  Ame dattara, shiai ga nai **deshō**
  *If it rains, there won't be a match, **will there?***

だろう・でしょう is also discussed in the chapter on auxiliary
suffixes (*see p. 181*).

Verbs

What is a verb?

A verb is a word which expresses an action or a process:

> I **watched** TV last night
> The door **opened**

A verb can also describe a state of affairs:

> The horse **is standing** in the field
> All the cups **are broken**

Properties of Japanese verbs

English verbs change their endings according to the person doing the action ('I go', 'she goes'), but this is not the case with Japanese verbs. Neither do they need a pronoun ('I', 'you', 'he', etc.) to show the grammatical subject. The subject of the sentence is usually clear from the context. This means that many of the examples given below have pronouns such as 'I' or 'she' in the English translations but not in the Japanese (see **pronouns**).

The main verb comes at the end of a Japanese sentence, although both verbs and verb phrases are also used in clauses within complex sentences. In this latter use they are often referred to as 'modifiers' because the verb or clause modifies the following noun or noun phrase (*see p. 209*).

Verb forms

Japanese verbs are usually spoken of as having 'forms', e.g. '～ます form' and '～ない form'. In fact, ～ます and ～ない are auxiliaries which are attached to particular stems of verbs, and are called **jodōshi** (助動詞) in Japanese. This book refers to 'forms' of verbs, in line with most textbooks, but also uses the term 'auxiliary' as an English equivalent of **jodōshi**. Auxiliaries are very important in Japanese, and they are considered in their own chapter (*see p. 181*).

All verbs have dictionary forms ending in one of the syllables from the う line of the kana chart (*see p. 255*). The possible endings are 〜う, 〜く, 〜ぐ, 〜す, 〜つ, 〜ぬ, 〜む, 〜ぶ, 〜る.

Verb stems

Japanese verbs have a series of stems to which suffixes are added. The following chart gives the stems together with their names, examples, and the most common suffixes attached to them.

The verbs used as examples are the ごだん verbs あう 'to meet', まつ 'to wait', かく 'to write', とる 'to take', はなす 'to speak', the いちだん verbs みる 'to see', 'to watch', たべる 'to eat', and the irregular verbs する 'to do' and くる 'to come'.

Chart of verb stems with common suffix elements

Japanese and English names (where commonly used) for stem	example	dictionary form	common structures based on this stem include . . .
conjunctive (pre-ます) stem	かき〜	かく	〜たい
	あい〜	あう	〜たい
	まち〜	まつ	〜ます (〜ません, 〜ました etc.)
れんようけい・連用形	とり〜	とる	
	はなし〜	はなす	(see **Conjunctive form**)
	み〜	みる	
	たべ〜	たべる	
	し〜	する	
	き〜	くる	
〜ない stem	かか〜	かく	〜ない
	あわ〜	あう	〜ない form

Japanese and English names (where commonly used) for stem	example	dictionary form	common structures based on this stem include . . .
みぜんけい・未然形	また〜	まつ	（さ）せる
	とら〜	とる	(see **causative**)
	はなさ〜	はなす	（ら）れる
	み〜	みる	(see **passive**)
	たべ〜	たべる	
	し〜	する	
	こ〜	くる	
dictionary form じしょけい・辞書形 also called しゅうしけい・終止形 or れんたいけい・連体形 The reason for having alternative names is that the dictionary form can be sentence final (＝しゅうしけい) or form part of a modifying clause and join to a following main clause (＝れんたいけい). Both forms are the same in modern Japanese, so じしょけい is the preferred term.	かく	かく	でしょう・だろう
	あう	あう	
			〜そう
			〜よう
			〜らしい
			〜みたい
	まつ	まつ	
	とる	とる	(see じょどうし p. 181)
			Also used to modify nouns
			(see **modifiers** p. 209)
	はなす	はなす	(see **Uses of the dictionary form**)
	みる	みる	
	たべる	たべる	
	する	する	
	くる	くる	

Japanese and English names (where commonly used) for stem	example	dictionary form	common structures based on this stem include . . .
かていけい・仮定形	かけ〜	かく	〜ば (conditional) (see **Conjunctive particles**)
	あえ〜	あう	
	まて〜	まつ	
	とれ〜	とる	
	はなせ〜	はなす	
	みれ〜	みる	
	たべれ〜	たべる	
	すれ〜	する	
	くれ〜	くる	
すいりょうけい・推量形	かこ〜	かく	
	あお〜	あう	〜う (see **volitional form**)
	まと〜	まつ	
	とろ〜	とる	
	はなそ〜	はなす	
	み〜	みる	〜よう
	たべ〜	たべる	
	しよ〜	する	
	こよ〜	くる	
めいれいけい・命令形 imperative	かけ	かく	
	あえ	あう	(see **Imperative form**)
	まて	まつ	
	とれ	とる	
	はなせ	はなす	
	みろ	みる	
	たべろ	たべる	
	しろ	する	
	こい	くる	

Japanese and English names (where commonly used) for stem	example	dictionary form	common structures based on this stem include . . .
〜てけい・テ形 〜て form	かいて	かく	〜ください
	あって	あう	〜いる
	まって	まつ	〜ある
	とって	とる	〜おく
	はなして	はなす	〜ください
	みて	みる	〜しまう
	たべて	たべる	〜もいい (see 〜て form)
	して	する	
	きて	くる	
〜たけい・タ形 〜た form	かいた	かく	〜ことがある
	あった	あう	〜ほうがいい
	まった	まつ	〜あと
	とった	とる	
	はなした	はなす	
	みた	みる	(see 〜た form)
	たべた	たべる	
	した	する	
	きた	くる	

Verb conjugation groups

Japanese verbs can be divided into two main groups according to how they conjugate (change the endings to indicate, for example, a negative or a past meaning). These groups are known as **ichidan** (一段) verbs and **godan** (五段) verbs. There are also two slightly irregular verbs which do not fit into these groups, する and くる.

いちだん verbs in the dictionary form end in a kana from the い or え line of the kana chart, followed by 〜る. The possible endings for いちだん verbs are 〜いる, 〜える, 〜しる, 〜せる, 〜ちる, 〜てる, 〜にる, 〜ねる, 〜びる, 〜べる, 〜みる, 〜める, 〜りる, 〜れる.

Verbs with other endings in the dictionary form are classified as ごだん verbs, except for the two irregular verbs する and くる.

The majority of verbs can be identified as either いちだん or ごだん verbs by their dictionary form ending, but note that there are some ごだん verbs ending in -eru or -iru, i.e. a kana from the え or い lines of the kana chart followed by る. A list of some of the most common of these is given after the basic conjugation charts. The best way to be certain of the conjugation of an unknown verb ending in -eru or -iru is to look in a good learner's dictionary (such as the Oxford Beginner's Japanese Dictionary) where the conjugation group of a verb is given.

ごだん verbs

The verbs in this group are sometimes called '-u verbs' in English, as the final -u of the romanized dictionary form is dropped before other endings are added. Other English terms found in text books are 'consonant stem verbs' and 'group one verbs'. The Japanese term **godan** (五段), meaning 'five-step', refers to the fact that the final kana of the dictionary form changes to another from the same row of the kana chart when making different forms, and these changes involve all five vowels. This is shown below with the verbs よむ・読む 'to read' and はなす・話す 'to speak':

読む	読まない	読みます	読める	読もう
yo**mu**	yo**ma**nai	yo**mi**masu	yo**me**ru	yo**mō**

話す	話さない	話します	話せる	話そう
hana**su**	hana**sa**nai	hana**shi**masu	hana**se**ru	hana**sō**

Conjugation chart for ごだん verbs

Note that the inclusion of a form in the chart does not necessarily mean that it is in common use, and some verbs may be rarely used in certain forms:

form	to meet	to write	to lend	to wait	to jump	to read	to take
dictionary	あう・会う	かく・書く	かす・貸す	まつ・待つ	とぶ・飛ぶ	よむ・読む	とる
～ます	あいます	かきます	かします	まちます	とびます	よみます	とります
conjunctive (pre-ます) stem	あい	かき	かし	まち	とび	よみ	とり
～たい	あいたい	かきたい	かしたい	まちたい	とびたい	よみたい	とりたい
～ない	あわない	かかない	かさない	またない	とばない	よまない	とらない
～て	あって	かいて	かして	まって	とんで	よんで	とって
～た	あった	かいた	かした	まった	とんだ	よんだ	とった
～たら	あったら	かいたら	かしたら	まったら	とんだら	よんだら	とったら
～たり	あったり	かいたり	かしたり	まったり	とんだり	よんだり	とったり
～ば	あえば	かけば	かせば	まてば	とべば	よめば	とれば
potential	あえる	かける	かせる	まてる	とべる	よめる	とれる
passive	あわれる	かかれる	かされる	またれる	とばれる	よまれる	とられる
causative	あわせる	かかせる	かさせる	またせる	とばせる	よませる	とらせる
causative-passive	あわせられる	かかせられる	not used	またせられる	とばせられる	よませられる	とらせられる
volitional	あおう	かこう	かそう	まとう	とぼう	よもう	とろう
imperative	あえ	かけ	かせ	まて	とべ	よめ	とれ
negative imperative	あうな	かくな	かすな	まつな	とぶな	よむな	とるな

Note that when a ごだん verb becomes potential or passive, it has an **-eru** ending. These forms are treated as new ごだん verbs and are conjugated into negative forms, conditional forms, etc., according to the pattern for いちだん verbs (see the sections on the passive *pp. 70–73* and potential *pp. 66–70*):

meaning	dictionary form (ごだん)	passive (いちだん)	potential (いちだん)
to buy	かう・買う	かわれる	かえる
to go	いく・行く	いかれる	いける
to read	よむ・読む	よまれる	よめる
to speak	はなす・話す	はなされる	はなせる
to return	かえる・帰る	かえられる	かえれる

いちだん verbs

The verbs in this group are often called '-ru verbs' in English, as the final 〜る of the dictionary form is dropped before other endings are added. Other terms are 'vowel stem verbs' and 'group two verbs'. In Japanese they are called **ichidan** (一段) verbs, meaning 'one step', referring to the fact that there is just one change needed to make other forms, with the final kana of the dictionary form being replaced by the suffix. This means that there is a consistent verb stem in all forms. This is illustrated below with the verbs たべる・食べる 'to eat' and みる・見る 'to see', 'to watch':

食べる	食べない	食べます	食べられる	食べよう
taberu	tabenai	tabemasu	taberareru	tabeyō

見る	見ない	見ます	見られる	見よう
miru	minai	mimasu	mirareru	miyō

Conjugation chart for いちだん verbs

All いちだん verbs have a dictionary form ending -**eru** or -**iru**, i.e. a kana from the え or い lines of the kana chart followed by る. Note that there are a few ごだん verbs which also have this ending (see below):

form	'to go out'	'to get up'
dictionary form	でかける・出かける	おきる・起きる
〜ます form	でかけます	おきます
conjunctive (pre-ます) form	でかけ	おき

form	'to go out'	'to get up'
～たい	でかけたい	おきたい
～ない form	でかけない	おきない
～て form	でかけて	おきて
～た form	でかけた	おきた
～たら	でかけたら	おきたら
～たり	でかけたり	おきたり
～ば	でかければ	おきれば
potential	でかけられる	おきれる
passive	でかけられる	おきられる
causative	でかけさせる	おきらせる
causative-passive	でかけさせられる	おきらせられる
volitional	でかけよう	おきよう
imperative	でかけろ	おきろ
negative imperative	でかけるな	おきるな

Irregular verbs する and くる

The verbs する, with a basic meaning of 'to do', and くる・来る 'to come' are slightly irregular and do not fit the pattern of いち だん and ごだん verbs. (There are also a very few irregularities in other verbs, and these are noted in the verb charts.) Verbs formed from a noun plus する, of which there are a great many, behave in the same way as する itself. For more on this, see the section on する at the end of this chapter.

Conjugation chart for くる・来る and する

dictionary form	くる・来る	する
～ます form	きます	します
conjunctive (pre-ます) form	き	し
～たい	きたい	したい
～ない form	こない	しない

dictionary form	くる・来る	する
～て form	きて	して
～た form	きた	した
～たら	きたら	したら
～たり	きたり	したり
～ば	くれば	すれば
volitional	こよう	しよう
imperative	こい	しろ or せよ
negative imperative	くるな	するな
potential	こられる	できる
passive	こられる・これる	される
causative	こさせる	させる
causative-passive	こさせられる	させられる

ごだん verbs which look like いちだん verbs

The following common verbs end in **-iru** or **-eru** but are ごだん verbs, and conjugate regularly according to their group. (There are other verbs like this, and to be certain of a verb's type a good dictionary should be consulted.)

いる・要る	to be necessary
かえる・帰る	to go home, to return
かぎる・限る	to be limited
きる・切る	to cut
しる・知る	to know
はいる・入る	to enter
はしる・走る	to run
しゃべる	to speak, to chatter
ける	to kick
すべる・滑る	to slip, to ski
まいる・参る	to come, to go, to visit

Different verbs with the same dictionary forms

There are a few common verbs which belong to different conjugations but which have the same dictionary forms. The use of kanji characters helps to distinguish them in writing:

dictionary form	ごだん	meaning	いちだん	meaning
きる	切る	to cut	着る	to wear, to put on
かえる	帰る	to return home	替える 換える 代える 変える	to change
いる	要る	to be necessary	（居る）	to exist
へる	減る	to decrease	経る	to pass (time)
しめる	湿る	to be damp	閉める	to close (the window etc.)
ねる	練る	to knead	寝る	to go to bed

The 〜ます form

The use of the auxiliary 〜ます is a feature of **keigo** (*see p. 213*), and makes the level of speech polite. For a discussion of politeness levels and the use of 〜ます versus plain forms, see the chapter on style (*p. 10*). The 〜ます form is made up of the conjunctive (pre- ます) stem and the auxiliary 〜ます, which can be made negative, past, past negative, etc.

Making the 〜ます form of ごだん verbs

To make the 〜ます form of ごだん verbs, the final kana of the dictionary form changes from the 〜う line of the kana chart to the 〜い line, and the auxiliary 〜ます is then added:

dictionary form	meaning	change in final kana	～ます form
あう・会う	to meet	う → い	あいます
もらう	to receive	う → い	もらいます
かく・書く	to write	く → き	かきます
いそぐ・急ぐ	to hurry	ぐ → ぎ	いそぎます
かす・貸す	to lend	す → し	かします
はなす・話す	to speak	す → し	はなします
まつ・待つ	to wait	つ → ち	まちます
しぬ・死ぬ	to die	ぬ → に	しにます
とぶ・飛ぶ	to fly	ぶ → び	とびます
よむ・読む	to read	む → み	よみます
とる	to take	る → り	とります
がんばる	to do one's best	る → り	がんばります

Making the ～ます form of いちだん verbs

The final ～る of the dictionary form is dropped, and the auxiliary ～ます is added:

dictionary form	meaning	with ～る dropped	～ます form
みる・見る	to see, to watch	み～	みます
おきる・起きる	to get up	おき～	おきます
たべる・食べる	to eat	たべ～	たべます
おしえる・教える	to teach, to tell	おしえ～	おしえます

Making the ～ます form of する and くる

The ～ます form of する is します. The ～ます form of くる is きます.

Conjugation of ～ます

The conjugation chart of ～ます is given below:

form	ending	example	meaning
non-past	〜ます	いきます	will go
past	〜ました	いきました	went
negative	〜ません	いきません	won't go
past negative	〜ませんでした	いきませんでした	didn't go
volitional	〜ましょう	いきましょう	let's go

There is also a 〜て form of 〜ます, with the ending 〜まして, but this is relatively rare. It is used to connect sentences in formal spoken situations:

- **すばらしいお土産をいただきまして、誠にありがとうございました**
  Subarashii omiyage o **itadakimashite**, makoto ni arigatō gozaimashita
  I am sincerely grateful for the marvellous present I **have received**

Other forms of 〜ます may be encountered on rare occasions, but the only common one not in the chart above is いらっしゃいませ, the expression frequently used by staff in shops and businesses to greet customers.

Use of 〜ます

The 〜ます form is generally used in conversation rather than writing (except in the case of letters, where **keigo** including 〜ます is common). It is used at the end of sentences only, and not in modifying clauses (*see p. 209*).

The auxiliary 〜ます makes sentences polite in style (see **style**), and so is very common in everyday conversational exchanges between adults who are not familiar with each other:

- **すみません。電話は近くにありますか**
  Sumimasen. Denwa wa chikaku ni **arimasu** ka
  Excuse me, **is there** a phone nearby?

- **どこから きましたか**
  Doko kara **kimashita** ka   Where do **you come** from?

- **オーストラリアから きました**
  Ōsutoraria kara **kimashita**   I'm/I **come** from Australia

- テレビを あまり見ません
  Terebi o amari **mimasen**   I **don't watch** much TV
- 妹に手紙を書きました
  Imōto ni tegami o **kakimashita**   I **wrote** a letter to my sister

〜ましょう is an equivalent of the volitional form (see below), and is used with the meaning 'Let's . . .':

- 一緒に行きましょう
  Issho ni **ikimashō**   **Let's go** together
- じゃ、そろそろ帰りましょう
  Ja, sorosoro **kaerimashō**   Right! **Let's go home**

〜ましょう can be followed by the question particle か to seek agreement with a proposal:

- お茶を入れましょうか
  O-cha o **iremashō ka**   Shall I make tea?

〜ません with the question particle か is a polite way of offering something or extending an invitation:

- コーヒーを飲みませんか
  Kōhii o **nomimasen ka**   Would you like a coffee?
- 一緒に行きませんか
  Issho ni **ikimasen ka**   Shall we go together?

The 〜たい form

This is an auxiliary that is attached to the conjunctive (pre-ます) stem, and gives the meaning of 'want to'. It is used to make statements about the speaker or writer. 〜たい is a sentence final form, and so does not need です in the plain style, although it is followed by です in the polite style (*see p. 10*):

- 来年日本に行きたいです
  Rainen Nihon ni **ikitai** desu
  I **want to go** to Japan next year
- それは楽しかったね。また行きたい
  Sore wa tanoshikatta ne. Mata **ikitai**
  That was fun. I **want to go** again!

The particle marking the desired object is usually が , but を is also found, especially where the feeling is very strong and an effort has to be made in order to bring about the desire:

- **今晩ラーメンが食べたいなあ**
  Konban **rāmen ga** tabetai nā
  Tonight I want to eat **ramen**

- **大学で生物学を勉強したい**
  Daigaku de **seibutsugaku o** benkyō shitai
  I want to study **biology** at university

Conjugation of 〜たい

たい conjugates in the same way as い adjectives to form negative, past, and past negative sentences, etc.:

form	meaning	ending	example
plain	want to	〜たい	いきたい
negative	don't want to	〜たくない	いきたくない
past	wanted to	〜たかった	いきたかった
past negative	didn't want to	〜たくなかった	いきたくなかった

- **あの映画がずっと見たかった**
  Ano eiga ga zutto **mitakatta**
  I have wanted to see that film for ages

- **七面鳥はもう食べたくない**
  Shichimenchō wa mō **tabetaku nai**
  I don't want to eat turkey any more

Uses of 〜たい

〜たい is used to talk about what the speaker or writer wants to do:

- **寿司が食べたいです**
  Sushi ga **tabetai** desu   I want to eat sushi

- **行きたくない**
  Ikitakunai   I don't want to go

Although statements with 〜たい may refer only to the speaker or writer, this form can be used to ask questions or make suppositions about other people:

- 疲れている様子だね。すぐ寝たいでしょう？
  Tsukarete iru yōsu da ne. Sugu **netai** deshō
  You look tired. I expect **you want to go** straight **to bed**, don't you?

- 喜多村先生は大学院に戻りたいですか
  Kitamura sensei wa daigakuin ni **modoritai** desu ka
  Do **you (Kitamura) want to go back** to graduate school?

〜たい can be used about people other than the speaker if there is a phrase suggesting report, supposition, or appearance, such as 'I heard that' or 'apparently':

- 早く食べたいでしょう
  Hayaku tabetai **deshō**   You want to eat early, I **suppose**?

- 彼女も行きたいって
  Kanojo mo ikitai **tte**   She says that she wants to go, too

- 梅沢君もロンドンで勉強したいそうです
  Umezawa kun mo Rondon de benkyō shitai **sō desu**
  I **heard that** Umezawa wants to study in London, too

〜たい cannot be used to make questions meaning 'Do you want to . . .?' It can occur with a following でしょう, or the question particle か, or be said with rising intonation, but in these cases it is asking for confirmation. For example, a mother looking at her child yawning might say もう ねたい？ 'You (obviously) want to go to bed, don't you?', but this is essentially a statement based on the evidence, rather than a question.

〜たがる

〜たがる is a combination of the auxiliaries 〜たい and 〜がる (see the section on adjectives of emotion, *pp. 102–104*). It is used to show that someone other than the speaker wants to do something:

- 山田さんは自分の過去について触れたがらない
  Yamada san wa jibun no kako ni tsuite **furetagaranai**
  Yamada **doesn't want** his past **brought up**

- 子供がずっと前から君に会いたがっているから遊びにきてね

  Kodomo ga zutto mae kara kimi ni **aitagatte iru** kara asobi ni kite ne

  The children **have been wanting to meet** you for ages, so please come and visit

〜がる conjugates as a ごだん verb.

The conjunctive (pre-ます) form/stem

The conjunctive (pre-ます) stem of ごだん verbs is made by changing the final kana from one in the う line of the kana chart to one in the い line. With いちだん verbs, it is made by removing the final る:

dictionary form	meaning	change in final kana	pre-ます form
ごだん verbs			
いく・行く	to go	く → き	いき
はいる・入る	to enter	る → り	はいり
よむ・読む	to read	む → み	よみ
まつ・待つ	to wait	つ → ち	まち
いちだん verbs			
たべる・食べる	to eat	remove final る	たべ
みる・見る	to see, to watch	remove final る	み

The conjunctive stem of する is し, and the conjunctive stem of くる is き.

Uses of the conjunctive (pre-ます) stem

This stem is used for adding 〜ます and other auxiliaries.

The conjunctive (pre-ます) stem with に + verb of motion

The conjunctive (pre-ます) stem can be used with the particle に and a verb of motion to express 'go and . . .', 'come in order to . . .', etc.:

- 今晩映画を見に行きたいです
  Konban eiga o **mi ni ikitai** desu
  I **want to go and see** a film tonight

- 明日、友達が遊びに来る
  Ashita, tomodachi ga **asobi ni kuru**
  A friend **is coming to visit** tomorrow

- ちょっとパンを買いに行ってくる
  Chotto pan o **kai ni itte kuru**
  I'm just **going to buy** some bread

The conjunctive (pre- ます) stem to join sentences

This form can be used in written language as an equivalent of the
～て form when joining sentences to show a sequence of events, or
a reason or cause. Notice that the names of individuals are given
without the suffix さん in this style:

- 江藤はタバコに火を点け、昨日のことを考えた
  Etō wa **tabako ni hi o tsuke**, kinō no koto o kangaeta
  Eto **lit a cigarette and** thought about the events of the
  previous day

- 斎藤は札幌へ行き、田川に会った
  Saitō wa **Sapporo e iki**, Tagawa ni atta
  Sato **went to Sapporo and** met Tagawa

The conjunctive (pre- ます) stem with なさい

なさい is a polite imperative meaning '(please) do . . .', and is
commonly used in classrooms and other semi-formal situations:

- ちょっと静かにしなさい
  Chotto shizuka ni **shi nasai**   Please be quiet!

なさい is sometimes abbreviated to な, but care should be taken
not to confuse this with the negative imperative (*see pp. 83–85*):

- ちょっと静かにしな
  Chotto shizuka ni **shi na**   Please be quiet!

The conjunctive (pre- ます) stem with ～かた・～方

A compound noun meaning 'way of . . . ing' is created by adding
the ending ～かた・～方:

- 書き方
  kakikata   *way of writing*

- 説明書に使い方が詳しく書いてあります
  Setsumeisho ni **tsukaikata** ga kuwashiku kaite arimasu
  Instructions for use are given in detail in the instruction manual

- この漢字の読み方を忘れてしまった
  Kono kanji no **yomikata** o wasurete shimatta
  I have forgotten the **way of reading** this kanji

The conjunctive (pre- ます) stem with 〜にくい and 〜やすい

The endings 〜にくい (or less commonly 〜つらい) and 〜やすい
mean 'difficult to . . .' and 'easy to . . .' respectively:

- バント先生の字が読みにくいです
  Banto sensei no ji ga **yominikui** desu
  Mr Bunt's handwriting **is difficult to read**

- この車は運転しやすい
  Kono kuruma wa **unten shiyasui**   This car **is easy to drive**

The conjunctive (pre- ます) stems of certain verbs can also be
used as nouns (*see p. 122*), for forming compound verbs
(*see pp. 85–87*), and in keigo (*see p. 213*).

     For the conjunctive (pre- ます) stem plus 〜そうだ, *see
pp. 182–183*. For conjunctive (pre- ます) stem plus 〜ながら,
see pp. 136–137.

The 〜て form

This is essentially a conjunctive form which allows the addition of
other verbs, phrases, or sentences. The structures thus produced
give a range of meanings which generally show a time or aspect
relationship (see **glossary**) between what is expressed by the verb
and the predicate (*see p. 5*) or clause that follows it. There are
numerous uses of the form, and various structures based on it.
Although usually taught as part of the conjugation
of verbs, it is best regarded as a conjunctive particle (*see p. 129*).

Making the ～て form of ごだん verbs

The method of making the ～て form depends on the final kana of the dictionary form. There are four groups: verbs ending in ～う, ～つ, ～る, verbs ending in ～む, ～ぶ, ～ぬ, verbs ending in ～す, and verbs ending in ～く, ～ぐ.

Verbs ending in ～う, ～つ, ～る

The final kana of the dictionary form is dropped, and って is added:

dictionary form	meaning	～て form
あう・会う	to meet	あって
おもう・思う	to think	おもって
まつ・待つ	to wait	まって
もつ・持つ	to hold, to have	もって
とる・取る・撮る	to take	とって
のる・乗る	to ride, to travel (on/by)	のって

The verbs とう・問う 'to ask', 'to enquire' and こう・請う・乞う 'to entreat', 'to beg' have the ～て forms とうて and こうて respectively. The ～て forms of these verbs are relatively uncommon.

Verbs ending in ～む, ～ぶ, ～ぬ

The final kana of the dictionary form is dropped, and んで is added:

dictionary form	meaning	～て form
よむ・読む	to read	よんで
ほほえむ・(微笑む)	to smile	ほほえんで
とぶ・飛ぶ	to fly	とんで
よろこぶ・喜ぶ	to rejoice, to be delighted	よろこんで
しぬ・死ぬ	to die	しんで

Verbs ending in ～す

The final す of the dictionary form is dropped, and して is added:

dictionary form	meaning	～て form
かす・貸す	to lend	かして
はなす・話す	to speak	はなして

Verbs ending in ～く, ～ぐ

A final く of the dictionary form is dropped, and いて is added.
A final ぐ is replaced by いで:

dictionary form	meaning	～て form
かく・書く	to write	かいて
はたらく・働く	to work	はたらいて
いそぐ・急ぐ	to hurry	いそいで
かぐ・嗅ぐ	to smell, to sniff	かいで

An important exception is the verb いく・行く 'to go', which has
the irregular ～て form いって.

Making the ～て form of いちだん verbs

The final ～る of the dictionary form is replaced with て:

dictionary form	meaning	～て form
みる・見る	to see, to watch	みて
おきる・起きる	to get up	おきて
たべる・食べる	to eat	たべて
つける・点ける	to turn on, to light	つけて

～て forms of する and くる

The ～て form of する is して. The ～て form of くる is きて.

Uses of the ～て form

～て joins sentences and clauses, so linking the verb with a
following word, clause, or sentence. Use of ～て shows an

aspectual relationship (see **glossary**) with what follows, usually indicating prior completion, but the meaning depends on the context. English translations of sentences with ～て forms can vary greatly, as shown below.

To show a sequence of actions

More than one ～て form can be used within one sentence to show a sequence of events or actions:

- 7 時に起きて、シャワーを浴びて、朝ご飯をたべました
  Shichi-ji ni **okite**, shawā o **abite**, asagohan o tabemashita
  I **got up** at seven, **had a shower and** ate breakfast

- 彼は車を止めて、地図を出した
  Kare wa **kuruma o tomete**, chizu o dashita
  He **stopped the car and** got out the map

To show a reason or cause

The first part of the sentence with a ～て form can show a reason or cause for what follows in the second part of the sentence:

- 盛岡さんは交通事故にあって、足に怪我をした
  Morioka san wa **kōtsūjiko ni atte**, ashi ni koga o shita
  Ms Morioka **had a traffic accident and** injured her leg

- 毎日外で働いて、風邪をひいてしまった
  Mainichi **soto de hataraite**, kaze o hiite shimatta
  I was **working outside** every day **and** ended up catching a cold

To show circumstances

The ～て form can be used to show the circumstances of an action, or the means of doing something:

- 彼女と手をつないで歩きました
  Kanojo to **te o tsunaide** arukimashita
  I walked **holding hands** with my girlfriend

- お箸を使ってご飯を食べました
  O-hashi o tsukatte gohan o tabemashita
  I ate the meal **using chopsticks**

To show manner of an action

The ～て form can show the manner in which something is done:

- **会社から歩いて帰りました**
  Kaisha kara **aruite** kaerimashita
  I came home from the office **on foot/I walked** home

- **仕事のあと急いで帰りました**
  Shigoto no ato **isoide** kaerimashita
  After work **I hurried** home

- **慌てて財布を捜しました**
  Awatete saifu wo sagashimashita
  I **frantically** searched for my wallet

To mark contrast

The 〜て form can be used to highlight a contrast with the
following part of the sentence:

- **僕はイギリスに帰って、彼女はフランスに残った**
  Boku wa Igirisu ni **kaette**, kanojo wa Furansu ni nokotta
  I **returned** to England **but** my girlfriend stayed in France

The 〜て form + いる

The 〜て form with いる can have various meanings, depending
on the type of verb with which it used. With verbs describing
actions that continue or can be repeated, the 〜て form plus いる
shows continuous or habitual action:

- **治輝君は友達と電話で話しています**
  Haruki kun wa tomodachi to denwa de **hanashite imasu**
  Haruki **is talking** to a friend on the phone

- **あそこで新聞を読んでいる人は鈴木さんです**
  Asoko de shinbun o **yonde iru** hito wa Suzuki san desu
  The person over there **reading** the paper is Suzuki

- **毎朝ジョギング（を）しています**
  Maiasa **jogingu (o) shite imasu**   I **jog** every morning

- **子供達は外で遊んでいる**
  Kodomotachi wa soto de **asonde iru**
  The children **are playing** outside

However, with verbs which describe momentary actions that
cannot be repeated, the 〜て form plus いる shows that the action
is completed:

- 外の自動販売機が壊れている
  Soto no jidōhanbaiki ga **kowarete iru**
  The vending machine outside is **broken**

- 映画はもう終わっているはずです
  Eiga wa mō **owatte iru** hazu desu
  The film should **have finished** by now

- 手紙が落ちている
  Tegami ga **ochite iru**
  The letter **has fallen down** (and is on the floor)

With verbs describing states and processes, the 〜て form with
いる shows that the state continues:

- 彼が今どこに居るか知っていますか
  Kare ga ima doko ni iru ka **shitte imasu ka**
  Do you know where he is now?

- ジョナサンが太っている
  Jonasan ga **futotte iru**
  Jonathan **has put on weight** (= is fat)

- 姉はお風呂に入っている
  Ane wa o-furo ni **haitte iru**   My sister **is** in the bath

- 梶原さんはニューヨークに住んでいます
  Kajiwara san wa Nyū Yōku ni **sunde imasu**
  Mr Kajiwara **is living** in New York

With positive predicates, 〜て with いる shows completion:

- 映画はもう終っている
  Eiga wa mō **owatte iru**   The film **has** already **finished**

- 木が倒れている
  Ki ga **taorete iru**   The tree **has fallen over**

- もう 電車が着いている
  Mō densha ga **tsuite iru**   The train **has** already **arrived**

In negative predicates, 〜て plus いない shows actions not yet
undertaken or completed:

- まだ食べていない
  Mada **tabete inai**   I **haven't eaten** yet

- 明日がテストなのにまだ勉強していません
  Ashita ga tesuto na no ni mada **benkyō shite imasen**
  There is a test tomorrow but I **haven't done any studying** yet

- まだ目を通していない書類はこっちです
  Mada **me o tōshite inai** shorui wa kotchi desu
  *These are the documents that I **have not** yet **looked through***

The adverb まだ '(not) yet' can sometimes be omitted:

- 使っていない切手はトレーに戻してください
  Tsukatte inai kitte wa torē ni modoshite kudasai
  *Please return **unused** stamps to the tray*

With some verbs, especially those indicating change and movement, the 〜ている form can be interpreted as both continuous action and a state, but the context (and use of adverbs) will usually determine which is appropriate:

- もしもし。すみませんが、今食べているところなんですよ。後でかけ直します
  Moshi moshi. Sumimasen ga, ima **tabete iru** tokoro nan desu yo. Ato de kakenaoshimasu
  *Hello? Sorry, but **we're eating** now. I'll call you back later*

- もう朝ご飯を食べています
  Mō asagohan o **tabete imasu**   *I've **already had** breakfast*

- 手紙が落ちている
  Tegami ga **ochite iru**
  *The letter **had fallen down** (onto the floor)*

- 最近株の値段が落ちている
  Saikin kabu no nedan ga **ochite iru**
  *The prices of shares **have been falling recently***

Both continuous actions and states can be talked about in the past, using 〜ていた・〜ていました.

- 丘の上から子供達を見ていた
  Oka no ue kara kodomotachi o **mite ita**
  *I **was watching** the children from the top of the hill*

- 日本に戻ったら桜の花が散っていた
  Nihon ni modottara sakura no hana ga **chitte ita**
  *When I returned to Japan, the cherry blossom **had fallen***

When 〜ている is part of a modifying clause, it often stays as 〜ている even with a past reference, as the tense of the whole sentence is shown by the final verb:

- 東京に住んでいるときは毎日外食をしていました

  Tokyo ni **sunde iru** toki wa mainichi gaishoku o shite imashita

  When I **lived** in Tokyo, I ate out every day

- 母はパリに住んでいるときよく美術館に行きました

  Haha wa Pari ni **sunde iru** toki yoku bijutsukan ni ikimashita

  When my mother **was living** in Paris, she often went to art museums

However, in situations where the emphasis is on the past in contrast to the present, 〜ていた is possible:

- アメリカに住んでいたときゴルフをよくやった

  Amerika ni **sunde ita** toki gorufu o yoku yatta

  When I **lived** in America I often played golf (but I don't now)

The verb いる which follows the 〜て form can be replaced by おる (humble) or いらっしゃる (honorific), depending on the speech level and style (*see p. 213 and p. 10*):

- 斎藤です。留守にしておりますので伝言をどうぞ

  Saitō desu. Rusu ni **shite orimasu** node dengon o dōzo

  This is Saito. I **am** out, so please leave a message

- 鈴木先生はこの辺に住んでいらっしゃいますか

  Suzuki sensei wa kono hen ni **sunde irasshaimasu** ka

  Do **you live** around here, Professor Suzuki?

Verbs which are usually or rarely used in the 〜ている form

Some verbs with implied continuous meanings tend to be used mostly in the 〜て form with いる. Among the most common of these are:

すむ・住む	→ すんでいる	to live (in)
けっこんする・結婚する	→ けっこんしている	to be married
もつ・持つ	→ もっている	to hold, to have
しる・知る	→ しっている	to know
うる・売る	→ うっている	to sell
はたらく・働く	→ はたらいている	to work
つとめる・勤める	→ つとめている	to work
おぼえる・覚える	→ おぼえている	to remember

- 彼が何を言ったか覚えていますか
  Kare ga nani o itta ka oboete imasu ka
  Do you remember what he said?

- ミラーさんは結婚しています
  Mirā san wa kekkon shite imasu   Ms Miller is married

The verb しる・知る 'to know' is used in the 〜て form with いる when positive, but not when negative:

- 佐藤先生の電話番号を知っていますか
  Satō sensei no denwa bangō o **shitte imasu** ka
  Do you **know** Professor Sato's phone number?

- いいえ、知りません。事務所で聞いてください
  Iie, **shirimasen**. Jimusho de kite kudasai
  No, I **don't** (know it). Please ask at the office

If a question with しる mentions previously unknown information, then the answer needs to be in the past negative form, and not the 〜て form with いる:

- 彼が　薫ちゃんと　付き合っているのを　知っていましたか
  Kare ga Kaoru chan to tsukiatte iru no o **shitte imashita ka**
  Did you know that he's going out with Kaoru?

- いいえ、知りませんでした
  Iie, **shirimasen deshita**   No. I **didn't know**

The verbs ある 'to exist', 'to be', 'to have', いる 'to exist', 'to be', and いる・要る 'to need' are not used in the 〜て form with いる.

Potential forms (see **potential form**) are not used with 〜ている. However, できる in the sense of 'to be completed', 'to be ready', can be used with 〜ている:

- ご飯が出来ている
  Gohan ga **dekite iru**   Dinner **is ready**

Verbs of motion in the 〜て form + いる

When いる follows the 〜て form of いく, くる, or かえる, it shows that a state is continuing, and is often translated into English with 'has gone', 'has come', 'has returned':

- 主人は会社に行っています
  Shujin wa kaisha ni **itte imasu**
  My husband **has gone** to work

- 主人はもう家に帰っている
  Shujin wa mō ie ni **kaette iru**
  My husband **has** already **come home**

In the sentence below, the in-laws have come (and are still here):

- 妻の家族が来ていて大変忙しいです
  Tsuma no kazoku ga **kite ite** taihen isogashii desu
  My wife's family **are here** so we are very busy!

The ～て form + verbs of giving and receiving

The verbs あげる 'I give', くれる '(someone) gives me', もらう 'receive', and other verbs of similar meaning are used with the ～て form when there is some sense of a benefit being given or received by the action taking place (see pp. 94–95)

   In the following sentences, the verb is translated as 'tell' in both cases, but the Japanese equivalents differ. Japanese requires a 'verb of benefit' to be used, especially when both the giver and the receiver of the action are in polite face-to-face discussion (first example), or where the speaker feels that she or he has benefited in some way (second example):

- アンヤの新しい住所を教えてあげる
  Anya no atarashii jūsho o **oshiete ageru**
  I **will tell** you Anja's new address

- アンヤの新しい住所を教えてくれるといいました
  Anya no atarashii jūsho o **oshiete kureru** to iimashita
  He said he would **tell** me Anja's new address

In the same way, the verb もらう 'to receive' is used following a ～て form to show that the speaker or writer has benefited by someone's action. This usage is often translated in English as 'get (someone) to . . .', or 'have someone do . . .':

- 学生に連絡先を書いてもらう
  Gakusei ni renrakusaki o **kaite morau**
  Get the students **to write** down their contact details

- 時間が心配ならもっと早く来てもらいましょう
  Jikan ga shinpai nara motto hayaku **kite moraimashō**
  If you're worried about time, **let's get** them **to come** earlier

- 田中さんに手紙の日本語をチェックしてもらう
  Tanaka san ni tegami no Nihongo o **chekku shite morau**
  I'll **get** Ms Tanaka **to check** the Japanese in my letter

Notice that the last sentence above may not be acceptable if Ms Tanaka is of higher status (such as the speaker's boss), or if she is actually present, in which case the verb is likely to be the more polite いただく (*see pp. 94–95* and *p. 213*):

- 田中さんに手紙の日本語をチェックしていただく
  Tanaka san ni tegami no Nihongo o **chekku shite itadaku**
  I'll **get** Ms Tanaka **to check** the Japanese in (my) letter

The following examples show other situations where the action of the verb is seen as beneficial to the speaker or listener, and so the ～て form is followed by a verb of giving or receiving:

- ペンを忘れてしまいました。貸してくれませんか
  Pen o wasurete shimaimashita. **Kashite kuremasen ka**
  I have forgotten my pen. Could you **lend me** one?

- 妻が今日珍しく弁当を作ってくれた
  Tsuma ga kyō mezurashiku bentō o **tsukutte kureta**
  Most unusually, my wife **made me** a boxed lunch today

- 辞書が2冊あるから一冊貸してあげる
  Jisho ga ni-satsu aru kara is-satsu **kashite ageru**
  I've got two dictionaries. I'll **lend you** one

- ちょっと来て、面白いものを見せてあげる
  Chotto kite, omoshiroi mono o **misete ageru**
  Come here a moment and I'll **show you** something interesting

When showing benefit with the verbs of giving and receiving, the benefit is not limited only to the speaker or listener directly, but can also refer to the relevant in-group and out-group (*see p. 7*):

- 先生が妹の日本語を誉めてくれた
  Sensei ga imōto no Nihongo o **homete kureta**
  The teacher **praised my sister's** Japanese

- 妹がバスでおばあちゃんに席を譲ってあげました

  Imōto ga basu de obāchan ni seki o **yuzutte agemashita**

  My sister gave her seat to an old lady on the bus

- 君のお陰で我が社の売上が上がった。よくやってくれた

  Kimi no o-kage de wagasha no uriage ga agatta. Yoku **yatte kureta**

  Thanks to you, our company sales have increased. You **have done** well for us

The ～て form + verbs of motion to describe processes

There is a special use of the verbs いく and くる after a verb in the ～て form to describe processes. The addition of いく to a ～て form, especially of なる 'to become', shows that an action or change is continuing:

- あの大学は年々と大きくなっていく

  Ano daigaku wa nennen to **ōkiku natte iku**

  That university **gets bigger** year by year

- 経済状態が深刻になっていった

  Keizaijōtai ga **shinkoku ni natte itta**

  The economic situation continued **to grow graver**

Similarly, the use of くる following a ～て form shows that a process has continued from a point in the past up to the present moment. Notice that the past form きた does not necessarily mean the whole sentence is past tense:

- 経済状態が深刻になってきた

  Keizai jōtai ga **shinkoku ni natte kita**

  The economic situation **has become grave**

- テ形の作り方がやっと分かってきた

  Te-kei no tsukurikata ga yatto **wakatte kita**

  I finally **understand** how to make the ～て form

There is also a use of ～て with くる to show that an action has just started:

- 試合が始まろうとした時に雨が降ってきた

  Shiai ga hajimarō to shita toki ni ame ga **futte kita**

  Just as the match was about to start **it began to rain**

The combination やってくる 'to appear', 'to show up' is very common, but is idiomatic:

- ちょうどそのとき竜也がやってきた
  Chōdo sono toki Tatsuya ga **yatte kita**
  Just at that moment Tatsuya **appeared**

The combination やっていく is also an idiom, and means 'get along (well) with . . .':

- 新しい会社で新しい仲間とうまくやっていきたいと思っている
  Atarashii kaisha nakama to umaku **yatte ikitai** to omotte iru
  I'm determined to **get along** well with my new colleagues at the new company

The 〜て form + しまう

The basic meaning of the verb しまう is 'to put away', as in the following example:

- 朝起きたら布団を押入れにしまう
  Asa okitara futon o oshiire ni **shimau**
  When we get up in the morning, we **put** the futons **away** in the cupboard

However, when it follows a 〜て form, しまう is used to indicate the completion of an action:

- レポートを書いてしまいましたか
  Repōto o **kaite shimaimashita** ka
  Have you **finished writing** your essay?

- この小説を全部読んでしまいました
  Kono shōsetsu o zenbu **yonde shimaimashita**
  I've **finished reading** this novel

- 文子さんはもう行ってしまった
  Ayako san wa mō **itte shimatta**   Ayako **has** already **left**

The use of a 〜て form plus しまう can also show that the speaker perceives the event negatively. This is similar to the colloquial English 'gone and . . .' as in 'You haven't gone and told him, have you?' or 'He's gone and drunk the whole bottle'. Whether to interpret 〜てしまう as showing completion or negative judgement, depends on the context:

- 今日の会議が1時からだとすっかり忘れてしまった
  Kyō no kaigi ga ichi-ji kara da to sukkari **wasurete shimatta**
  I completely **forgot** that today's meeting was from 1 o'clock!

- ごめんね。彼にもう言ってしまった
  Gomen ne. Kare ni mō **itte shimatta**
  Sorry. I've already **told** him (and I shouldn't have)

In the spoken language, 〜ちゃう as a contracted form of 〜てしまう is very common. Verbs with a 〜て form of 〜んで have the contracted form じゃう:

- 全部食べちゃう
  Zenbu **tabechau**   I will **eat** it all

- ビールをたくさん飲んじゃった
  Biiru wo takusan **nonjatta**   I **drank** loads of beer

The 〜て form + みる

The use of the verb みる 'to see' after a 〜て form is equivalent to the English 'try to . . . and see what happens':

- これを食べてみてください
  Kore o **tabete mite** kudasai   Please **taste** this **and see**

- 宿題を新しいコンピュータで打ってみた
  Shukudai o atarashii konpyūta de **utte mita**
  I **tried using** the computer to do my homework

- 一度だけでもいいから中国へ行ってみたい
  Ichido dake demo ii kara Chūgoku e **itte mitai**
  Even if it's only once, I want **to go** to China **and see what it's like**

The 〜て form + ある

The basic meaning of the verb ある is 'to exist'. The use of a 〜て form with ある shows that something was affected by an action, and it still exists in that state. This structure occurs mostly with transitive verbs (*see pp. 87–91*), but notice that the particle used is が to show a subject, rather than を to mark a direct object:

- 窓が開けてある
  Mado ga **akete aru**   The window **is open**

- 宿題が黒板に書いてある
  Shukudai ga kokuban ni **kaite aru**
  The homework **is written** on the blackboard

～てある often occurs with the adverb もう 'already':

- 夕飯をもう作ってある
  Yūhan wo **mō tsukutte aru**   I **have already made** dinner

The particle を in the sentence above shows that the emphasis is on the person who made dinner. The particle が could also be used, in which case the emphasis would be on dinner being ready:

- 夕飯がもう作ってある
  Yūhan ga mō tsukutte aru   **Dinner's** already made

The agent (the person who does the action) is not usually explicitly stated, but implied by the context.

The ～て form + おく

The basic meaning of the verb おく・置く is 'to put'. The ～て form with おく shows that an action is done to prepare something for future use:

- ビールを冷やしておきます
  Biiru o **hiyashite okimasu**   I will **chill** the beer

- 僕の名前の漢字を書いておきます
  Boku no namae no kanji o **kaite okimasu**
  I'll **write down** my name in kanji (for you)

- 明日の試験のために勉強しておかなければならない
  Ashita no shiken no tame ni **benkyō shite okanakereba naranai**
  I **must study** in order to be ready for the exam tomorrow

- 荷物をドアの近くに置いておいてください
  Nimotsu o doa no chikaku ni **oite oite** kudasai
  Please **put** the bags by the door

Compare the following pairs of sentences which show the difference between ～てある and ～ておく:

- 弟の誕生日のプレゼントを買っておきます
  Otōto no tanjōbi no purezento o **katte okimasu**
  I **will buy** my brother a birthday present (in advance)

- 弟の誕生日のプレゼントが買ってあります
  Otōto no tanjōbi no purezento ga **katte arimasu**
  I **have bought** my brother's birthday present

- 地図をかいておいてあげますよ
  Chizu o **kaite oite** agemasu yo
  I'll **draw** a map for you (to take along)

- もう地図がかいてありますよ
  Mō chizu ga **kaite arimasu** yo   The map **is ready**

～て form + から

から after a ～て form shows that the action of the verb is completed before a subsequent event or action begins:

- 食事が終ってから話しましょう
  Shokuji ga **owatte kara** hanashimashō
  Let's talk about it **after we finish** the meal

- 帰国してから就職活動に入りました
  Kikoku shite kara shūshoku katsudō ni hairimashita
  After I returned home (to my own country), I started looking for a job

～て form + は + いけない・ならない・だめ（だ）

This structure expresses negative obligation 'must not . . .':

- たばこを吸ってはいけない
  Tabako o **sutte wa ikenai**   You **mustn't smoke**

- 1人だけで行ってはだめだよ
  Hitori dake de **itte wa dame da** yo
  You **mustn't go** on your own!

See also ～なくてはいけない and なければならない・なければ
いけない under ～ない below.

～て form + は

This is often used when making suggestions 'how about . . . ?':

- それなら同時に2つ頼んではどうですか
  Sore nara dōji ni futatsu **tanonde wa** dō desu ka
  In that case, why not **order** two at the same time?

The どうですか can be implied and omitted:

- 今日はだめだな。では明日行っては？
  Kyō wa dame da na. Dewa ashita **itte wa**
  Well, it's no good today, then. OK, **how about going** tomorrow?

〜て form + も

The addition of も to a 〜て form gives a structure meaning 'even if . . .':

- がんばっても 1 日ではできないよ
  Ganbatte mo ichinichi de wa dekinai yo
  Even if I really work at it, I can't do it in one day

- フェリー代を払ってもフランスでワインを買うほうが安い
  Ferii dai o **haratte mo** Furansu de wain o kau hō ga yasui
  Even after paying for the ferry, wine is cheaper in France

The addition of いい gives a structure used to ask or grant permission:

- 電話を使ってもいいですか
  Denwa o **tsukatte mo ii** desu ka   May I use the phone?

- どうぞ食べてもいいよ
  Dōzo **tabete mo ii** yo   You may start eating

For （なく）て followed by も, see below under なくても.
For more on も, see the chapter on particles (*pp. 167–169*).

The 〜ない form

This is the negative form, and is made by adding the auxiliary 〜ない to a verb stem. 〜ない is a conjugating part of speech, i.e. it alters its endings to show negatives and other forms. (For more information on auxiliaries, *see p. 181*.)

Making the 〜ない form of ごだん verbs

The final kana of the dictionary form of ごだん verbs changes from the 〜う line to the 〜あ line before adding 〜ない. Verbs ending in 〜う in their dictionary form change this to 〜わ (rather than 〜あ). There is one very important irregularity: the verb ある has the 〜ない form of ない (rather than あらない). The following chart shows the changes, with examples:

dictionary form	meaning	change in final kana		～ない form
あう・会う	to meet	う →	わ	あわない
もらう	to receive	う →	わ	もらわない
かく・書く	to write	く →	か	かかない
いそぐ・急ぐ	to hurry	ぐ →	が	いそがない
かす・貸す	to lend	す →	さ	かさない
はなす・話す	to speak	す →	さ	はなさない
まつ・待つ	to wait	つ →	た	またない
しぬ・死ぬ	to die	ぬ →	な	しXない
とぶ・飛ぶ	to fly	ぶ →	ば	とばない
よむ・読む	to read	む →	ま	よまない
とる・取る・撮る	to take	る →	ら	とらない
がんばる	to do one's best	る →	ら	がんばらない
ある	to exist, to be, to have	(irregular)		ない

Making the ～ない form of いちだん verbs

The final ～る of the dictionary form of いちだん verbs is replaced with ～ない:

dictionary form	meaning	～ない form
みる・見る	to see, to watch	みない
おきる・起きる	to get up	おきない
たべる・食べる	to eat	たべない
つける・付ける・点ける	to attach, to turn on, to light	つけない

Conjugation of ～ない

～ない conjugates by dropping the final い before adding endings to mark the past tense and other forms, such as ～たら and ～ば:

- 何も言わなかった
  Nani mo **iwanakatta**　　I **didn't say** anything

- **バスが後１０分こなかったら**タクシーで行きましょう
  Basu ga ato jup-pun **konakattara** takushii de ikimashō
  If the bus **doesn't come** in 10 minutes, let's get a taxi

- **明日手紙が来なければ**電話します
  Ashita tegami ga **konakereba** denwa shimasu
  If the letter **doesn't come** tomorrow, I will telephone

For more on 〜ば and 〜たら, see **conjunctive particles**.

〜ず as an alternative to 〜ない

The ending 〜ず instead of 〜ない is an older form of negative that is still quite commonly used:

- **週末は家に帰らず、ずっと会社にいました**
  Shūmatsu wa ie ni **kaerazu** zutto kaisha ni imashita
  He was in the office the whole weekend, **without going home** at all

The formation of the negative of する in this way is irregular, being せず:

- **クリスマスデコレーションをせず、２５日を迎えました**
  Kurisumasu dekorēshon o **sezu** ni-jū-go-nichi o mukaemashita
  We had Christmas Day **without putting up** any decorations

The ending 〜ず is commonly followed by に to mean 'without . . . ing'. For examples, see the section on 〜ないで below.

Uses of the 〜ない form

This form is used for negative sentences in the plain style (*see p. 10*):

- **私はアルコールを飲まない**
  Watashi wa arukōru o **nomanai**   I **don't drink** alcohol

- **ズボンとジャケットが合わない**
  Zubon to jaketto ga **awanai**
  The trousers and jacket **don't match**

Like the dictionary form, the 〜ない form can also be used in a modifying clause in complex sentences (*see p. 209*):

- **毎日ピアノをちゃんと練習しない人は上手にならない**
  Mainichi piano wo chanto **renshū shinai hito** wa jōzu ni naranai
  People who don't practise the piano properly every day will not improve!

- **分からないときは**僕に聞いてください
Wakaranai toki wa boku ni kiite kudasai
Please ask me **when you don't understand** (something)

Constructions using 〜ない

〜なくて

The form 〜なくて can be used as a negative equivalent of the
〜て form (see 〜て **form**). The 〜なくて ending shows a cause or
reason, often shown in English translations with 'because' or 'as':

- ギリスではやっぱり電車が**来なくて**困りました
Igirisu dewa yappari densha ga **konakute** komarimashita
I was in trouble **because** the train **didn't come** – as you'd expect
in England!

- 食べ物が**なくて**、大変だった
Tabemono ga **nakute**, taihen datta
There was a problem **because there was no** food

〜なくても

The addition of も to 〜なくて gives a structure meaning 'even if
. . . is not', 'even without . . .':

- 原田さんが**来なくても**しょうがない、会議を始めましょう
Harada san ga **konakute mo** shō ga nai, kaigi o hajimemashō
Even if Harada **isn't here,** that's too bad! Let's start the
meeting

- 研が**なくても**よく切れる包丁です
Toganakute mo yoku kireru hōchō desu
This knife will cut well **even if you don't sharpen it**

〜なくてはいけない

The form 〜なくてはいけない indicates that something is
compulsory:

- 写真を撮りたければ前もって**きかなくてはいけない**
Shashin o toritakereba maemotte **kikanakute wa ikenai**
If you want to take photos, **you must ask** in advance

The 〜なくてはいけない element is often compressed to 〜なく
ちゃ in informal spoken language:

- 行かなくちゃ
  Ikanakucha　　I must go

〜なくてもいい and 〜なくてよかった

〜なくてもいい is a structure used to express 'don't have to . . .', 'it isn't necessary to . . .', 'it's OK without . . .':

- 忙しいなら行かなくてもいいです
  Isogashii nara **ikanakute mo ii** desu
  You **don't have to go** if you're busy

- 嫌いなものがあったら、食べなくてもいいです
  Kirai-na mono ga attara, **tabenakute mo ii** desu
  If there are things you don't like, you **don't have to eat** them

This is sometimes abbreviated to 〜なくていい in the spoken language:

- 食べなくていい
  Tabenakute ii　　You don't have to eat it

As a question with ですか (polite style), 〜なくてもいい means 'Is it all right not to . . . ?', and can be translated as 'Do I have to . . . ?':

- 明日行かなくてもいいですか
  Ashita ikanakute mo ii desu ka
  Is it OK not to go tomorrow?/Do I have to go tomorrow?

This use can also be marked in informal speech by intonation rather than a question particle:

- 行かなくていい？
  Ikanakute ii?　　Do I have to go?

〜なくてよかった

The phrase 〜なくてよかった is a structure used to express the meaning 'I am glad that . . . didn't . . .':

- 雨が降らなくてよかった
  Ame ga **furanakute yokatta**　　I'm glad it didn't rain

- あの飛行機に乗らなくてよかったね。ハイジャックされたんだって
  Ano hikōki ni **noranakute yokatta** ne. Haijakku sareta n da tte
  I'm glad we didn't take that plane. They're saying it was hijacked!

なければならない and なければいけない

When the conditional 〜なければ is followed by the negative form of なる 'to become', or いける 'to go well', the phrase has the meaning of 'must' or 'have to'. There is no difference in meaning between the two, but なる tends to be used more in writing. なる and いける can be in the polite style or the plain style:

- 明後日出張で東京まで行かなければなりません
  Asatte shutchō de Tokyo made **ikanakereba narimasen**
  I **have to go** to Tokyo on a business trip the day after tomorrow

- 6時までに終わらなければならない
  Roku-ji made ni **owaranakereba naranai**
  We **must be finished** by 6 o'clock

- この間借りた本を返さなければいけません
  Kono aida karita hon o **kaesanakereba ikemasen**
  I **must give back** the book I borrowed the other day

The 〜なければならない element is often compressed to 〜なきゃ in informal spoken language, and followed by further information:

- もう6時だ。行かなきゃ間に合わない
  Mō roku-ji da. **Ikanakya** ma ni awanai
  It's already 6 o'clock! I **must go** or I'll be late

〜なければ + よかった

This structure means 'I wish I hadn't . . .' or 'If only . . . hadn't happened':

- 新しいコンピュータがすぐダメになった。買わなければよかった
  Atarashii konpyūta ga sugu dame ni natta. **Kawanakereba yokatta**
  (My) new computer quickly broke down. I **wish I hadn't bought** it!

〜ないで

This expression, which is related to 〜て, can mean 'without . . . ing':

- 何も食べないで家へ帰りました
  Nani mo **tabenaide** ie e kaerimashita
  I went home **without eating** anything

- 漢字を使わないで住所を書きます
  Kanji o **tsukawanaide** jūsho o kakimasu
  I will write the address **without using** kanji

The 〜ないで ending can be followed by expressions of request:

- 心配しないでください
  Shinpai **shinaide kudasai**   **Please don't** worry

- まだ見ないでください
  Mada **minaide kudasai**   **Don't look** yet!

- 危ないところへ行かないでほしい
  Abunai tokoro e **ikanaide hoshii**
  I **don't want** you **to go** anywhere dangerous

This usage is so common that the remainder of the sentence can often be omitted, and implied by the context:

- 食べないで
  Tabenai de   Don't eat (it)!

- 忘れないで
  Wasurenai de   Don't forget!

A more formal alternative to 〜ないで is the old literary negative 〜ず with the particle に:

- 忘れずに
  Wasurezu ni   Don't forget!

- 田中が何も考えずに床からたばこを拾った
  Tanaka ga nani mo **kangaezu ni** yuka kara tabako o hirotta
  Without thinking, Tanaka picked up the cigarettes from the floor

The 〜た form

The 〜た form shows completion, and that actions occurred in the past. The formation is as for the 〜て form, but with a final 〜た rather than 〜て, and 〜だ rather than 〜で (see 〜て form).

Making the 〜た form of ごだん verbs

The formation of the 〜た form depends on the final kana of the dictionary form. There are four groups: verbs ending in 〜う,

～つ, ～る, verbs ending in ～む, ～ぶ, ～ぬ, verbs ending in ～す, and verbs ending in ～く, ～ぐ.

Verbs ending in ～う, ～つ, ～る

The final kana of the dictionary form is dropped, and った is added:

dictionary form	meaning	final kana dropped	～た form
あう・会う	to meet	あ～	あった
おもう・思う	to think	おも～	おもった
まつ・待つ	to wait	ま～	まった
もつ・持つ	to hold, to have	も～	もった
とる・取る・撮る	to take	と～	とった
のる・乗る	to ride, to travel (on, by)	の～	のった

The verbs とう・問う 'to ask', 'to enquire', and こう・請う・乞う 'to entreat', 'to beg' have ～た forms of とうた and こうた, respectively. The ～た forms of these verbs are relatively uncommon.

Verbs ending in ～む, ～ぶ, ～ぬ

The final kana of the dictionary form is dropped, and んだ is added:

dictionary form	meaning	final kana dropped	～た form
よむ・読む	to read	よ～	よんだ
ほほえむ・微笑む	to smile	ほほえ～	ほほえんだ
とぶ・飛ぶ	to fly	と～	とんだ
よろこぶ・喜ぶ	to rejoice, to be delighted	よろこ～	よろこんだ
しぬ・死ぬ	to die	し～	しんだ

Verbs ending in 〜す

The final す of the dictionary form is dropped, and した is added:

dictionary form	meaning	final kana dropped	〜た form
かす・貸す	to lend	か〜	かした
はなす・話す	to speak	はな〜	はなした

Verbs ending in 〜く, 〜ぐ

The final く of the dictionary form is dropped, and いた is added. A final ぐ is replaced by いだ:

dictionary form	meaning	final kana dropped	〜た form
かく・書く	to write	か〜	かいた
はたらく・働く	to work	はたら〜	はたらいた
いそぐ・急ぐ	to hurry	いそ〜	いそいだ
かぐ・嗅ぐ	to smell, to sniff	か〜	かいだ

The only irregularity is that the verb いく 'to go' has the 〜た form いった (and not いいた).

Making the 〜た form of いちだん verbs

The final る of the dictionary form is dropped, and た is added:

dictionary form	meaning	る dropped	〜た form
おきる・起きる	to get up	おき〜	おきた
たべる・食べる	to eat	たべ〜	たべた

Uses of the 〜た form

The 〜た form is used for past sentences in the plain style, and shows that an action has been completed:

- 昨日映画を見た
  Kinō eiga o **mita**   I **saw** a film yesterday

- 磯部さんは大学を卒業して外務省に入った
  Isobe san wa daigaku o sotsugyō shite gaimushō ni **haitta**
  Isobe graduated from university and **joined** the foreign ministry

- 天野さんは転職して銀行員になった
  Amano san wa tenshoku shite ginkōin ni **natta**
  Amano changed jobs and **became** a bank clerk

- ジョナサンとあっちゃんが９２年に結婚した
  Jonasan to At-chan ga kyū-jū-ni-nen ni **kekkon shita**
  Jonathan and Atsuko **married** in 1992

- 遠藤さんは仕事を辞めて小説を書いた
  Endō san wa shigoto o yamete shōsetsu o **kaita**
  Endo gave up work and **wrote** a novel

- 夕飯ができた
  Yūhan ga **dekita**   Supper **is ready!**

The 〜た form can be used within complex sentences as part of a modifying clause (*see p. 209*).

- 大学で勉強した統計学がやっと役に立った
  Daigaku de benkyō shita tōkeigaku ga yatto yaku ni tatta
  The statistics course I studied at university finally came in useful

- ズコブ映画監督は日本で見た能を作品に取り入れた
  Zukobu eiga kantoku wa **Nihon de mita nō o** sakuhin ni toriireta
  The film director Zhukov incorporated **the Noh Theatre he had seen in Japan** into his work

The 〜た form is also used for the instant when something is noticed, realized, or discovered:

- 確かにこのポケットに財布を入れたんだけど ...。　　あぁ！あった！
  Tashika kono poketto ni saifu o ireta n da kedo ... Ah, **atta!**
  I was sure I put the wallet in this pocket ... Ah, **here it is!**

- 速く、速くドアが閉まるぞ。やった！
  Hayaku, hayaku doa ga shimaru zo. **Yatta!**
  Quickly, quickly! The door's about to shut! We **made it!**

〜た + から

When から follows the 〜た form, it makes the situation described by the verb the reason or cause for what follows. (Care should be taken not to confuse this with 〜て + から, discussed above):

- 食堂が閉まったから近くのレストランで食べましょう
  Shokudō ga **shimatta kara** chikaku no resutoran de tabemashō
  The dining hall is **closed, so** let's eat at a restaurant nearby

〜た + ほうがいい

This idiom, based on the 〜た form, is used for making suggestions and giving advice:

- 今晩勉強したほうがいいよ。明日試験があるから
  Konban benkyō **shita hō ga ii** yo. Ashita shiken ga aru kara
  You **had better study** tonight as there's an exam tomorrow

- 機械の調子が悪い。止めたほうがいい
  Kikai no chōshi ga warui. **Tometa hō ga ii**
  The machine is not working properly. **It's best to switch it off**

- 歌舞伎を見られるいいチャンスだから思い切って行ったほうがいい
  Kabuki o mirareru ii chansu dakara omoikitte **itta hō ga ii**
  It's a good chance to see Kabuki (theatre) so we really **should go**

〜た and 〜ている to express completion

Both 〜た and 〜ている can be used to indicate completed actions. The first example below emphasizes the state of 'being in bed', and the second example emphasizes the completed action of 'having gone to bed':

- かおるはもう寝ている
  Kaoru wa mō **nete iru**   Kaoru's already **gone to bed**

- かおるは１０時に寝た
  Kaoru wa jū-ji ni **neta**   Kaoru **went to bed** at 10

With verbs which describe actions, 〜ている usually indicates continuing action:

- 健太は今ご飯を食べている
  Kenta wa ima gohan o **tabete iru**   Kenta **is eating**

However, in some cases a verb describing an action can express both continuing action and completion with 〜ている:

- 健太はもうご飯を食べている
  Kenta wa mō gohan o **tabete iru**
  Kenta **has** already **eaten**/Kenta **is** already **eating**

- あそこの家はクリスマスツリーを飾っている
  Asoko no ie wa kurisumasu tsurii o **kazatte iru**
  That family **have decorated** the Christmas tree/That family **are decorating** the Christmas tree

See the section on the 〜て form + いる above for more examples.

〜たり, 〜たり + する

A common construction based on the 〜た form is with 〜たり, 〜たり plus する. This is used to give representative actions from a wider selection, and carries the sense of '. . . and so on'. There are usually at least two different actions mentioned:

- 昨日ビデオを見たり、テニスをしたりしました
  Kinō bideo o **mitari**, tenisu o **shitari shimashita**
  Yesterday I **watched** videos, **played** tennis and **so on**

- 週末ジャックは大抵ファミコンをしたり、雑誌を読んだりしている
  Shūmatsu Jakku wa taitei famikon o **shitari**, zasshi o **yondari shite iru**
  At weekends, Jack usually **plays** on the computer and **reads** magazines, **etc.**

However, sometimes there can be just a single instance of 〜たり:

- 雑誌を読んだりして彼女の帰りを待っていた
  Zasshi o **yondari shite** kanojo no kaeri o matte ita
  I **read** magazines **and so on** while I waited for her to come home

This structure is also used with actions of opposite meaning which alternate:

- 泣いたり、わらったりしました
  Naitari warattari shimashita   I was **laughing and crying**

- ドアを開けたり、閉めたりしないでください
  Doa o **aketari shimetari shinaide** kudasai
  Stop opening and closing the door

～たら

This is a conjunctive particle that is used to join sentences, and add the meaning 'if' or 'when' to the first clause. It is formed by adding ら to the ～た form of a verb:

- 明日博美ちゃんに会ったら、これを渡してください
  Ashita Hiromi chan ni **attara** kore o watashite kudasai
  If/When you see Hiromi tomorrow, please give her this

For more information on ～たら, refer to the section on conjunctive particles (*p. 129*).

～ば

ば is a conjunctive particle used to join sentences and make the first a condition. It can often be translated with 'if'. ～ば is also used in certain idiomatic constructions such as ～なければ (ならない) and ～ばよかった (see ～ない and **conjunctive particles**). It is formed by changing the final kana of the dictionary form to the え line of the kana chart, e.g. る → れ, or す → せ, and then adding ば:

dictionary form	meaning	change in final kana	～ば form
はなす・話す	to talk	す → せ＋ば	はなせば
まつ・待つ	to wait	つ → て＋ば	まてば

The ～ば conditional

The use of ～ば is dealt with more fully in the section on conjunctive particles (*p. 129*).

The potential form

Potential verbs show that someone can do something or that something is possible.

Making the potential form of ごだん verbs

The potential form of ごだん verbs is made by changing the last kana of the dictionary form from the う line to the え line of the kana chart and adding る:

dictionary form	meaning	change in final kana	potential form
かう・買う	to buy	う → え	かえる
いく・行く	to go	く → け	いける
よむ・読む	to read	む → め	よめる
とる・取る	to take	る → れ	とれる

Making the potential form of いちだん verbs

The potential form of いちだん verbs is made by removing the last kana of the dictionary form, and adding 〜られる. In spoken Japanese, 〜られる is often contracted to 〜れる:

dictionary form	meaning	final kana dropped	potential form
たべる・食べる	to eat	たべ〜	たべられる
かりる・借りる	to lend	かり〜	かりられる

Conjugation of potential verbs

A verb in the potential form becomes a new verb in its own right, with 〜ない, 〜た, 〜ます, conditional, and 〜て forms, etc. Potential verbs conjugate regularly as いちだん verbs. The chart below shows some of the possible variations in the potential verb かえる・買える 'to be able to buy', which has been formed from the verb かう・買う 'to buy':

form	Example	meaning
negative	かえない	can't buy
〜ます	かえます	can buy
past	かえた	could buy
past negative	かえなかった	couldn't buy
〜て	かえて	could buy, and . . .

The potential forms of する and くる

The potential of する is できる. The potential of くる is こられる (often contracted to これる in spoken Japanese). できる can be used with certain nouns, such as the names of languages, sports, musical instruments, etc., to indicate ability:

- ピアノができます
  Piano ga **dekimasu**   I **can play** the piano

- カーカムさんは日本語ができる
  Kākamu san wa Nihongo ga **dekiru**
  Mr Kirkham **can speak** Japanese

Verbs that do not have potential forms

The following verbs are not generally used in the potential form:

わかる・分かる	to understand
しる・知る	to know
ある	to exist, to have, to be
いる・要る	to be necessary
いる・(居る)	to exist, to be

Intransitive verbs describing states, such as those listed in the chart of transitive and intransitive verbs (*see pp. 87–91*), are not generally used in the potential form.

Uses of the potential form

Potential verbs show that a person etc. can do something, or that something is possible:

- 香港でコンピュータが安く買えます
  Honkon de konpyūta ga yasuku **kaemasu**
  Computers **can be bought** cheaply in Hong Kong

- 自分の名前を片仮名で書けめますか
  Jibun no namae o katakana de **kakemasu ka**
  Can you write your name in katakana?

The negative of a potential verb shows that someone can't do something, or that something is not possible:

- おばあさんは病気で来られない
  Obāsan wa byōki de **korarenai**
  Grandma **can't come** because she's ill

- いいえ、漢字が読めないんですよ
  Iie, kanji ga **yomenai** n desu yo   No, I **can't read** kanji
- それは信じられない
  Sore wa **shinjirarenai**   That's unbelievable/I **can't believe** it!

Although a direct object is usually indicated by the particle を, with potential verbs the particle が is generally used (see **particles**). Compare the following sentences:

- ジョナサンは納豆が食べられますか
  Jonasan wa **nattō ga** taberaremasu ka
  Can you eat **natto** (fermented beans), Jonathan?
- 毎朝和食を食べます
  Maiasa **washoku o** tabemasu
  I eat **Japanese food** every morning

The potential of みる・見る and きく・聞く・聴く

The potential forms of みる and きく are みられる and きける. These forms imply that an effort needs to be made to see or hear something:

- ロンドンで日本の映画も見られます
  Rondon de Nihon no eiga mo **miraremasu**
  In London, you **can** even **see** Japanese films
- 日本にいても BBC ニュースが聞ける
  Nihon ni ite mo bii bii shii nyūsu ga **kikeru**
  Even (if you are) in Japan you **can hear** the BBC news

みられる is used to talk about the occurrence of phenomena or circumstances:

- 「さけ・鮭」という言葉はアイヌ語からきたと見られる
  'Sake' to iu kotoba wa Ainugo kara kita to **mirareru**
  The word 'sake' (= 'salmon') **is seen** as having come from the Ainu language

The form 〜とみられている indicates a provisional judgement:

- 火事の原因はたばこの吸殻だと見られている
  Kaji no genin wa tabako no suigara da to **mirarete iru**
  A cigarette end **seems to have been** the cause of the fire

The intransitive verbs みえる 'be visible' and きこえる 'be audible' suggest that something can be seen or heard without any effort, or that this is inevitable in a certain situation (*see pp. 87–91*):

- 皆さん、黒板の字が見えますか
  Minasan, kokuban no ji ga **miemasu ka**
  Can everyone **see** the writing on the blackboard?

- もうちょっと大きい声で話してください。よく聞こえません
  Mō chotto ōkii koe de hanashite kudasai. Yoku **kikoemasen**
  Please speak more loudly. I **can't hear** you very well

- もうちょっと近づくと聞こえるはずだ
  Mō chotto chikazuku to **kikoeru** hazu da
  If we go a bit closer, we should **be able to hear**

There is also a way of expressing possibility with ことができる following the dictionary form of a verb. For more on this, see the section on こと (*see p. 126 and p. 206*).

The passive form

In a sentence with an active verb, the subject performs an action, but when the verb is passive, the subject of the sentence has some kind of action performed on it.

active verb: The dog **ate** the sausage.
passive verb: The sausage **was eaten** by the dog.

Making the passive form

The passive is formed with the auxiliary（ら）れる. All ごだん verbs change the final kana of the dictionary form to the あ line, and then add れる. (Verbs ending in う change it to わ and add れる.) いちだん verbs drop the final る and then add られる:

dictionary form	meaning	change in final kana	passive form
ごだん verbs			
とる・取る	to take	る → ら	とられる
いう・言う	to say	う → わ	いわれる
かく・書く	to write	く → か	かかれる
いちだん verbs			
たべる・食べる	to eat	る → ら	たべられる
しる・知る	to know	る → ら	しられる

The passive of する is される, and the passive of くる is こられる.

Uses of the passive form

The passive can be a counterpart of an active sentence, and therefore similar to the English active and passive sentences below:

- **安部さんは山田さんをぶちました**
  Abe san wa Yamada san o **buchimashita**
  Mr Abe **hit** Mr Yamada!

- **山田さんは安部さんにぶたれました**
  Yamada san wa Abe san ni **butaremashita**
  Mr Yamada **was hit** by Mr Abe!

In the active sentence, Mr Yamada is the direct object, marked with を, but becomes the subject, marked by は, in the passive sentence. Mr Abe is the subject, marked with は, in the active sentence, but becomes the agent in the passive sentence, marked with に.

The agent does not need to be mentioned if it is not important:

- **東大寺は７５１年に建てられた**
  Tōdai-ji wa nana-hyaku go-jū-ichi-nen ni **taterareta**
  Todai Temple **was built** in 751AD

Where the agent is shown in passive sentences, it can be marked with either に or によって without a significant difference in meaning, although the latter is more formal. If a passive is used to say who wrote books, films, music, etc., then によって is required, although the passive is not used in this way as much as it is in English:

- このすばらしいセレナーデはモーツァルトによって作曲された
  Kono subarashii serenāde wa **Mōtsuaruto ni yotte** sakkyoku sareta
  This wonderful serenade was composed **by Mozart**

The particle から can also be used as an equivalent of 'by' when an item, request, etc. comes from the agent:

- 警察から捜査の協力をたのまれた
  Keisatsu kara sōsa no kyōryoku o tanomareta
  My cooperation in the investigation was requested **by the police**

Things made of/from . . .

The passive is not generally used to describe what things are made from. Instead, the particle で is used where the material does not change in form, but where the material does change in form, either から or で can be used. Notice that the choice of kanji for the verb つくる in the following examples reflects this:

- 尺八は竹で作る
  Shakuhachi wa **take de** tsukuru
  Shakuhachi (Japanese flutes) are made **of wood**

- 酒は米から造る
  Sake wa **kome kara** tsukuru   Sake is made **from rice**

The indirect passive

The passive in Japanese can be used to suggest that something is perceived negatively, a use that has no real equivalent in English. This indirect passive use is sometimes called the 'adversative' or 'suffering' passive. The direct object of the active sentence is not converted into a subject, but retains the particle を and is used with a passive verb. The agent is marked with the particle に:

- スリに財布を盗まれました
  Suri ni saifu o nusumaremashita
  My wallet was stolen by a pickpocket

* **子供にコンピューターを壊された**
  Kodomo ni konpyūtā o kowasareta
  The children broke my computer

The agent can sometimes be omitted if the context makes it clear. In the following example, it is not stated exactly who trod on my feet, although it was clearly fellow passengers:

* **僕は電車で三回も足を踏まれた**
  Boku wa densha de san-kai mo ashi o fumareta
  When I was on the train, my feet were trodden on three times!

The negative perception of an event expressed with an indirect passive is sometimes clear from the use of expressions such as たいへん 'it's terrible', or こまった 'I'm troubled':

* **母に入院されて困った**
  Haha ni nyūin sarete komatta
  It was awful when my mother went into hospital

In many cases, the reason for the negative nuance can be deduced easily from the circumstances:

* **こんな忙しいのに部下に休まれた**
  Konna isogashii no ni buka ni yasumareta
  Although we're so busy, my staff took time off (and so I had more work!)

* **雨に降られた**
  Ame ni furareta   *I got wet in the rain!*

* **彼女とキスしているところをおふくろに見られたよ**
  Kanojo to kisu shite iru tokoro o ofukuro ni mirareta yo
  I was kissing my girlfriend and my mum saw us!

In the following example, the English is close to the feel of the Japanese passive:

* **3年前に妻に逃げられた**
  San-nen mae ni tsuma ni nigerareta
  My wife ran out on me three years ago!

The passive is also used to express respect (*see p. 213*).

The causative form

The causative form indicates permission or compulsion. The name 'causative' comes from the fact that someone or something 'causes' something to be done, and verbs in this form are sometimes translated as 'make (someone) do (something)' or 'get (someone) to do (something)'. It is made by adding the auxiliary （さ）せる to a verb stem.

Making the causative form of ごだん verbs

For ごだん verbs, the final kana of the dictionary form changes to the あ line, and せる is added:

dictionary form	meaning	change in final kana	causative form
あう・会う	to meet	う → わ	あわせる
いく・行く	to go	く → か	いかせる
はなす・話す	to speak	す → さ	はなさせる

Making the causative form of いちだん verbs

For いちだん verbs, the final る of the dictionary form is replaced by させる:

dictionary form	meaning	remove last kana	causative form
たべる・食べる	to eat	たべ〜	たべさせる
みる・見る	to see, to watch	み〜	みさせる
かりる・借りる	to borrow	かり〜	かりさせる

Making the causative form of する and くる

The causative of する is させる. The causative of くる is こさせる.

Conjugation of the causative form

A verb in the causative form becomes a new verb in its own right, with 〜ない, 〜た, 〜ます, conditional, and 〜て forms, etc.

These causative verbs conjugate regularly as いちだん verbs. This is illustrated in the following chart with いく 'to go' and たべる 'to eat' as examples:

	dictionary form	*negative*	～ます *form*	～た *form*	*past negative*	～て *form*
ごだん verbs	～せる	～せ ない	～ (ます)	～せた	～せな かった	～せて
example	いかせる	いかせ ない	いかせ ます	いか せた	いかせな かった	いか せて
いちだん verbs	～させる	～させ ない	～させ (ます)	～さ せた	～させな かった	～さ せて
example	たべさ せる	たべさ せない	たべさ せます	たべさ せた	たべさせ なかった	たべさ せて

Uses of the causative form

The use of the causative to show compulsion relates to the relative status of the people involved. Generally it is used by older people about those who are younger, and by people in senior positions about their juniors:

- 子供をお使いに行かせました

  Kodomo o o-tsukai ni **ikasemashita**

  I **made** the kids **go** on an errand

- たくさんミスがあって済みませんでした。以後部下に慎重にチェックをさせます

  Takusan misu ga atte sumimasen deshita. Igo buka ni shinchō ni **chekku sasemasu**

  I am sorry about all the errors. I **will get** (my) staff **to check** carefully from now on

In the following example, the relationship is general rather than personal:

- 国がどういう政策で新卒業生を就職させるのでしょうか

  Kuni ga dō iu seisaku de shin-sotsugyōsei o **shūshoku saseru** no deshō ka

  What kind of policies should the state use to **get** new graduates **into employment**?

In some circumstances it is better to avoid the causative because of its connotations of relative status or authority. The 〜て form with a verb of giving or receiving is often more appropriate:

- 彼女に手紙の日本語を見てもらう
  Kanojo ni tegami no Nihongo o **mite morau**
  I **will get** my girlfriend **to check** the Japanese in the letter

Permission with the causative

Although the basic meaning is 'make (someone) do (something)', the causative can also express the granting of permission:

- 皿洗いは僕にさせてください
  Sara arai wa boku ni **sasete kudasai**
  Let me do the washing up

- 子供にハリー・ポッターを読ませた
  Kodomo ni Harii Pottā o **yomaseta**
  I **made/let** my kids **read** the 'Harry Potter' novel

- 父はパーティに行かせてくれなかった
  Chichi wa pātii ni **ikasete kurenakatta**
  Dad **didn't let** me **go** to the party

Sometimes the use of words and phrases such as むりやり 'against someone's will', or すきなだけ 'as much as one likes', can clarify whether a causative implies compulsion or permission:

- 子供に無理やり食べさせた
  Kodomo ni **muriyari tabesaseta**   I **forced** the children **to eat**

- 子供に好きなだけ食べさせた
  Kodomo ni **suki na dake tabesaseta**
  I **let** the children **eat** as much as they wanted

Use of particles with causative verbs

In sentences with a transitive verb, the particle に is used to mark the person being made to do something:

- 子供にピアノの練習をさせる
  Kodomo ni piano no renshū o saseru
  I will make **the children** do (their) piano practice

A direct object (marked with を) may not be present, but simply implied:

- **ゴミを捨てた人々に（散らばっている紙を）拾わせる**
  Gomi o suteta hitobito ni (**chirabatte iru kami o**) hirowaseru
  I will make the people who dropped the litter clean it (**the scattered paper**) up

With intransitive verbs, the person being made to do something can be marked with を or に:

- **父は僕に犬を散歩させた**
  Chichi wa **boku ni** inu o sanpo saseta
  Dad got **me** to walk the dog

- **部長は鈴木君を会議に行かせた**
  Buchō wa **Suzuki kun o** kaigi ni ikaseta
  The senior manager got **Suzuki** to go to the meeting

If に is used, the action taken by the person affected must be something that they themselves intended, e.g. 'I' intended to take the dog for a walk anyway, but Suzuki probably didn't intend to go to the meeting.

If there is a direct object with を in the same clause, the person affected must be marked by に:

- **先生が学生に「サラダ記念日」を読ませた**
  Sensei ga **gakusei ni** 'Sarada Kinenbi' o yomaseta
  The teacher made **the students** read 'Salad Anniversary'

Causative + いただく

The ～て form of a causative verb followed by the verb いただく 'to receive (a favour)' is commonly used as a polite request for permission. The form ～いただけませんか is used to seek permission directly, and ～いただきたい（んです）is for more indirect use:

- **来週の金曜日休ませていただけませんか**
  Raishū no kinyōbi **yasumasete itadakemasen ka**
  Could you allow me to have next Friday as a holiday?

- 英語圏のお客様が多いので英語で話させていただきたい
  Eigoken no o-kyakusama ga ōi node Eigo de **hanasasete
  itadakitai**
  As there are many guests from the English-speaking world,
  I **would like to address you** in English

〜す as an alternative to 〜せる

There is another pattern for forming a causative which may be
encountered, using 〜さす instead of させる for いちだん verbs
and する, and changing the last kana of the dictionary
form to the あ line and adding す for ごだん verbs:

- 6時までにこどもを食べさしてください
  Roku-ji made ni kodomo o **tabesashite kudasai**
  Please get the children **to eat** by six o'clock
- 息子を大学に行かすつもりだ
  Musuko o daigaku ni **ikasu** tsumori da
  I intend to **have** my daughter **go** to university

The causative-passive form

The causative-passive shows that someone or something was
made to do something, and can suggest that this is or was
disagreeable (*see pp. 72–73*). It can often be translated as
'be made to . . .'

Making the causative-passive form

The causative-passive is formed by the addition of the passive
auxiliary （ら）れる to the conjunctive (pre-ます) stem of a
causative verb:

dictionary form	causative	conjunctive (pre-ます) stem of causative	causative-passive
いく・行く	いかせる	いかせ	いかせられる
たべる・食べる	たべさせる	たべさせ	たべさせられる

Conjugation of causative-passives

The conjugation of the causative-passive is shown in the chart below, using いく 'to go' and たべる 'to eat' as examples (some forms may be relatively uncommon):

	dictionary form	negative	～ます form	～た form	past negative	～て form
いちだん verbs	～せ られる	～せら れない	～せられ (ます)	～せら れた	～せられな かった	～せら れて
example	いかせ られる	いかせら れない	いかせ られます	いかせ られた	いかせられ なかった	いかせら れて
ごだん verbs	～させ られる	～させら れない	～させられ (ます)	～させ られた	～させられ なかった	～させ られて
example	たべさせ られる	たべさせ られない	たべさせら れます	たべき せられた	たべさせら れなかった	たべさ せられて

The causative-passive of する is させられる. The causative-passive of くる is こらせられる.

Uses of the causative-passive

The causative-passive is used to show that someone is made to do something. The unpleasant nature of being made to do things is usually evident:

- 子供のとき、いつも帰ったらすぐ宿題をさせられた
  Kodomo no toki itsumo kaettara sugu shukudai o **saserareta**
  When I was a child, I **was** always **made to do** my homework as soon as I got home

- 私は2時間も待たせられた
  Watashi wa ni-jikan mo **mataserareta**
  I was **made to wait** for two full hours!

- 母に部屋を片付けさせられる
  Haha ni heya o **katazukesaserareru**
  I will **be made to clean** my room by my mother

- 僕は貧血気味だったので毎日母にほうれん草を食べさせられた

  Boku ha hinketsugimi datta node mainichi haha ni hōrensō o **tabesaserareta**

  I was slightly anaemic, so my mother **made me eat** spinach every day

The causative-passive is not used if the speaker feels there is some benefit in being made to do something. (In the example above, the speaker's dislike of spinach is more significant than its benefit.) In such a case, a verb of receiving is added to the 〜て form of the causative verb (*see pp. 47–49*):

- 病院で看護婦の清水さんに歩かせてもらった

  Byōin de kangofu no Shimizu san ni **arukasete moratta**

  At the hospital, nurse Shimizu **got me to walk**

The volitional form

The volitional form is primarily used to propose an action, or to suggest doing something together with one or more others, and in this sense it is often translated as 'Let's . . .' It is also used in situations relating to decisions.

Making the volitional form of ごだん verbs

The volitional form of ごだん verbs is made by changing the last kana of the dictionary form to the お line of the kana chart, and adding う:

dictionary form	meaning	change in final kana			volitional form
いう・言う	to say	う	→ お	＋ う	いおう
いく・行く	to go	く	→ こ	＋ う	いこう
はなす・話す	to speak	す	→ そ	＋ う	はなそう
まつ・待つ	to wait	つ	→ と	＋ う	まとう
よむ・読む	to read	む	→ も	＋ う	よもう
とる・取る	to take	る	→ ろ	＋ う	とろう

Making the volitional form of いちだん verbs

The volitional form of いちだん verbs is made by removing the last
kana of the dictionary form and adding よう:

dictionary form	meaning	final kana dropped	volitional form
たべる・食べる	to eat	たべ〜	たべよう
ねる・寝る	to go to bed, to sleep	ね〜	ねよう
おきる・起きる	to get up	おき〜	おきよう
みる・見る	to see, to watch	み〜	みよう

Making the volitional form of する and くる

The volitional of する is しよう. The volitional of くる is こよう.

Uses of the volitional form

The volitional form shows the speaker's proposed intention:

- 駅前に喫茶店がある。あそこで会おう
  Ekimae ni kissaten ga aru. Asoko de **aō**
  There's a coffee shop in front of the station. **Let's meet** there

- もう行こう
  Mō iko   Let's go

The addition of the particle か can add to the nuance of suggestion:

- もう行こうか
  Mō ikō ka   Shall we go?

This can sometimes be an offer of help (see pp. 47–49):

- 読んであげようか
  Yonde **ageyō** ka   Shall I read it **to you**?

The polite-style equivalent of the volitional is 〜ましょう, and
this is very common, especially for offers (see the section on the
〜ます form above):

- じゃ、なんについて話しましょうか
  Ja nan ni tsuite **hanashimashō ka**
  Well, what **shall we talk** about?

- では頂きましょうか
  Dewa **itadakimashō ka**   Right, **shall we** (start to) **eat**?

The volitional is often used with 〜と　おもう・と思う, literally
'I think I'll . . .'. It can sometimes be translated into English as
'have decided':

- 来年の夏日本へ行こうと思います
  Rainen no natsu Nihon e **ikō to omoimasu**
  I **have decided to go** to Japan next year

- 今年一生懸命勉強しようと思っている
  Kotoshi isshōkenmei **benkyō shiyō to omotte iru**
  I'**ve decided to study** hard this year

- フランスへ行こうと思っていたけど結局どこへも行かな
  かった
  Furansu e **ikō to omotte ita** kedo kekkyoku doko e mo ikanakatta
  I **had/intended to go** to France, but in the end I didn't go
  anywhere

When the intention of the speaker is less fixed, the particle か can
be used before とおもう:

- 来年の夏日本へ行こうかと思います
  Rainen no natsu Nihon e **ikō ka to omoimasu**
  I **am wondering whether to go** to Japan next summer

The volitional form can be used with the question particle か,
or just marked with rising intonation, when seeking agreement
(*see p. 33*):

- １２時過ぎだ。もう寝ようか
  Jūni-ji sugi da. Mō neyō ka   It's after 12. Shall we go to bed?

- １２時過ぎだよ。もう寝よう
  Jūni-ji sugi da yo. Mō neyō   It's after 12. Let's go to bed!

When used with 〜とする, the volitional form shows that an
unsuccessful attempt was made, or that something happened just
as the attempt was being made:

- 読もうとしたが難しすぎて読めなかった
  Yomō to shita ga muzukashisugite yomenakatta
  I **tried to read** it but it was too difficult (= I couldn't)

- 彼女にキスしようとすると兄が部屋に入ってきた
  Kanojo ni **kisu shiyō to suru** to ani ga heya ni haitte kita
  I **was just about to kiss** her when my brother came into the room

The imperative and negative imperative

Imperatives are forms used for giving commands.

Making the imperative form of ごだん verbs

The imperative of ごだん verbs is formed by changing the final kana of the dictionary form to the え line of the kana chart:

dictionary form	meaning	change in final kana	imperative form
いう・言う	to say	う → え	いえ
いく・行く	to go	く → け	いけ
はなす・話す	to speak	す → せ	はなせ
まつ・待つ	to wait	つ → て	まて
よむ・読む	to read	む → め	よめ
とる・取る	to take	る → れ	とれ

Making the imperative form of いちだん verbs

The imperative of いちだん verbs is formed by changing the final る to ろ:

dictionary form	meaning	Imperative form
たべる・食べる	to eat	たべろ
ねる・寝る	to go to bed, to sleep	ねろ
おきる・起きる	to get up	おきろ
みる・見る	to see, to watch	みろ

Making the imperative form of する and くる

The imperative of する is either しろ or the less common せよ.
The imperative of くる is こい.

Making the negative imperative

The negative imperative is formed in the same way for all verbs: the dictionary form is followed by な. (Note that there is also a structure using the pre- ます form + な which is used for requests and commands. *See p. 37.*)

dictionary form	meaning	negative imperative form
たべる・食べる	to eat	たべろな
はなす・話す	to speak	はなすな

Uses of the imperative and negative imperative

The imperative can sound very rough and angry, so requests and instructions are normally given using other forms, such as 〜て + ください (see above). The imperative is restricted to giving orders in urgent situations, or where there is a clear hierarchy, e.g. when a parent speaks to a child:

* 早く起きろ
  Hayaku **okiro**   Hurry up and **get up**!

* こっち（へ）こい
  Kotchi (e) **koi**   **Come** here!

The imperative of がんばる 'to do one's best' is often used to shout encouragement, e.g. to a team at sports matches:

* 頑張れ
  Gambare   Go for it!

The negative imperative is used for urgent instructions and exhortations on signs and posters:

* 触るな。危ない
  Sawaru na. Abunai   **Don't touch**! Danger

* 焦るな。安全運転のルールを守れ
  Aseru na! Anzen unten no rūru o mamore
  Don't hurry. Drive according to the safety rules!

There are other, less abrupt-sounding structures, such as the pre-ます form + なさい , which are used for giving orders in most situations (*see p. 37*).

Compound verbs

A number of Japanese verbs are made up of elements from two verbs. The first is usually the conjunctive (pre-ます) stem. Some examples are given below:

盛る　＋　上がる　＝　盛り上がる
moru　+　agaru　=　moriagaru
to pile up　to go up　to swell up, to rise

働く　＋　過ぎる　＝　働きすぎる
hataraku　+　sugiru　=　hatarakisugiru
to work　to be excessive　to overwork

取る　＋　消す　＝　取り消す
toru　+　kesu　=　torikesu
to take　to extinguish　to cancel

There are a number of verbs that can regularly be added to conjunctive forms to give new compound verbs. Verbs showing movement in particular directions ('upwards', 'downwards', 'inwards', etc.) are very common:

とりあげる・取り上げる	to accept (a plan, etc.)
ひきおろす・引き下ろす	to pull downwards/to unseat
かきいれる・書き入れる	to fill in (a form, etc.)

The following list shows some of the elements most commonly used in compounds, some of which have several meanings:

ending	meaning	example	meaning of example
〜あう・ 〜合う	to be in accord with	はなしあう・ 話し合う	to speak together
おわる・ 終る	to finish	よみおわる・ 読み終わる	to finish reading
かえす・ 返す	to return (something)	くりかえす・ 繰り返す	to repeat
かえる・ 換える	to change	いいかえる・ 言いかえる	to rephrase
かかる	(several meanings)	よりかかる・ 寄りかかる	to lean on, to be supported
かける	(several meanings)	はなしかける・ 話しかける	to speak to, to call out to
きれる・ 切る	to be cut	たべきれない・ 食べきれない	to be unable to eat completely
こむ・混む	to crowd in	はいりこむ・ 入りこむ	to enter
すぎる・ 過ぎる	to exceed	たべすぎる・ 食べすぎる	to eat too much
そこなう・ 損なう	to fail	のりそこなう・ 乗りそこなう	to miss (a train or bus)
だす・出す	to start	あめが ふりだした・ 雨が降り出した	it started to rain
つける・ 付ける	to attach	とりつける・ 取り付ける	to attach
つづける・ 続ける	to continue	はなしつづける・ 話しつづける	to keep on speaking
なおす・ 直す	to repair, to mend	やりなおす	to redo
なれる・ (馴れる)	to be used to	ききなれる・ 聞きなれる	to be used to hearing
はじめる・ 始める	to start	たべはじめる・ 食べはじめる	to start to eat

ending	meaning	example	meaning of example
まわる・回る	to rotate	あるきまわる・歩き回る	to walk around
もどす・戻す	to return (something)	とりもどす・取り戻す	to put back
わすれる・忘れる	to forget	ききわすれる・きき忘れる	to forget to ask

Transitive and intransitive verbs

A transitive verb is one which has a direct object ('I finished the book'), while an intransitive verb does not have a direct object ('The lecture finished').

The English verb 'to open' can be used both transitively and intransitively in the same form, but Japanese requires the transitive verb あける (開ける) for the first example below and the intransitive verb あく (開く) for the second. Notice that the direct object of the transitive verb is marked with the particle を, while the intransitive verb has a subject marked with the particle が (*see pp. 154–156*):

- 窓を開けました
  Mado o **akemashita**   I **opened** the window

- ドアがゆっくりと開きました
  Doa ga yukkuri to **akimashita**   The door **opened** slowly

The situation is similar with 'to begin':

- 食事を始めましょう
  Shokuji o **hajimemashō**   Let's **begin** the meal

- 映画が8時に始まります
  Eiga ga hachi-ji ni **hajimarimasu**   The film **begins** at 8 o'clock

Both transitive and intransitive verbs can sometimes appear without the particles を or が where context makes the meaning clear. They may also have the particles は or も which suppress を or が (see **particles**):

- 皆さんおそろいのようですのでそろそろ始めましょうか
  Mina san osoroi no yō desu no de sorosoro hajimemashō ka
  It looks like we are all here, so shall (we) begin?

- 私は外国の切手も集めています
  Watashi wa gaikoku no **kitte mo** atsumete imasu
  I collect foreign **stamps as well**

- 心臓は止まっているが、細胞はまだ生きている
  Shinzō wa tomatte iru ga, **saibō wa** mada ikite iru
  The heart has stopped, but **the cells** are still alive

- セール前だから値段はまだ下がらないよ
  Sēru mae dakara **nedan wa** mada sagaranai yo
  It's before the sales, so **the prices** won't drop yet

Common transitive and intransitive verb pairs

Some of the most common pairs of transitive and intransitive verbs are given in the chart below:

transitive	English equivalent	intransitive	English equivalent
あける・開ける	to open	あく・開く	to open
あげる・上げる	to raise	あがる・上がる	to rise
あつめる・集める	to collect	あつまる・集まる	to collect, to gather
いれる・入れる	to put in	はいる・入る	to enter, to come in
うる・売る	to sell	うれる・売れる	to be sold
おこす・起こす	to wake (someone) up	おきる・起きる	to wake up
おとす・落とす	to drop	おちる・落ちる	to drop, to fall
おろす	to let (someone) out, to drop off (transport)	おりる	to get off (transport)

transitive	English equivalent	intransitive	English equivalent
おる・折る	to break, to snap	おれる・折れる	to break, to snap
かえる・変える・代える・換える・替える	to change	かわる・変わる・代わる・換わる・替わる	to change
かける	to phone, to hang (something) up	かかる	to be phoned, to be hung up
かたづける・(片付ける)	to tidy up	かたづく	to be tidied up
きく・聞く	to listen to	きこえる・聞こえる	to hear
きる・切る	to cut	きれる・切れる	to be cut
こぼす	to spill	こぼれる	to be spilt
こわす・壊す	to break	こわれる・壊れる	to break
さげる・下げる	to lower to clear (the table), to withdraw (money)	さがる・下がる	to come down, to step back
する	to do, to make	なる	to become, to happen
そだてる・育てる	to bring up	そだつ・育つ	to be brought up
だす・出す	to take out (and other meanings)	でる・出る	to go out (and other meanings)
たすける・助ける	to help, to save	たすかる・助かる	to be helped, to be saved
ちかづける・近づける	to bring/draw (something) close	ちかづく・近づく	to approach

transitive	English equivalent	intransitive	English equivalent
つける・付ける つける・点ける	to attach, to light	つく・付く つく・点く	to be attached, to be lit
つづける 続ける	to continue	つづく・続く	to continue
とどける・届ける	to deliver	とどく・届く	to be delivered, to arrive
とめる・止める	to stop	とまる・止まる	to stop
ながす・流す	to flush	ながれる・流れる	to flow
のこす・残す	to leave	のこる・残る	to remain
のせる・乗せる	to give (someone) a ride	のる・乗る	to ride in/on
はじめる・始める	to start	はじまる・始まる	to start
ぶつける	to hit (accidentally)	ぶつかる	to be hit (accidentally)
ふやす・増やす	to increase	ふえる・増える	to increase
へらす・減らす	to decrease	へる・減る	to decrease
みつける・見つける	to find, to discover	みつかる・見つかる	to be found, to be discovered
みる・見る	to watch	みえる・見える	to be visible, to seem
わかす・沸かす	to boil (water)	わく・沸く	to boil
わる・割る	to break, to crack	われる・割れる	to break, to crack

- 探していたものがようやく見つかった
  Sagashite ita mono ga yōyaku **mitsukatta**
  The thing I was looking for has finally **turned up**

- この猫を見つけた人はすぐに電話をください
  Kono neko o **mitsuketa** hito wa sugu ni denwa o kudasai
  Whoever **finds** this kitten should telephone us straight away

- 果てしなく森が続く
  Hateshinaku mori ga **tsuzuku**
  The forest **continued** endlessly

- 今年もテニスのレッスンを続けます
  Kotoshi mo tenisu no resson o **tsuzukemasu**
  I will **continue** tennis lessons this year

Meanings and uses of する

The meaning of the verb する is often given as 'to do', but English translations of sentences with する can vary widely. The basic meaning is that something, or someone, causes a state or an action to occur.

Noun + する

A large number of nouns referring to actions, such as サッカー 'soccer', ジョギング 'jogging', べんきょう 'study', and でんわ 'telephone', can be made into verbs by the addition of する. Many of the verbs so derived use the particle を to mark the noun as the direct object:

- 学校が終ったら僕と聡はサッカーをする
  Gakkō ga owattara boku to Satoshi wa **sakkō o suru**
  Satoshi and I **play soccer** after school

- 毎朝ジョギングを　します
  Maiasa **jogingu o shimasu**   I **will jog** every morning

- 清君は宿題をしています
  Kiyoshi kun wa **shukudai o shite imasu**
  Kiyoshi **is doing his homework**

However, in some cases the verb does not have a direct object marked with を, and can appear as a single unit of noun + する:

- ６時にピーターに電話しました
  Roku-ji ni Piitā ni **denwa shimashita**
  At 6 o'clock I **called** Peter

- ３時間以上運転するといつも疲れてしまいます
  San-jikan ijō **unten suru** to itsumo tsukarete shimaimasu
  I always get tired if I **drive** for more than three hours

If there is some modifying element in front of the noun, then を must be used (*see p. 206*):

- 試験の勉強をする
  shiken no benkyō o suru
  study for an exam (= do some **study for an exam**)

- ご飯の準備をする
  gohan no junbi o suru
  prepare a meal (= do some **preparation for a meal**)

Certain verbs such as あいする・愛する 'to love', せっとくする・説得する 'to persuade', and りかいする・理解する 'to understand' are never used with を between the noun and する. For more on uses of the particle を, see the relevant section in the chapter on particles (*p. 149*).

Adjective + する

する is often used to mean 'to make' with adjectives. The adjectives are in the adverbial forms (*see pp. 106–107 and 119–120*), with い adjectives ending in 〜く and な adjectives followed by に:

- 部屋をきれいにした
  Heya wo **kirei ni shita**
  I **made** the room **tidy**/I **tidied** the room

- テストをもっと難しくしましょう
  Tesuto wo motto **muzukashiku shimashō**
  Let's **make** the test more **difficult**!

- 部屋を暖かくした
  Heya o **atatakaku shita**
  I turned the heating up (**warmed** the room)

'To wear', 'to put on'

する is used with words for fashion accessories such as jewellery and watches to mean 'to put on', 'to wear' (note that there are other verbs which also translate as 'to wear' for use with items of clothing):

- 父は珍しくネクタイをした
  Chichi wa mezurashiku **nekutai o shita**
  Unusually, dad **wore a tie**

- 腕時計はしません
  Udedokei wa shimasen   I **don't wear** a watch

する with sound symbolism

A number of Japanese adverbs imitate sounds, or symbolize non-audible actions and states by according them particular sounds or groups of sounds. There is no real equivalent of this in English except sound imitation ('woof woof' etc.) and sound association, e.g. the 'cr-' in words like 'crisp', 'crunch', 'crack', 'creak', etc. Many of these adverbs can be used with する (see **adverbs**):

- どきどきする
  dokidoki suru   to be anxious/afraid

- ぼうっとする
  bōtto suru   to daydream

- いらいらしている
  iraira shite iru   to be irritated

'To decide'

する following に can show a decision:

- 君は何にしますか
  Kimi wa nan **ni shimasu ka**   What are you **going to order?**

- 私は天ぷら定食にします
  Watashi wa tenpura teishoku **ni shimasu**
  I'm going to have the tempura set meal

- 夏休みはフランスに行くことにしました
  Natsu-yasumi wa Furansu ni iku koto **ni shimashita**
  We decided to go to France for our summer holiday

- アルコールを飲まないことにした
  Arukōru o nomanai koto **ni shita**
  I **decided** not to drink alcohol

For more on ことにする, *see pp. 211–212.*

'To taste', 'to smell', etc.

Sensations such as taste and smell can be indicated by する:

- ガスの臭いがする
  Gasu no **nioi ga suru**   I **smell** gas

- グレープフルーツの味がした
  Gurēpufurūtsu no **aji ga shita**   It **tasted** of grapefruit

- 昨日はここにあった気がする
  Kinō wa koko ni atta **ki ga suru**
  I **have a feeling** that it was here yesterday

'To cost'

The cost of items can be expressed with する:

- のカメラは８万円する
  Kono kamera wa hachiman-en **suru**
  This camera **costs** 80,000 yen

Verbs of giving and receiving

The use of certain verbs of giving and receiving depends on who is giving and who is receiving. The basic verb for 'to give' is あげる・上げる when the speaker is giving to someone else, and くれる when someone else is giving to the speaker. The words for 'I' and '(to) me' are given in the English translations below, but equivalents are not needed in Japanese as the choice of verb shows who is giving:

- 母に本を上げます
  Haha ni hon o **agemasu**   I **will give** a book to my mother

- 母が本をくれました
  Haha ga hon o **kuremashita**   My mother **gave** me a book

The use of these verbs can be extended to refer to the in-group and out-group. For example, in the sentence below the speaker describes the event from his sister's viewpoint, with くれる (*see p. 7*):

- 田辺さんが妹に本をくれました
  Tanabe-san ga imōto ni hon o **kuremashita**
  Mrs Tanabe **gave** my sister a book

The particle marking the indirect object with あげる and くれる is に:

- この絵を鷹取さんに上げたい
  Kono e o **Takatori san ni** agetai
  I'd like to give this picture **to Ms Takatori**

The verb 'to receive' is もらう, and the indirect object can be expressed with either the particle に or the particle から (see **particles**):

- 父に鞄をもらいました
  Chichi ni kaban o moraimashita
  I received a bag **from my father**

- 誕生日に父から車をもらいました
  Tanjōbi ni **chichi kara** kuruma o moraimashita
  On my birthday I received a car **from my father**

There are other verbs for 'give' and 'receive' which are more polite or humble in style (see **keigo** *p. 213*).

The verb やる (which usually means 'to do') means 'to give' when the recipient is of lower status than the giver, e.g. human to animal, or father to child:

- 犬に餌をやった？
  Inu ni esa o **yatta**?   Have you **given** the dog his food?

- 大学入試に受かったら１０万円やるぞ
  Daigaku nyūshi ni ukattara jū-man-en **yaru** zo
  If you pass the university entrance exam, I'll **give** you 100,000 yen!

For more information of verbs of giving and receiving, *see* ~て **form + verbs of giving and receiving**, *pp. 47–49*.

Adjectives

What is an adjective?

An adjective is a word such as 'big', 'quiet', or 'easy' which adds extra information about a noun. Both Japanese and English adjectives can come before the noun ('an **honest** politician', '**heavy** books', the **black** cat'), but both can also appear at the end of a sentence or phrase, separated from the nouns they describe ('The flowers are **beautiful**.')

Types of adjective

Japanese adjectives belong to one of two groups: い adjectives and な adjectives.

い adjectives

The adjectives in this group, known as **keiyōshi** (形容詞), are often called 'い adjectives' in English as their dictionary form always ends with the hiragana い. Adjectives of this type end in **-ai**, **-ii**, **-ui**, or **-oi**. There are no い adjectives ending **-ei**.

Plain and polite styles of い adjectives

When い adjectives occur at the end of a sentence, they can be followed by です to make the style more polite, especially when there are sentence-ending particles such as よ or ね, or the sentence is joined to another by a conjunction. The final です is omitted in the plain style (see **keigo** and **style**):

にほんの　えいがは　おもしろいですね (polite style)
にほんの　えいがは　おもしろいね (plain style)
Japanese films **are interesting**, aren't they?

きのうみた　えいがは　おもしろかったです (polite style)
きのうみた　えいがは　おもしろかった (plain style)
The film I saw yesterday **was interesting**

い adjectives do not change their form or need です when used in front of a noun:

- これは新しい車です
  Kore wa **atarashii kuruma** desu   This is a **new car**

- 奥村さんは優しい人です
  Okumura san wa **yasashii hito** desu
  Ms Okumura is **a kind person**

Changes in the form of い adjectives

Like verbs, い adjectives change their endings (or 'conjugate') to indicate, for example, a negative ('not hot') or past meaning ('was hot'). The stem, or part of the word before the final い, does not change:

- イギリスの夏はそんなに暑くない
  Igirisu no natsu wa sonna ni **atsukunai**
  English summers **are not so hot.**

- 昨日は暑かった
  Kinō wa **atsukatta**   Yesterday **was hot**

The conjugation of い adjectives is shown in the table below in the plain style. For details on the use of 〜たら、〜ば、〜なくて, etc., see the appropriate sections on these forms in the chapter on verbs.

form	い adjective	meaning
dictionary form	おいしい	delicious
negative	おいしくない	not delicious
past	おいしかった	was delicious
past negative	おいしくなかった	wasn't delicious
〜くて	おいしくて	delicious and . . . (joins two or more adjectives)
〜なくて	おいしくなくて	not delicious and. . . .
〜く	おいしく	deliciously
〜たら	おいしかったら	when/if delicious
〜なかったら	おいしくなかったら	when/if not delicious
〜ば	おいしければ	if it is delicious
〜なければ	おいしくなければ	if it isn't delicious

よい as alternative form of いい

The common adjective いい 'good' has the alternative form よい, with no difference in meaning. The various forms of いい are all derived from よい, e.g. よくない, よかった, よかったら.

- 天気はよかったですか
  Tenki wa **yokatta** desu ka   *Was the weather good?*

Adjectives ending 〜て + も

This structure means 'even if it is (not) . . .':

- おいしくてもそんなにたくさん食べてはいけない
  Oishikute mo sonna ni takusan tabete wa ikenai
  Even if it's tasty, you shouldn't eat so much of it!

- 朝はそんなに暑くなくても日焼け止めを持っていこう
  Asa wa sonna ni **atsuku nakute mo** hiyakedome o motte ikō
  Even if it's not so hot in the morning, we'll take the sunscreen!

- コーヒーは暑くても冷たくてもいいです
  Kōhii wa **atsukute mo tsumetakute mo** ii desu
  I don't mind if the coffee is hot or cold

The equivalent for な adjectives is でも (see だ・です).

    For more on 〜て and 〜なくて with も and with いい, see the sections on 〜て and 〜ない（なくて）in the chapter on verbs.

い adjectives with 〜すぎる

The verb すぎる (過ぎる) 'to exceed' can be added to the stem of an い adjective to give the meaning 'too . . .':

- 寿司が食べたいけど高すぎる
  Sushi ga tabetai kedo **taka-sugiru**
  I want to eat sushi but it's too expensive

- 大きすぎるから入れない
  Ōki-sugiru kara hairenai   *It's too big so it won't go in!*

な adjectives

The second group of adjectives are the **keiyōdōshi** (形容動詞),
commonly called 'な adjectives' in English as they need the
addition of a final な when used in front of the nouns they describe.
They are often listed in glossaries and vocabularies
with な in brackets, e.g.:

しんせつ（な）	kind
しずか（な）	quiet

When な adjectives occur at the end of a sentence they do not
need な, but they do need だ・です to complete the sentence
(see だ・です). Compare the following pairs of sentences:

- ショウ先生は親切です
  Shō sensei wa **shinsetsu desu**   Shaw sensei is kind

- ショウ先生は親切な人です
  Shō sensei wa **shinsetsu-na hito desu**
  Shaw sensei is a kind person

- 街が静かでした
  Machi wa **shizuka deshita**   The town was quiet

- 静かな街を歩くのが好きです
  Shizuka-na machi o aruku no ga suki desu
  I like walking the quiet (streets of the) town

Changes in だ・です with な adjectives

Unlike い adjectives, な adjectives do not change their form to
show past tense, negative meaning, etc. Instead it is the following
auxiliary だ・です which conjugates (see p. 15 and p. 181):

form	な adjective	meaning
predicative (used after noun)	しずか（だ）	quiet
attributive (used in front of noun)	しずかな	quiet
negative	しずかじゃない	not quiet
past	しずかだった	was quiet

form	な adjective	meaning
past negative	しずかじゃなかった	wasn't quiet
〜くて	しずかで	quiet and . . . (joins two or more adjectives)
〜なくて	しずかじゃなくて	not quiet and . . .
adverbial	しずかに	quietly
〜たら	しずかだったら	when/if quiet
〜なかったら	しずかじゃなかったら	when/if not quiet
〜ば	しずかなら（ば） しずかであれば	if it is quiet
〜なければ	しずかでなければ	if it isn't quiet

Plain and polite styles of な adjectives

With な adjectives, it is the form of the following だ・です that shows the style of the sentence (*see p. 10*):

まちは　しずかです (polite style)
まちは　しずかだ (plain style)
The town **is quiet**

まちは　しずかでした (polite style)
まちは　しずかだった (plain style)
The town **was quiet**

な adjectives which end in い

There are some words which end in い even though they are な adjectives, not い adjectives. Such words all end in -ei. The most common are:

きれい（な）・奇麗（な）　　　pretty, clean, tidy
しつれい（な）・失礼（な）　　　rude
ゆうめい（な）・有名（な）　　　famous

Compare the following pair of sentences:

● 鎌倉の大仏は有名です
Kamakura no Daibutsu wa **yūmei** desu
The great Buddha at Kamakura is **famous**

- 銀座のデパートで有名な女優をみました
  Ginza no depāto de **yūmei-na joyū** o mimashita
  I saw **a famous actress** at a Ginza department store

い adjectives with alternative な forms

There are a few い adjectives which have alternative forms in
front of a noun. These forms have a final な in place of い, although
they are not な adjectives. The most common of these alternative
forms are おおきな and ちいさな:

- 大きなテレビだ
  Ōki-na terebi da   That's **a big TV**!

- 子供のとき田舎の小さな村に住んでいた
  Kodomo no toki inaka no **chiisa-na mura** ni sunde ita
  When I was a child I lived in **a small village** in the country

Using two or more adjectives together

When something is described with more than one adjective, there
are changes to the ending of the first one used. When this is an
い adjective, the い is dropped and 〜くて is added:

- このレストランは安くておいしい
  Kono resutoran wa **yasukute** oishii
  This restaurant is **cheap and** good

- 大きくて古い家
  Ōkikute furui ie   **a big**, old house

- 彼女は頭がよくて面白いひとです
  Kanojo wa atama ga **yokute** omoshiroi hito desu
  She's **a clever**, funny person

When a な adjective comes first, it is followed by で, a form of
だ・です (*see p. 15*):

- 先生は静かでやさしい
  Sensei wa **shizuka de** yasashii   The teacher **is quiet and** kind

- バーは賑やかで煙たい
  Bā wa **nigiyaka de** kemutai   The bar is **busy and** smoky

A few な adjectives which refer to types of things rather than qualities, such as さまざま 'all kinds of' and いろいろ 'various', do not make these changes in front of other adjectives:

* 様々な若い人が話し合えるチャンスです
  Samazama-na wakai hito ga hanashiaeru chansu desu
  It's a chance for **all kinds of young people** to be able to meet and chat

* 色々な珍しい食べ物を出してくれた
  Iroiro-na mezurashii tabemono o dashite kureta
  They served me **various unusual foods**

When the two adjectives are in contrast, e.g. 'expensive but inferior', 'kind but stupid', then they are not used in the way described above, but instead are joined with a conjunction such as が 'but':

* あのレストランはやすいが、全然おいしくないと思う
  Ano resutoran wa **yasui ga zenzen oishiku nai** to omou
  That restaurant is **cheap but I don't** think **the food is good**

Describing feelings

There is a group of い adjectives referring to emotions which can be used freely to express the emotions of the speaker or writer, but not the feelings of third parties. The most common members of this group of adjectives are:

うれしい・嬉しい	glad
かなしい・哀しい	sad
さびしい・寂しい	lonely
いたい・痛い	painful
こわい・怖い	frightening, frightened
おそろしい・恐ろしい	frightening
なつかしい・懐かしい	nostalgic, reminiscent of
くるしい・苦しい	painful, distressing
ほしい・欲しい	desiring, wanting

Describing the emotions of other people

Other people's emotions are often described in terms of assumptions based on hearsay, or appearance, or some

other evidence, and so are qualified with phrases such as
'She looks . . .', 'He sounds . . .', 'He said that . . .':

- 犬が死んで哀しかったでしょう
  Inu ga shinde **kanashikatta deshō**
  You **must have been very sad** when the dog died

- 松雄さんは嬉しそうだ
  Matsuo san wa **ureshi-sō da**   Matsuo **looks delighted**

- 彼女は悲しいらしい
  Kanojo wa **kanashii rashii**
  She's **apparently (extremely) sad**

Adjectives of emotion can normally be used freely in questions:

- 頭が痛いか
  Atama ga **itai** ka
  Does your head **hurt**?/Do you have a headache?

- 犬が恐いですか
  Inu ga **kowai** desu ka   Are you **frightened** of dogs?

Describing emotions with 〜がる

Other people's emotions can sometimes be described directly
if the suffix 〜がる is added to the stem of the adjective:

- かまれたら子供が犬を怖がる
  Kamaretara kodomo ga inu o **kowagaru**
  The children **will be frightened** of dogs if they get bitten

Adjectives used with 〜がる tend to be in the 〜て + いる form
when describing a current situation:

- 子供が犬を怖がっている
  Kodomo ga inu o **kowagatte iru**
  The children **are frightened** of dogs

- ジョナサンは新しいパソコンを欲しがっている
  Jonasan wa atarashii pasokon o **hoshigatte iru**
  Jonathan **wants** a new computer

The な adjective いや 'unpleasant' takes the 〜がる ending to
make the common verb いやがる 'to loathe', 'to be reluctant to':

- 田中家の息子は学校を嫌がっている
  Tanaka-ke no musuko wa gakkō o **iyagatte iru**
  The Tanakas' son **hates** school / The Tanakas' boy **is reluctant** (to go to) school

Describing emotions with the 〜た form

For events in the past, the 〜た form of an adjective of emotion is sometimes used even of third parties:

- 正義の浮気で真弓ちゃんはとても悲しかった
  Masayoshi no uwaki de Mayumi chan wa totemo **kanashikatta**
  Mayumi **was deeply saddened** by Masayoshi's infidelity

Use of ほしい

This adjective of emotion, meaning 'desiring', 'wanting', has a special use when it follows the 〜て form of a verb (*see p. 38*). In this case it means that the speaker wants someone to do (or not do) something:

- 明日またこの時間にきて欲しい
  Ashita mata kono jikan ni **kite hoshii**
  I **want you to come** again at the same time tomorrow

- 触らないで欲しい
  Sawaranaide hoshii   I **don't want you to touch it**

Comparative and superlative

Japanese adjectives do not have special forms for comparative or superlative, unlike some English adjectives ('hotter', 'deeper', 'coldest', 'highest'). Instead they add extra words.

The comparative

To say that something is, for example, 'bigger' or 'more expensive' than something else, the item to which it is compared is marked with the particle より, and the adjective itself does not change:

- 東京はロンドンより大きいです
  Tōkyō wa **Rondon yori ōkii** desu
  Tokyo is **bigger than London**

- 寿司より安いものを食べましょう
  Sushi yori yasui mono o tabemashō
  *Let's eat something **cheaper than sushi***

- 富士山よりきれいな山がない
  Fujisan yori kirei-na yama ga nai
  *There's no mountain **more beautiful than Mt Fuji***

- 日本語はドイツ語より簡単だ
  Nihongo wa **Doitsugo yori kantan** da
  *Japanese is **simpler than German***

Questions giving two choices

In questions where two choices are offered, such as 'Which is more expensive, London or Tokyo?', the choices are marked with the particle と, and the question word どちら (or どっち in informal speech) is used:

- 東京と、ロンドンと、どちらが高いですか
  Tokyo to Rondon to dochira ga takai desu ka
  Which is more expensive, Tokyo or London?

- 日本語と、スペイン語と、どっちが　おもしろい？
  Nihongo to Supeingo to dotchi ga omoshiroi?
  *Which is more interesting, **Japanese or Spanish?***

The answer is given by adding のほうが to the chosen alternative, plus the appropriate adjective:

- 東京のほうが高いです
  Tōkyō **no hō ga takai** desu   *Tokyo is **the more expensive***

- 日本語のほうがおもしろい
  Nihongo **no hō ga omoshiroi**
  *Japanese is **the more interesting** (language)*

Comparisons with くらい, ほど, and もっと

Comparisons such as 'as cold as ice' can be expressed with くらい (or ぐらい), meaning 'extent', 'level', following the noun with which is being used for comparison. In negative constructions (e.g. 'not as hot as last summer'), the particle ほど is used:

- ロンドンは東京ぐらい高い
  Rondon wa **Tōkyō gurai takai**
  *London is **as expensive as Tokyo**!*

- ロンドンの物価は東京ほど高くない
  Rondon no bukka wa **Tōkyō hodo takaku nai**
  London prices are **not as high as Tokyo (prices)**!

The adverb もっと 'more' can also be used to show comparison:

- ロンドンは高かったが、東京はもっと高いですよ
  Rondon wa takakatta ga Tōkyō wa **motto takai** desu yo
  London was expensive but Tokyo is (even) **more expensive**!

The superlative

The superlative is the form of the adjective which expresses the highest degree, such as 'biggest', 'most beautiful', 'most expensive'. The Japanese equivalent of 'most' is いちばん (一番), literally 'number one', and is placed in front of the adjective:

- 世界で一番高い車は何ですか
  Sekai de **ichi-ban takai** kuruma wa nan desu ka
  What is **the most expensive** car in the world?

- 日本の1番有名な山は富士山です
  Nihon no **ichi-ban yūmei-na** yama wa Fujisan desu
  The **most famous** mountain in Japan is Mt Fuji

Questions giving three choices

In questions where three or more choices are offered, these choices are marked with the particle と, and the question word どれ is used:

- 日本語と、スペイン語と、ロシア語と、どれが難しいですか
  Nihongo to Supeingo to Roshiago to dore ga muzukashii desu ka
  Which is most difficult, **Japanese, Russian, or Spanish?**

| Adverbial use of adjectives

Adjectives can be used in front of a verb to describe a state resulting from an action or a process. In such cases, the 〜く form of い adjectives is used, and に is added to な adjectives. This use is adverbial and is discussed in more detail in the chapter on adverbs (*see pp. 119–120*):

- 塩を入れるともっとおいしくなりますよ
  Shio o ireru to motto **oishiku narimasu** yo
  It will **taste** even **better** if you put some salt in

- 6時過ぎは急に寒くなる
  Roku-ji sugi wa kyū ni **samuku naru**
  After 6 o'clock it suddenly **gets cold**

- 事故の後は大変でしたが元気になりました
  Jiko no ato wa taihen deshita ga **genki ni narimashita**
  It was hard after the accident but **I've got better**

- この靴を履くともっときれいに見える
  Kono kutsu o haku to **motto kirei ni mieru**
  It will **look** even **prettier** if you wear these shoes (with it)

- もうちょっと大きく書いてください
  Mō chotto **ōkiku kaite** kudasai   Please **write** a little **larger**

Adjectives with irregular forms

おなじ・同じ

The な adjective おなじ, meaning 'the same', is slightly irregular.
At the end of a sentence it requires だ・です, but it does not need
な when it appears in front of a noun:

- 娘の名前が同じだ
  Musume no namae ga **onaji da**
  My daughter's name is **the same** (as yours)

- イギリスと日本はその面で同じだ
  Igirisu to Nihon wa sono men de **onaji da**
  In that respect the UK and Japan are **the same**

- 君は僕と同じ大学だ
  Kimi wa boku to **onaji daigaku** da
  You and I are at the **same university**

- 同じ人が三回も来ました
  Onaji hito ga san-kai mo kimashita
  The **same person** came three times

The form おなじく is used to combine sentences:

- 渡辺さんは佐藤さんと同じく留学生だ
  Watanabe san wa **Satō san to onajiku** ryūgakusei da
  *Watanabe is an exchange student, **the same as Sato (is)***

ちかく・近く, とおく・遠く, and おおく・多く

The three い adjectives ちかい, とおい, and おおい are not commonly used before nouns. Instead, the alternative noun forms ending in 〜く are used. The particle の is needed to join them to the following nouns:

- 近くのスーパー
  chikaku no sūpā   *a **nearby** supermarket*

- 遠くの町
  tōku no machi   *a **distant** town*

- 多くの人
  ōku no hito   ***many** people*

However, the 〜い adjective tends to be used if there is also another element included in the description:

- 家から遠いスーパーまで行かないとワインを買えないんだ
  Uchi kara tōi sūpā made ikanai to wain o kaenai n da
  *Unless we go to a supermarket **a long way from home**, we can't buy wine*

- レストランが多いところに行きましょう
  Resutoran ga ōi tokoro ni ikimashō
  *Let's go to a place **where there are lots of restaurants***

Note that when とおい 'distant' and ちかい 'close' are used to refer to time rather than physical distance, the 〜くの forms are not used:

- 遠い昔
  tōi mukashi   *a long, long time ago*

- 近い将来がんで死ぬ人が減るだろう
  Chikai shōrai gan de shinu hito ga heru darō
  *Perhaps in **the near future**, the number of people dying of cancer will decrease*

すくない・少ない and すこし・少し

The adjective すくない 'few', 'a little' cannot be used before a noun. Instead, すこし 'small amount' is used. As すこし is a noun, it needs the particle の to join it to the following noun:

- 英語がとても上手な日本人が少ない
  Eigo ga totemo jōzu-na nihonjin ga **sukunai**
  The number of Japanese people with good English **is small**

- 少しのアルコールで顔が直ぐ赤くなる
  Sukoshi no arukoru de kao ga sugu akaku naru
  My face gets red with just **a little** alcohol

Noun forms from adjectives

Some い adjectives have noun forms that are made by removing the final い and adding さ or み:

い adjective	meaning	noun	meaning
おおきい	big	おおきさ	size
おもい	heavy	おもさ	weight
あまい	sweet	あまみ	sweetness

For more information, see **nouns** p. 122.

Other types of adjectival expression

As well as い and な adjectives, there are other ways to describe the qualities and nature of things which would require an adjective in an English equivalent. These are dealt with in more detail in the section on modifiers, but examples of the two main ways are given here.

Nouns joined by the particle の

A noun or noun phrase followed by the particle の can be used to describe the noun which follows it:

- 日本の車
  Nihon no kuruma   a **Japanese** car

- 日本語の教科書
  Nihongo no kyōkasho   a **Japanese language** textbook

- 外国の選手も東京マラソンに参加しています
  Gaikoku no senshu mo Tōkyō marason ni sanka shite imasu
  Foreign athletes are taking part in the Tokyo Marathon too

Plain form of verbs

Verb expressions in plain forms such as 〜た, 〜ない, and
〜ている, etc., can describe a noun and function as modifiers
(*see p. 209*):

- 食べられない物
  taberarenai mono   **inedible** things

- 開いている窓
  aite iru mado   an **open** window

- 笑っている子供
  waratte iru kodomo   **laughing** children

- べたべたした手
  betabeta shita te   **sticky** hands

- 会議の後ジョナサンはがっかりした顔で帰ってきた
  Kaigi no ato Jonasan wa **gakkari shita kao** de kaette kita
  After the meeting Jonathan returned **looking downcast**

Adverbs

What is an adverb?

An adverb is used to give extra information about verbs, adjectives, and other adverbs. In English, adverbs often end in '-ly', e.g. 'he walked **slowly**', '**extremely** happy'. There are also other forms, e.g. 'walk **fast**', '**very** happy', '**quite** often'. For further information, see **glossary**.

Position of adverbs

Unlike English, Japanese adverbs always come before the word or phrase to which they apply:

とても　あつい	**very** hot
よく　いきます	**often** go
ゆっくり　あるきます	walk **slowly**

Types of adverb

Japanese adverbs can be subdivided into groups describing time, quantity and degree, and manner. Adverbs are also used to introduce a judgement, statement, or opinion.

Adverbs of time

Adverbs of time include such words as さいきん 'recently', あさ '(in the) morning', and よく 'often', as well as other words for time of day, the seasons, and days of the week, etc. Many of these words (including さいきん and あさ) are actually nouns used as adverbs:

- 朝6時に起きます
  Asa roku-ji ni okimasu   I get up at 6 **in the morning**

- 最近子供でさえ携帯電話を持っていますよ
  Saikin kodomo desae keitai denwa o motte imasu yo
  Recently even children have mobile phones

- 先生は東京へよくいらっしゃいますか
  Sensei wa Tōkyō e **yoku** irasshaimasu ka
  (Teacher!) Do you **often** go to Tokyo?

Use of に with adverbs of time

Clock times used adverbially require the particle に ('in', 'on', 'at'):

- 8時半に会いましょう
  Hachi-ji han ni aimashō   Let's meet **at 8:30**

The particle に can be used with adverbs which indicate fixed times, although it is often omitted:

- 木曜日（に）会議があります
  Mokuyōbi (ni) kaigi ga arimasu
  On Thursday I have a meeting

- 第2土曜日（に）行きません
  Dai-ni doyōbi (ni) ikimasen
  I don't go **on the second Saturday** (of the month)

Words of relative time (i.e. those where the time is relative to when the statement is made), such as けさ 'this morning' and きのう 'yesterday', do not generally take the particle に when they are used as adverbs:

- 来週フランスへ行きます
  Raishū Furansu e ikimasu   I'm going to France **next week**

- 昨日おばあちゃんから電話がかかってきた
  Kinō obāchan kara denwa ga kakatte kita
  Gran called me **yesterday**

- 今朝また朝寝坊をしてしまった
  Kesa mata asanebō o shite shimatta
  I overslept again **this morning**

Words with the prefix まい〜 'every' are also adverbs of relative time and so do not take に:

- 毎朝ジョギングをしている
  Maiasa joggingu o shite iru   I jog **every morning**

- 毎晩お酒を飲むのはいけないよ
  Maiban o-sake o nomu no wa ikenai yo
  You really shouldn't drink **every night**!

For more on time expressions, see **numbers, counting, time, dates**
p. 191.

Adverbs of quantity and degree

Adverbs of quantity and degree include とても 'very', すこし
'a little', and たくさん 'many', 'a lot of':

- とても難しい
  totemo muzukashii   **very** difficult

- 人がたくさんいます
  Hito ga **takusan** imasu   There are **lots of** people

- まだお寿司が少しありますよ
  Mada o-sushi ga **sukoshi** arimasu yo
  There's still **a little** sushi left

Adverbs of manner

Adverbs of manner, which show the way in which an action is
carried out, include ゆっくり 'slowly', and すっかり 'completely':

- もうちょっとゆっくり話してください
  Mō chotto **yukkuri** hanashite kudasai
  Please speak more **slowly**

- 買い物に行くのをすっかり忘れました
  Kaimono ni iku no o **sukkari** wasuremashita
  I **completely** forgot to do the shopping!

Other types of adverb

Other adverbs are used to introduce the speaker's judgement
or opinion (どうも 'somehow or other', もちろん 'of course'),
a request by the speaker (もし 'if, in that case'), or to emphasize
a request or hope (ぜひ):

- もし車で行くならあの大きいダンボルを持っていってくれませんか
  Moshi kuruma de iku nara ōkii danboru o motte itte kuremasen ka
  If you're going by car could you take the big box for me?

- このごろどうも様子がおかしい
  Kono goro **dōmo** yōsu ga okashii
  Recently his appearance has been **somehow** strange

- もちろん彼は彼女が本当のことを言ったと思わなかった
  Mochiron kare wa kanojo ga hontō no koto o itta to omowanakatta
  Of course he didn't think that she had told the truth

- 是非遊びに来て下さい
  Zehi asobi ni kite kudasai   You **really must** come and visit

Adverbs requiring a negative predicate

Some adverbs can only be used with a negative predicate
(*see* p. 5.) The most common of these are given below:

かならずしも・必ずしも '(not) necessarily'

- 外国人は必ずしも英語ができるとは限らない
  Gaikokujin wa **kanarazushimo** eigo ga dekiru to kagira**nai**
  It doesn't **necessarily** follow that all foreigners speak English

さっぱり '(not) at all'

- さっぱり分かりません
  Sappari wakari**masen**   I don't understand **at all**

ぜんぜん・全然 '(not) at all', '(none) at all'

- 頑張ったけど全然できなかった
  Ganbatta kedo **zenzen** deki**nakatta**
  I tried hard but I couldn't do it **at all**

In colloquial speech, ぜんぜん is sometimes used with a positive
predicate:

- 全然大丈夫だ
  Zenzen daijōbu da   It's **perfectly** OK

Also note that ぜんぜん can be used with words with a strong
negative meaning within a positive predicate:

- この時計は全然だめです
  Kono tokei wa **zenzen dame** desu
  This watch has **completely had it**!

なかなか

There is no straightforward translation for なかなか, but it suggests
difficulty and lack of success:

- 三回もやってみたけどなかなか出来ません
  Sankai mo yatte mita kedo **nakanaka dekimasen**
  I've tried it three times but I **just can't** do it

にどと・二度と '(not) again', 'never'

- ここには２度と来ないよ
  Koko ni wa **2-do to** konai yo   I am **never** coming here again!

めったに 'rarely', 'seldom'

- めったに本を読まない
  Mettani hon o yoma**nai**   I **rarely** read books

ろくに 'unsatisfactorily', 'inadequately'

- ろくに弟と話す時間がなかった
  Rokuni otōto to hanasu jikan ga **nakatta**
  I didn't **even** have time to talk to my brother!

Adverbs requiring a positive predicate

A few adverbs can only be used in a sentence with a positive
predicate (*see p. 5*). These include かならず・必ず 'without fail,
definitely', and ぎりぎり 'barely':

- 必ず６時前に着てください
  Kanarazu 6-ji mae ni kite kudasai
  Please **be sure to** arrive before 6 o'clock

- 駅まで道がとても込んでいたがぎりぎり終電に間に合った
  Eki made michi ga totemo konde ita ga **girigiri** jūden ni maniatta
  The street to the station was so crowded I was **barely** in time for
  the last train

Adverbs which change meaning with positive and negative predicates

Some adverbs have different meanings depending on whether the sentence has a positive or negative predicate. For example, まだ means 'still' with a positive predicate, but 'not yet' with a negative predicate:

- まだ食べています
  Mada tabete imasu   I am **still** eating

- まだ食べていない
  Mada tabete i**nai**   I haven't eaten **yet**

Other common adverbs with these changes in meaning are given below:

adverb	meaning with positive forms	meaning with negative forms
あまり	so (much/greatly) that	not very
いっさい・一切	all, everything	not at all
ぜんぜん・全然	completely	not at all
どうも	very much	not very much, in some way or other (implies inadequacy)
とても	very	can't, not at all
なかなか	quite, very, considerably	hardly, just can't (implies little success in spite of effort)
べつに・別に	separately	not especially
ほとんど	almost all, mostly	hardly any, almost none
まだ	still	not yet
もう	already	not any more, not any longer
しばらく	for a long time	not for a long time

Compare the following pairs of sentences which show the differences in usage:

あまり

- あまりに寂しくて泣いてしまいました
  Amari ni sabishikute naite shimaimashita
  I felt **so** lonely that I cried

- この本はあまりおもしろくないです
  Kono hon wa **amari** omoshiro**kunai** desu
  This book isn**'t very** interesting

ほとんど

- これらの学生はほとんど東南アジアからです
  Korera no gakusei wa **hotondo** Tōnan Ajia kara desu
  Almost all these students are from South-East Asia

- アイヌ語を話せるひとはほとんどいません
  Ainu-go o hanaseru hito wa **hotondo imasen**
  There are **hardly any** people who can speak the Ainu language

もう

- 子供達はもう寝ています
  Kodomotachi wa **mō** nete imasu
  The children have **already** gone to bed

- ピアノがもう弾けません
  Piano ga **mō** hike**masen**   I can't play the piano **any more**

Adverbs used with conditional forms

Some adverbs, such as もし and たとえ meaning 'if', occur with conditional forms (e.g. ～たら), or with structures with conditional meanings (e.g. ～ても) (see **verbs** and **conjunctive particles**). The adverbs introduce the conditions which follow them:

- もし田中さんに会ったらこの手紙を渡してください
  Moshi Tanaka san ni at**tara** kono tegami o watashite kudasai
  If you meet Mrs Tanaka, please give her this letter

- たとえ車で行っても、遅くなりますよ
  Tatoe kuruma de itt**e mo**, osoku narimasu yo
  Even if I go by car, I'll still be late

Adverbs used with tentative expressions or requests

Some adverbs expressing probability are used with tentative expressions such as でしょう. Amongst these are あるいは 'or', たぶん 'perhaps, maybe', and きっと 'definitely':

- 多分こないでしょう
  Tabun konai deshō   **Maybe** she's not coming

- 来年きっと合格するでしょう
  Rainen **kitto** gōkaku suru **deshō**
  He will **definitely** pass (the exam) next year, (don't you agree?)

Words which symbolize the sound or manner of an action

Japanese has numerous words which imitate sounds, or describe the way something is done, or symbolize psychological states and feelings by their sound. Many words of this type can be used as adverbs to describe the manner in which something happens. They are often joined to the following verb or predicate by the particle と:

- 犬がワンワンと鳴いていた
  Inu ga **wanwan to** naite ita
  The dog was barking ('**woof woof**')

- ドッスンと落ちた
  Dossun to ochita   It dropped **with a crash**

- 枝がパッキンと折れた
  Eta ga **pakkin to** oreta   The branch snapped **with a crack**

- 父はかっと怒った
  Chichi wa **katto** okotta   Dad **flew into** a temper

- かばが口をがばっと開けた
  Kaba ga kuchi o **gabatto** aketa
  The hippopotamus opened its mouth **wide**

There are also many adverbs of this type which do not require と
to join with the following verb or predicate:

- 彼は日本語をぺらぺらしゃべれる
  Kare wa Nihongo o **perapera** shabereru
  He can speak Japanese **fluently**

- 彼女が僕の手をしっかり握った
  Kanojo ga boku no te o **shikkari** nigitta
  She gripped my hand **firmly**

- 電車の中に通勤客がぎっしり詰まっていた
  Densha no naka ni tsūkinkyaku ga **gisshiri** tsumatte ita
  The commuters were **jam**-packed inside the train

- 自分が一体どこにいるかさっぱり分からなかった
  Jibun ga ittai doko ni iru ka **sappari** wakaranakatta
  I had **absolutely** no idea where I was

- ゆっくり読んでください
  Yukkuri yonde kudasai   Please read it **slowly**

Adverbials derived from adjectives

In phrases such as はやく　たべる 'eat quickly', and しずかに
よむ 'read quietly', the words 'quickly' and 'quietly' describe the
manner of eating and reading. Japanese adverbials of this type are
derived from adjectives, and in this way they are similar to the
English '-ly' suffix in words such as 'quickly' and 'easily'. Some
examples are given below, but they are strictly part of the
conjugation and use of adjectives (*see pp. 106–107*).

い adjectives change the final い to く:

- みんな、こっちへ早く来なさい
  Minna kotchi e **hayaku kinasai**   **Come** here **quickly**, everyone!

- 明日また遅く来るでしょう
  Ashita mata **osoku kuru** deshō
  He'll probably **come late** again tomorrow!

Note that ちかく・近く 'close' and とおく・遠く 'far' are nouns and take the particle に when used adverbially. These words and their uses are discussed in more detail in the chapter on adjectives (*see p. 108*):

- 家族は近くに住んでいます
  Kazoku wa **chikaku ni** sunde imasu   My family live **nearby**

な adjectives add the particle に:

- 彼女は積極的にボランティアをやっています
  Kanojo wa **sekkyokuteki ni** borantia o yatte imasu
  *She does her voluntary work **enthusiastically***

- お祖父ちゃんは毎朝元気に運動している
  Ojiichan wa maiasa **genki ni** undō shite iru
  *Grandad does his exercises **energetically** every morning*

Other adverbs and adverbials

Certain common expressions are adverbial, and among these are ざんねんながら 'regrettably', もしかすると, もしかしたら 'probably, perhaps' (with a tentative ending), and ただいま 'I'm back!, just now':

- 残念ながら、今日はダメです
  Zannennagara, kyō wa dame desu
  Unfortunately, *it's impossible today*

- もしかすると、雨が降るかもしれません
  Moshikasuruto, ame ga furu **kamo shiremasen**
  Perhaps *it's going to rain*

- Husband: 只今！   Wife: お帰りなさい
  Tadaima   *I'm home!*   O-kaeri nasai   *Welcome back*

Comparative and superlative of adverbs

The comparative of adverbs is similar to the comparative of adjectives (*see p. 104*).

Comparative of adverbs

In English, the comparative of an adverb is formed with the word 'more' or with the addition of the suffix '-er':

*Could you speak **more quietly**, please?*
*She studies **harder** than I do*

With Japanese, the item to which the comparison is being made is marked with より, and the adverb itself doesn't change:

- 彼女は私よりよく練習します
  Kanojo wa **watashi yori yoku** renshū shimasu
  *She practises **more often** than I do*

- この機械のお陰でホームベーキングは前より簡単にできる
  Kono kikai no o-kage de hōmu bēkingu wa **mae yori kantan ni** dekiru
  *Home baking can be done **more easily than before**, thanks to this machine*

Some adverbs and adverbials of degree can also be used to modify adverbs to show comparisons:

- もっと優しくしてください
  Motto yasashiku shite kudasai   *Please be **more gentle***

- もうちょっと早く起きてほしい
  Mō chotto hayaku okite hoshii   *I want you to get up **earlier***

Superlative of adverbs

The superlative of adjectives in English is formed with the word 'most' or with the addition of the suffix '-est':

*She speaks Japanese **the most** fluently of all of us.*
*Who can run **the fastest**?*

The Japanese equivalent of 'most' is いちばん・一番, literally 'number one', which is placed in front of the adverb:

- 我が家では弟は一番早く布団から起きだします
  Waga ya dewa otōto wa **ichiban hayaku** futon kara okidashimasu
  *In our family, my little brother always gets up **earliest** in the morning.*

- 一番楽にお金を稼ぐ方法はなんでしょう？
  Ichiban raku ni o-kane o kasegu hōhō wa nan deshō
  *I wonder what is **the easiest** way of earning money?*

Nouns

What is a noun?

A noun is a word which names people ('child', 'teacher'), or places ('station', 'Tokyo'), or things ('apple', 'bus'). The names of abstract qualities and emotions are also nouns ('beauty', 'happiness').

Characteristics of Japanese nouns

Unlike many other languages, Japanese nouns do not have grammatical gender (masculine, feminine, neuter), and do not decline, i.e. change their forms to express grammatical relationships. The grammatical role of a noun in a sentence is determined by the particle which follows it (*see p. 149*). Nouns require だ・です to form a predicate (*see p. 5*):

- 田中さんは日本人です

  Tanaka san wa **nihonjin desu**   Mr Tanaka **is (a) Japanese**

Plural nouns

Japanese does not generally have a plural form for nouns. In English, a final -s distinguishes 'book' from 'books', but in Japanese the noun ほん can mean both 'book' and 'books'. This means that it is sometimes unclear whether a Japanese noun should be translated as an English singular or plural, and in such cases only the context can help determine which is appropriate:

- 本はどこですか

  Hon wa doko desu ka

  Where is **the book**?/Where are **the books**?

- すみません。赤い本を渡してちょうだい

  Sumimasen. **Akai hon** o watashite chōdai

  *Would you pass me **the red book**, please?*

- 本棚に本がたくさんある

  Hondana ni **hon ga takusan** aru

  *There are **lots of books** in the bookcase*

A plural meaning can also be identified by using a number and a counter (*see p. 191*).

Plural suffixes

A very few nouns, all of which refer to people, can be shown to be plural by adding the suffixes 〜たち and 〜ら, although these words can have a plural meaning even without the suffixes. Note that the suffix 〜ら can be impolite and is best avoided, except in the word かれら 'they', 'them':

わたしたち	we, us
がくせいたち	students, the students
こどもたち	children, the children
せんせいたち	teachers
かれら	they, them
やつら	they, them (impolite)

The suffix 〜たち is often used when referring back to a noun already mentioned. In such situations, English often uses 'the', as with 'the students' in the example below:

- 学生が 800 人いました。僕がマイクに近寄ると学生達は立ちました

  Gakusei ga happyaku-nin imashita. Boku ga maiku ni chikayoru to **gakuseitachi** wa tachimashita

  *There were 800 **students** there. When I approached the microphone **the students** stood up*

Plural by duplication

There are a few Japanese nouns where plural meanings are formed by repeating a singular noun:

ひとびと・人々	people
しまじま・島々	islands
ところどころ・所々	here and there
たびたび・度々	many times, often

Nouns formed from adjectives

In English, a suffix can often be added to adjectives to form nouns, e.g. 'wide → width', 'weak → weakness', and the same is true of Japanese.

〜さ

The suffix 〜さ can be added to the stem of some adjectives to give noun meanings:

adjective	meaning	derived noun	meaning
おおきい・大きい	big	おおきさ	size
おもい・重い	heavy	おもさ	weight
ひろい・広い	wide	ひろさ	width, scale
かなしい・悲しい	sad	かなしさ	sadness

〜み

There are also a few nouns formed by adding the suffix 〜み to an adjective stem:

adjective	meaning	derived noun	meaning
あまい・甘い	sweet	あまみ	sweetness
くるしい・苦しい	painful	くるしみ	pain, anguish

Colours

Some nouns for colours are the same as the adjectives but minus the final い:

あか・赤	red
くろ・黒	black
あお・青	green/blue
きいろ・黄色	yellow

Some colours only have a noun form (むらさき・紫 'purple', みどり・緑 'green'), and these are often used with the suffix いろ 'colour'. They are joined to the following word with の:

- 緑色のセーター
  midori-iro no sētā
  a **green** sweater

Nouns formed from verbs

Sometimes the conjunctive (pre-ます) stem of a verb can be used as a noun. The following examples all derive from verbs, and there are many others (see **conjunctive (pre-masu) form**):

かえる	to return	→	かえり・帰り	return, homecoming
むく	to face	→	むき・向き	direction
つづく	to continue	→	つづき・続き	continuation
おわる	to finish	→	おわり・終り	conclusion, finish
このむ	to like, to prefer	→	このみ・好み	taste, preference
ちぢむ	to shrink	→	ちぢみ・縮み	shrinking

Nouns with special functions

A small number of nouns can have a structural function in certain cases. There are some examples below to show how the meanings of the nouns change in this use, but for more information, refer to the section on nominalization (*see p. 206*).

とき

This is used after the plain forms of verbs and adjectives, with expressions of time:

アメリカへ	いったとき	when I went to America
	たべるとき	when I eat/when eating
	あついとき	when it's hot
	わかいとき	when I was young

とき can also be used following another noun, to which it is joined by the particle の:

- 子供のときよく恐竜の絵を描きました
  Kodomo no toki yoku kyōryū no e o kakimashita
  When I was a child, I often drew pictures of dinosaurs

こと

Japanese uses こと 'abstract thing' after the plain forms of verbs to form a noun phrase, and this can often be translated into English with an '-ing' ending (e.g. 'watching', 'going'):

- テレビを見ることが好きです
  Terebi o **miru koto** ga suki desu   I like **watching** TV

- 学校へ行かないことはよくないよ
  Gakkō e **ikanai koto** wa yoku nai yo
  Not going to school is a bad thing (to do)

When こと comes after the 〜た form of a verb, it has the special use of referring to a past experience (*see p. 60 and p. 206*):

- 馬に乗ったことがありますか
  Uma ni **notta koto** ga arimasu ka
  Have you ever ridden a horse?

ところ

Although the noun ところ means 'place', it can be used after the plain forms of verbs to refer to an event which is just about to happen or has just happened. In this use it refers to a point in time:

- 出かけるところです
  Dekakeru tokoro desu   I'm **just about to go out**

- 夕飯を食べたところです
  Yūhan o **tabeta tokoro** desu   I have **just eaten**

With a 〜ている structure, ところ emphasizes being 'in the middle of . . .' something:

- いま電話しているところだからちょっと待ってね
  Ima **denwa shite iru tokoro** dakara chotto matte ne
  Just a minute - I'm **on the phone**

とおり・通り

とおり, meaning 'way, street', is used after the dictionary form or 〜た form of a verb, or after a noun with の, to talk about the method of doing something or way in which something happens:

- 私が言う通りにしなさい
  Watashi ga **iu tōri** ni shi nasai   Please do **as I tell you**

- 僕がいった通りだ
  Boku ga **itta tōri** da   It's just **as I said**

- 説明書の通りに組み立てる
  Setsumeisho no tōri ni kumitateru
  Assemble **as per the instructions**

はず

はず is used after the plain forms of verbs or adjectives to show that there is a likelihood or expectation of something happening:

- もうすぐ着くはずです
  Mō sugu **tsuku hazu** desu   They **should be here** shortly

- 田中さんは明日来ないはずです
  Tanaka san wa ashita **konai hazu** desu
  I'm **fairly sure** that Tanaka **won't be coming** tomorrow

ため

ため shows the purpose or result of an action. It can follow the plain forms of verbs:

- 日本へ行くのが勉強するためです
  Nihon e iku no wa **benkyō suru tame** desu
  The reason for going to Japan **is to study**

- これは印刷をするための機械です
  Kore wa **insatsu o suru tame** no kikai desu
  This is a machine **for printing**

ため can also be used after another noun when joined by the particle の:

- 台風のため、木が倒れた
  Taifū no tame, ki ga taoreta
  A tree was brought down **as a result of the typhoon**

- 病気のため欠席しました
  Byōki no tame kesseki shimashita
  I did not attend, **owing to illness**

For ために, *see pp. 144–145*.

よう

To talk about how something seems to be, よう 'appearance' is used, following the plain forms of verbs and adjectives:

- 世界的に日本語が話せる人が増えているようだ
  Sekai-teki ni Nihongo ga hanaseru hito ga **fuete iru yō** da
  It seems that the number of people worldwide who can speak Japanese **is increasing**

- 日本語で話しかけたが、分からないようだった
  Nihongo de hanashikaketa ga, **wakaranai yō** datta
  I spoke to her in Japanese but she didn't **seem to understand**

For ように, *see pp. 146–147*.

Nouns with the polite prefixes お and ご

The style of a sentence can be changed to a more formal or polite register by using the prefixes お or ご with certain nouns. For more on this subject, refer to the chapter on **keigo** (*p. 213*).

Nouns used as adverbs

Some Japanese nouns can also be used as adverbs (*see p. 111*). This is most common with nouns referring to relative time such as あした 'tomorrow', and せんしゅう 'last week' etc., and with nouns of quantity such as たくさん 'a lot (of)'. The following sentences show the word あした used first as a noun, and then as an adverb:

- 明日の授業は隣りの教室です
  Ashita no jugyō wa tonari no kyōshitsu desu
  Tomorrow's class will be in the room next door

- 申し訳ないですが明日来られません
  Moshiwake nai desu ga **ashita koraremasen**
  I'm very sorry, but (I) **can't come tomorrow**

Conjunctions and conjunctive particles

What is a conjunction?

Conjunctions link words, phrases, or clauses. English conjunctions include 'and', 'but', and 'however', and some appear in pairs ('neither . . . nor . . .'). Subordinating conjunctions such as 'that', 'in order to', 'if', and 'because' link main and subordinate clauses.

Japanese equivalents of English conjunctions 'and', 'both', 'or', and 'neither' are particles (for と meaning 'and', や, も, and か, see **particles**). Some of the conjunctions given below can also be described as noun and particle combinations. Others are conjunctive particles, which are often considered as forms of verbs and adjectives. In addition, all of the 〜て form group of endings, e.g. 〜て, 〜ないで, 〜なくて, で, etc., are conjunctions in that they link phrases and sentences. These are discussed in the chapters on verbs and adjectives.

Conjunctive particles

There are several particles which are conjunctions in terms of their function, but which are usually described in textbooks as either forms of verbs (or adjectives), or as particles. Two of them, 〜たら and 〜ば, cause changes in the form of the verb or adjective to which they are attached. They are included in the charts of forms for verbs and adjectives.

〜たら

〜たら consists of the 〜た form of the verb or adjective followed by ら. It joins clauses together and shows that one action begins before another action. In the following sentence, going to Japan precedes the visit to Kyoto:

- 日本へ行ったら京都に行きたい
  Nihon e **ittara** Kyōto ni ikitai
  When / if I go to Japan, I want to go to Kyoto

The English translation of this sentence can be with 'when' or 'if', depending on whether or not a trip to Japan is being planned. A wide range of relative time relationships can be expressed with ~たら, and there may be a choice as to the use of 'if' or 'when' (or indeed some other phrasing) in English:

- 食べ終ったら電話します
  Tabeowattara denwa shimasu
  I will call you **when I finish eating**

- こんど日本へ行ったら温泉に行こう
  Kondo Nihon e **ittara** onsen ni ikō
  Next time **we go** to Japan, let's go to an onsen (hot spring)

- 彼が帰っていたら電気が点いているはずだ
  Kare ga **kaette itara** denki ga tsuite iru hazu da
  If he is (has come) home, the lights should be on

Note that よかったら, from いい・よい 'good', means 'if you like':

- よかったら、もっと食べてください
  Yokattara, motto tabete kudasai
  Please eat some more **if you like**!

~たら in questions and suggestions

There is a common use of ~たら in 'what should I do?' questions and in making suggestions in response, as illustrated by the following examples:

- 日本語をもっと早く学習するにはどうしたらいいですか
  Nihongo o motto hayaku gakushū suru ni wa **dō shitara ii** desu ka
  What should I do to learn Japanese faster?

- 日本のテレビドラマを見たらどうですか
  Nihon no terebi dorama o **mitara dō desu ka**
  How **about watching** Japanese TV dramas?

~たら with negative clauses

The addition of ~たら to negatives of verbs and ~い adjectives changes the ~ない ending to ~なかったら:

- 分からなかったら日本人の友達に聞いてください
  Wakaranakattara Nihonjin no tomodachi ni kiite kudasai
  When/If you don't understand, please ask a Japanese friend

- この電車に乗らなかったら田中さんに会えませんよ
  Kono densha ni **noranakattara** Tanaka san ni aemasen yo
  If we don't get on this train, we won't be able to meet Tanaka

- あまりおもしろくなかったら、帰りましょう
  Amari **omoshiroku nakattara** kaerimashō
  If it's not very **interesting**, let's go home!

- 寒くなかったら外で食べる
  Samuku nakattara soto de taberu
  If it's not cold, we'll eat outside

～ば

～ば is a conjunction which expresses a condition, and is
sometimes referred to as 'the conditional form' or 'the ～ば form'
of い adjectives and verbs. The addition of ～ば requires a change
in the final kana of the verb or い adjective. Adjectives change the
final ～い to ～ければ:

dictionary form	meaning	final ～い dropped	～ば
さむい・寒い	cold	さむ～	さむければ
やさしい	gentle, kind	やさし～	やさしければ

Verbs change the final kana of the dictionary form to the え line of
the kana chart:

dictionary form	meaning	change in final kana	+ ～ば
おこる・起こる	to occur	る → れ	おこれば
よむ・読む	to read	む → め	よめば
いく・行く	to go	く → け	いけば
はなす・話す	to speak	す → せ	はなせば
まつ・待つ	to wait	つ → て	まてば

dictionary form	meaning	change in final kana	+ 〜ば
あう・会う	to meet	う → え	あえば
いそぐ・急ぐ	to hurry	ぐ → げ	いそげば
たべる・食べる	to eat	る → れ	たべれば
みる・見る	to see, to watch	る → れ	みれば
する	to do	る → れ	すれば
くる・来る	to come	る → れ	くれば

Uses of 〜ば

The two clauses linked with 〜ば show a relationship where the first action or situation must occur in order for the second statement or action to be true. In the following sentence, a car must be used in order to complete the journey in 90 minutes:

- 車で行けば 90 分かかる
  Kuruma de **ikeba** kyū-jup-pun kakaru
  If you go by car, it takes 90 minutes

In the examples below, the CDs must be cheap before the speaker will consider buying any, and it must be raining before a decision is made to cancel the match:

- CD は安ければ買います
  Shiidii wa **yasukereba** kaimasu
  If CDs **are cheap**, I'll buy some

- 雨が降れば試合が中止になる
  Ame ga fureba shiai ga chūshi ni naru
  If it rains, the match will be cancelled

If the 〜ば clause holds true, then the other event becomes true:

- 明日晴れればハイキングに行きましょう
  Ashita **harereba** haikingu ni ikimashō
  If it's fine tomorrow, let's go hiking

〜ば with negative conditions

The addition of 〜ば to negatives of verbs and い adjectives changes the 〜ない ending to 〜なければ and the condition established with 〜ば becomes negative:

dictionary form	meaning	～ない form	～なければ
い adjectives			
さむい・寒い	cold	さむくない	さむくなければ
やさしい	gentle, kind	やさしくない	やさしくなければ
verbs			
おこる・起こる	to occur	おこらない	おこらなければ
よむ・読む	to read	よまない	よまなければ
いく・行く	to go	いかない	いかなければ
たべる・食べる	to eat	たべない	たべなければ
みる・見る	to see, to watch	みない	みなければ
する	to do	しない	しなければ
くる・来る	to come	こない	こなければ

- ＣＤは安くなければ買いません
  Shiidii wa **yasukunakereba** kaimasen
  If CDs **aren't cheap**, I won't buy any

- 佐藤さんが来なければ３人で試合をやるしかない
  Satō san ga **konakereba** san-nin de shiai o yaru shika nai
  If Sato **doesn't come**, there's nothing for it but to play the match with three people

- 明日手紙が来なければ電話します
  Ashita tegami ga **konakereba** denwa shimasu
  If the letter **doesn't come** tomorrow, I'll telephone

See also the section on the ない form in the chapter on verbs where idiomatic uses of ～なければ are discussed, and ほど in the chapter on particles for ～ば ～ほど.

～ばよかった

This is an idiomatic structure meaning 'I wish that . . .':

- もっと勉強すればよかった
  Motto **benkyō sureba** yokatta   **I wish I'd studied** more!

Comparison of ～ば and ～たら

Sometimes there will be little or no difference in meaning between sentences joined with ～ば and sentences joined with ～たら. In the two sentences below there is only a slight difference in nuance: the first (～ば) indicates that the air conditioning should be used only at times when the weather is hot, and the second (～たら) shows a time relationship where hot weather precedes putting on the air conditioning:

* 暑ければエアコンを点けてください
  Atsukereba eakon o tsukete kudasai
  If it's hot, please turn on the air conditioning

* 暑かったらエアコンを点けてください
  Atsukattara eakon o tsukete kudasai
  If it's hot, please turn on the air conditioning

The second half of the sentence can be a request (as above) or a statement:

* 授業が早く終れば電話します
  Jugyō ga hayaku **owareba** denwa shimasu
  If the class finishes early, I will ring

* 授業が早く終ったら電話電話します
  Jugyō ga hayaku **owattara** denwa shimasu
  If the class finishes early, I will ring

However where there is a request, suggestion, or command in the main clause and the subordinate clause is volitional (something the subject decides to do), ～たら is used:

* 今度マンチェスターへ来たら電話してください
  Kondo Manchesutāe **kitara** denwa shite kudasai
  Please ring me when you next come to Manchester

Where the subject of both clauses is the same and the main clause is past tense then ～たら is used for the preceding event where the time relationship to what follows is central:

* 空港に着いたらパスポートがないとすぐ気づいた
  Kūkō ni **tsuitara** pasupōto ga nai to sugu Kidzuita
  When I arrived at the airport I realized straight away that I didn't have my passport

However, if the main clause is an intentional action by the subject, then rather than showing 'when . . .' by ～たら, the two clauses are combined with a ～て form meaning 'and':

- 空港に着いてすぐ電話した
  Kūkō ni **tsuite** sugu denwa shita
  I **arrived** at the airport **and** phoned straight away

と

The use of と shows a natural and inevitable link between what happens in the first clause and what follows in the next. This means that English translations may feature 'and', 'if', or 'when':

- このボタンを押すと機械が動き始める
  Kono botan o **osu to** kikai ga ugokihajimeru
  Push this button **and** the machine starts/**If you push** this button, the machine starts

- 夜になるとお化けが出てくる
  Yoru ni **naru to** obake ga dete kuru
  Ghosts come out **when it gets** dark

と is also used when an event has occurred or a discovery been made unexpectedly because of something described in the first clause:

- ドアを開けると知らない男の人が立っていた
  Doa o **akeru to** shiranai otoko no hito ga tatte ita
  I **opened** the door and found a stranger standing there

- 公園へ行くと友達がいた
  Kōen e **iku to** tomodachi ga ita
  When I went to the park, I ran into a friend

The clause that follows と cannot be a request or command, or express the intention of the speaker. For these kinds of clauses ～たら is used.

～なら

なら is often described as a noun equivalent of the ～たら and ～ば forms of verbs and adjectives. なら is part of the conjugation of だ・です. Its function is to confirm a condition, and it is often explained as meaning 'if . . . is the case, then . . .', as in the following examples:

- 街まで行くのなら郵便局にも行ってくれる？
  Machi made **iku no nara** yūbinkyoku ni mo itte kureru?
  If you're going to town, could you go to the post office for me?

- あまり時間がないならいい
  Amari jikan ga **nai nara** ii
  If you haven't got much time, then it's OK (not to go to the post office)

〜なら is used after the plain forms of verbs and adjectives, and also after nouns and な adjectives. With noun and な adjective sentences, there is no need for だ・です or な, as なら is itself a conjugated form of だ・です:

- 寿司ならとろが一番だ
  Sushi nara toro ga ichi-ban da
  If you want sushi, then 'toro' is the best!

- 元気なら行ける
  Genki nara ikeru   *If I feel well enough, I'll be able to go*

With verbs and い adjectives, the use of the particle の is optional:

- カメラを買う（の）ならビックカメラへ行きましょう
  Kamera o **kau (no) nara** Bikku Kamera e ikimashō
  If you want to buy a camera, let's go to the Bikku Camera store

- 出かける（の）なら卵も買ってきてください
  Dekakeru (no) nara tamago mo katte kite kudasai
  If you are going out, please buy (me) some eggs

- 寒い（の）なら暖房を入れましょう
  Samui (no) nara danbō o iremashō
  If you are cold, let's put the heating on

〜なら is often used in conversations to confirm information, as in the phrase じゃ それなら 'Well, if that's the case . . .'

Other types of conjunction

〜ながら

The basic meaning of 〜ながら is 'while . . . ing', and it shows that two things are happening at the same time. It follows the conjunctive (pre-ます) form of the verb (*see p. 36*):

- 食べながらテレビを見ました
  Tabenagara terebi o mimashita
  I watched TV **while eating**

- 傘をさしながら自転車に乗るのは危ない
  Kasa o sashinagara jitensha ni noru no wa abunai
  It's dangerous to ride a bicycle **with an umbrella up**!

〜まま

まま is a noun which is often used as a conjunction, following either the 〜た form or 〜ない form of a verb. It shows that the state described is left as it is, remaining unchanged at the time of an action. The implication is that this is wrong or inappropriate. When it follows a negative verb, the meaning is 'without . . . ing':

- 電気を点けたまま寝た
  Denki o **tsuketa mama** neta   I went to bed **with the lights on**

- 勘定を払わないまま店をでた
  Kanjō o **harawanai mama** mise o deta
  I left the restaurant **without paying** the bill

し

し shows that the clause it follows is one of a number of possible statements. In the example below, し implies that a lack of money is only one of numerous reasons why life is hard at the moment:

- お金がないし、生活は大変だ
  O-kane ga **nai shi**, seikatsu wa taihen da
  I **don't have** any money, **and** life is tough

The sentence below indicates that there are various reasons to consider Japanese grammar as not being difficult:

- 日本語は複数形がないし、文法が難しくないですよ
  Nihongo wa **fukusūkei ga nai shi**, bunpō ga muzukashiku nai desu yo
  Japanese **has no plural forms (and so on), so** the grammar's not difficult

し can be used several times to list reasons in support of a statement or suggestion, and so conveys a strong overtone of 'amongst other things':

- 子供が疲れているし、腹が減ったし、もう帰りましょう
  Kodomo ga **tsukarete iru shi**, **hara ga hetta shi**, mō kaerimashō
  The kids **are tired, and they're hungry (and so on), so** let's go
  home

- 佐藤さんはまじめだし、経験があるし、この仕事にぴった
  りだ
  Satō san wa **majime da shi, keiken ga aru shi**, kono shigoto ni
  pittari da
  Sato **is steady enough, he's got experience, and so on**. He's
  perfect for this job

それから

それから is used for 'and then ...', 'after that', 'furthermore',
and also as a question to ask for more information:

- 東京に３日いてそれから京都へ行きます
  Tokyo ni mikka ite **sore kara** Kyoto e ikimasu
  We will be in Tokyo for three days, **and then** go to Kyoto

- それから？
  Sore kara?   And?/And then?/And what?

- それから何をしましたか
  Sore kara nani o shimashita ka
  What did you do **after that**?

それで

それで shows a reason or cause, and so can often be translated as
'therefore', 'so', 'that's why':

- きのうまで韓国へ出張で行っていた。それでいなかったんだ
  Kinō made Kankoku e shutchō de itte ita. **Sore de** inakatta n da
  I was in Korea on a business trip until yesterday. **That's why**
  I wasn't around

それでは

This is a version of それで used at the beginning of a sentence to
refer back to something which has been mentioned previously,
and to highlight it as a topic ('then, in which case ...'):

- 明日は無理か。それではあさってにしよう
  Ashita wa muri ka. **Sore de wa** asatte ni shiyō
  So tomorrow's impossible? **Then** *let's do it the day after*

It is also commonly used to bring classes to a close, or otherwise signal a conclusion, similar to the English 'well, then!':

- それではまた来週
  Sore de wa mata raishū
  Well, **then,** *I'll see you again next week*

- それではそろそろ失礼します
  Sore de wa sorosoro shitsurei shimasu   *Well, I must be going*

それとも

それとも is used to present alternatives, and means 'or':

- 日本語は難しいですか。それともやさしいですか
  Nihongo wa muzukashii desu ka. **Sore tomo** yasashii desu ka
  Is Japanese difficult? **Or** *is it easy?*

それなら

This refers back to what has just been said, and means 'if that's the case, then . . .':

- 医者の証明があるんですか。それなら授業に休んでもいいよ
  isha no shōmei ga aru n desu ka. **Sore nara** jūgyō ni yasunde mo ii yo
  You've got a doctor's note? **In that case,** *you don't have to come to the lesson*

- 前の彼が行くんですか。それなら絶対に行かない
  Mae no kare ga iku n desu ka. **Sore nara** zettai ikanai
  My ex-boyfriend's going? **In that case,** *there's no way I'm going!*

そして

そして joins sentences with the meaning 'and' or 'and then':

- 日本語はやさしいです。そして面白いです
  Nihongo wa yasashii desu. **Soshite** omoshiroi desu
  Japanese is easy, **and** *it's interesting*

- 6時に着きました。そして主人に電話しました
  Roku-ji ni tsukimashita. **Soshite** shujin ni denwa shimashita
  I arrived at 6 o'clock. **Then** I called my husband

すると

This links sentences to show what happened next, and can be
translated as 'whereupon . . .', 'then . . .' It can also introduce
a conclusion based on the previous sentence, in the sense of
'in which case . . .':

- 去年会社に入った。すると妙実にであった
  Kyonen kaisha ni haitta. **Suru to** Taemi ni deatta
  I joined the company last year. **Then** I met Taemi

- 彼は子供のときフランスに住んでいたんでしょ？するとフ
  ランス語ができるでしょう
  Kare wa kodomo no toki Furansu ni sunde ita n desho. **Suru to**
  Furansugo ga dekiru deshō
  He lived in France when he was a child? **In that case**, he can
  probably speak French

が

が connects two clauses with the meaning 'but' or 'although':

- 母は日本人ですが私は日本語があまり話せません
  Haha wa Nihonjin desu **ga**, Nihongo ga amari hanasemasen
  Although my mum is Japanese, I can't speak much Japanese

- 井上さんは明日いますが、あさってから出張です
  Inoue san wa ashita imasu **ga**, asatte kara shutchō desu
  Mrs Inoue will be here tomorrow, **but** from the next day she's away
  on a business trip

It is very common to use が at the end of a sentence to soften the
tone. This is especially true when favours are being asked or
refused, or information and permission sought. In this use,
the second clause is left unexpressed and must be inferred:

- すみませんが
  Sumimasen **ga**   Excuse me, **but** . . .

- 明日の晩友達のパーティに行きたいが
  Ashita no ban tomodachi no pātii ni ikitai **ga**
  Tomorrow night I'd like to go a friend's party (**may I?**)

- ちょっとお伺いしたいんですが
  Chotto o-ukagai shitai n desu **ga**
  I'd like to ask **(for some information, please)**

- それはそうですが
  Sore wa sō desu **ga**   Well, yes, that's right, **but** . . .

けれども, けれど, けど, だけど

These conjunctions and some other variations are spoken
language equivalents of が, meaning 'but', 'although'. けど is
very informal. They are sometimes used at the beginning of a
sentence or clause to qualify something previously said:

- このアパートは駅に近くて便利だ。けれどもうるさい
  Kono apāto wa eki ni chikakute benri da. **Keredomo** urusai
  This apartment is convenient as it's close to the station.
  However, it's noisy!

- 明日行きたいけれど、明後日テストがある。どうしよう？
  Ashita ikitai **keredo**, asatte tesuto ga aru. Dō shiyō
  I'd like to go tomorrow, **but** there's a test the day after! What
  should I do?

- あいつは馬鹿だ。けど人はいいよね
  Aitsu wa baka da. **Kedo** hito wa ii yo ne
  He's a bit of an idiot, **but** he's friendly

- パブへ行きたい。だけど、お金がない
  Pabu e ikitai. **Dakedo**, o-kane ga nai
  I want to go to the pub, **but** I don't have any money

のに

のに has two uses. One use is to show purpose. This usage is
related to the particle に used for purpose (*see p. 161*), and
to the conjunctive (pre-ます) form + に (*see below and pp. 36–37*):

- このコンピュータはウィンドウズ２０００日本語版が入っ
  ているので日本語でレポートを書くのに使えます
  Kono konpyūta wa Uindōzu ni-sen Nihongo-ban ga haitte iru node
  Nihongo de repōto o **kaku no ni** tsukaemasu
  This computer has the Japanese version of Windows (*propr.*)
  2000, so it can be used **for writing** reports in Japanese

- 電子辞書は勉強するのに役立つ
  Denshi-jisho wa **benkyō suru no ni** yakudatsu
  Electronic dictionaries are useful **for studying**

The second use of the のに structure is to link an action or event with an unexpected outcome:

- 早く行ったのに間に合わなかった
  Hayaku itta **no ni** ma ni awanakatta
  In spite of going early, I wasn't in time

Sometimes the second element is left unstated, in which case the のに ending has the nuance of a complaint, such as 'in spite of the fact that . . .' or 'even though . . .':

- せっかく夕飯を作ったのに
  Sekkaku yūhan o tsukutta **no ni**
  Even though I made dinner specially (you didn't come!)

～ても

The ～て form of a verb or adjective followed by も shows that the second element is not what might be expected from the first element, and so is similar to the English 'although', 'even if . . .':

- 夜遅くても電話してください
  Yoru **osokute mo** denwa shite kudasai
  Even if it's late at night, please call me

- 雨が降っても行きます
  Ame ga futte mo ikimasu   *I'll go* **even if it rains**

- あなたが悪くなくても、謝ってくれませんか
  Anata ga **waruku nakute mo**, ayamatte kuremasen ka
  Even if you are not in the wrong, could you please say sorry?

See also the sections on uses of the ～て form in the chapters on verbs (*p. 38*) and adjectives (*p. 98*). Nouns and な adjectives are followed by でも (see below).

でも

でも is an equivalent of the ～て form + も (*see p. 54*), but used with nouns:

- 子供でもできる
  Kodomo demo dekiru   **Even a child** can do it

- 日曜日でも、あの店は開いています
  Nichiyōbi demo, ano mise wa aite imasu
  That store is open **even on Sundays**

There is also a common use of でも to mark an example in a suggestion:

- コーヒーでもいかがですか？
  Kōhii demo ikaga desu ka
  Would you like **a coffee or something**?

～から

～から marks a clause as giving a reason for what follows:

- 明後日試験ですから、勉強しなければならない
  Asatte **shiken desu kara**, benkyō shinakereba naranai
  I have to study, **because there's an exam** the day after tomorrow

- 僕はもう読んだから、貸してあげる
  Boku wa **mō yonda kara**, kashite ageru
  I've **already read it, so** I'll lend (it) to you

- 夜は寒くなるから、ジャケットを忘れないでください
  Yoru wa **samuku naru kara**, jaketto o wasurenaide kudasai
  It gets cold at night, **so** don't forget your jacket

- 電車が遅れているから、まだ家に着いていないだろう
  Densha ga **okurete iru kara**, mada ie ni tsuite inai darō
  Because **the trains are late**, he's probably not reached home yet

The order of clauses can be reversed:

- 心配しないでください。お医者さんもうすぐ来るから
  Shinpai shinaide kudasai. O-isha san mō sugu kuru **kara**
  Don't worry (**because**) the doctor will be here soon

There is also a particle から (*see p. 170*).

ので

Following the plain or polite forms of verbs and adjectives,
～ので indicates a reason or cause:

- 安くなりましたので買いましょうか
  Yasuku narimashita no de, kaimashō ka
  It's been reduced, so shall we buy it?

- もう食べたので何も要らない
  Mō tabeta no de nani mo iranai
  I've already eaten, **so** I don't need anything

〜ので is linked to preceding nouns and な adjectives with な:

- 今日は雨なので明日にしよう
  Kyō wa **ame na no de** ashita ni shiyō
  As it's raining today, let's do it tomorrow

- ここは有名なので記念写真を撮ります
  Koko wa **yūmei na no de** kinen-shashin o torimasu
  This is a **well-known** spot, **so** I'll take a souvenir photograph

Both 〜ので and 〜から can mark a reason or cause, but 〜ので differs from 〜から in that it is not used for responding to 'Why . . . ?' questions, and does not follow 〜だろう・でしょう.

ため

ため is a noun that can be used to join two clauses to express cause or reason (*see pp. 127–128*):

- ほかに意見がないため会議が早めに終った
  Hoka ni **iken ga nai tame** kaigi ga hayame ni owatta
  There were no other opinions, so the meeting finished early

- 明日から出張へ行くため、今日この仕事を終わらせなければならない
  Ashita kara **shutchō e iku tame**, kyō kono shigoto o owarasenakereba naranai
  I'm going on a business trip tomorrow, **so** I must get this work finished today

- 交通事故のため今朝は渋滞した
  Kōtsu jiko no tame kesa wa jūtai shita
  We were delayed (in a traffic jam) this morning **because of an accident**

ために

This shows the target of an action, and so is often translated as 'for (the purpose of)'. ために follows nouns and the plain or polite forms of verbs. When following a noun, it requires the particle の:

- 来年日本へ行くために貯金しています
  Rainen **Nihon e iku tame ni** chokin shite imasu
  I am saving money **in order to go to Japan** next year

- 今の仕事はあまり好きじゃないが、家族のために頑張っている
  Ima no shigoto wa amari suki ja nai ga, **kazoku no tame ni** ganbatte iru
  I don't like my current job, but I am doing my best **for the family's sake**

ために can also show cause or reason:

- 台風のために木がたくさん倒れている
  Taifū no tame ni ki ga takusan taorete iru
  Many trees have fallen **because of the typhoon**

For orders, requests, and judgements of probability, から or ので must be used instead of ために to show cause or reason:

- 試験問題を配りますので静かにしなさい
  Shiken mondai o **kubarimasu no de** shizuka ni shi nasai
  I **am going to hand** out the exam question paper, **so please be quiet**

Conjunctive (pre-ます) form/stem + に

The use of this structure to describe purpose is also discussed in the section on uses of the conjunctive (pre-ます) stem in the chapter on verbs (*see pp. 36–37*).

With に + verb of motion

The conjunctive (pre-ます) stem can be used with the particle に and a verb of motion to give an expression meaning 'go and . . .', 'come in order to . . .', etc.:

- 今晩映画を見に行きたいです
  Konban eiga o **mi ni ikitai** desu
  I want to **go and (= in order to) see** a film tonight

- 明日、友達が遊びに来る
  Ashita, tomodachi ga **asobi ni kuru**
  A friend **is coming to visit** tomorrow

- **ちょっとパンを買いに行ってくる**
  Chotto pan o **kai ni itte kuru**
  I'm just **going to buy** some bread

To join clauses

This form can be used in formal (usually written) language as an equivalent of the 〜て form when joining clauses to show a sequence of events, or a reason or cause:

- **江藤はタバコに火を点け、昨日のことを考えた**
  Eto wa tabako ni **hi o tsuke**, kinō no koto o kangaeta
  Eto **lit** a cigarette **and** thought about the events of the previous day

- **斎藤は札幌へ行き、田川に会った**
  Saitō wa Sapporo e **iki**, Tagawa ni atta
  Sato **went** to Sapporo **and** met Tagawa

〜ように

This structure is used to show that the action in the main clause must occur for the action in the subordinate clause to come about. It is commonly used with negatives:

- **間違わないようによく見てください**
  Machigawanai yō ni yoku mite kudasai
  Watch carefully **so that you don't make a mistake**

- **荷物を忘れないようにご注意ください**
  Nimotsu o wasurenai yō ni go-chūi kudasai
  Please take care **not to forget your bags**

It can also be used with positives:

- **江尻さんに明日来るように言っておいてください**
  Ejiri san ni ashita **kuru yō ni** itte oite kudasai
  Please tell Ms Ejiri **to come** tomorrow

ように is common with なる to mean that something becomes possible:

- **やっと日本の新聞が大体読めるようになりました**
  Yatto nihon no shinbun ga daitai **yomeru yō ni narimashita**
  At last I am more or less **able to read** a Japanese newspaper

* 仲間同士と自由に話せるようになりたい
  Nakama dōshi to jiyū ni hanaseru **yō ni naritai**
  *I **want to be able to** speak easily with my colleagues*

ようにする

ように with する shows action to be taken so that something does or does not occur:

* 学生がこの部屋に入らないようにしてください
  Gakusei ga kono heya ni hairanai **yō ni shite** kudasai
  *Please **make sure that** the students do not enter this room*

ようにしている

This structure indicates that an action is habitually taken:

* 毎朝 30 分日本語の勉強をするようにしています
  Maiasa sanjup-pun nihongo no benkyō o suru **yō ni shite imasu**
  *I (**make it a point to**) study Japanese for 30 minutes every morning*

Noun phrase + ように

よう is a noun (see **nouns**) and is joined to preceding noun phrases with の:

* 日本人のように話せるけど、実はタイ人ですよ
  Nihonjin no yō ni hanaseru kedo jitsu wa taijin desu yo
  *He speaks **like a Japanese** but actually he is Thai*

* いつものように校長先生に挨拶した
  Itsumo no yō ni kōchō sensei ni aisatsu shita
  *I greeted the head teacher **as usual***

Conjunctions of time

The following nouns are used as conjunctions to show a time relationship between two clauses. All of these follow plain forms of verbs and adjectives. まえ, とき, and あいだ can be used with negatives as well as positives.

～あと, ～あとで 'after'

あと follows a ～た form:

- 映画を見た後、食事に行きます

  Eiga o **mita ato**, shokuji ni ikimasu

  After we've seen the film, we'll go for dinner

～まえ, ～まえに 'before'

- 大学へ行く前、ミルクを飲みます

  Daigaku e **iku mae**, miruku o nomimasu

  I drink milk *before I leave* for university

～とき, ～ときに 'while, when'

- 子供のときに本をたくさん読んでもらった

  Kodomo no toki ni hon o takusan yonde moratta

  When I was a kid, I had lots of books read to me

～あいだ, ～あいだに 'while, during'

- 冬休みの間にスキーが上手になりました

  Fuyu-yasumi no aida ni sukii ga jōzu ni narimashita

  I got quite good at skiing *over the winter holiday*

～まで, ～までに 'by, until'

- 6時まで勉強しました

  Roku-ji made benkyō shimashita

  I studied *until 6 o'clock*

- 月曜日までに宿題をしなければなりません

  Getsuyōbi made ni shukudai o shinakereba narimasen

  I have to do the homework *by Monday*

～うちに 'during', 'while' (with a positive), 'before', 'while' (with a negative)

- 暖かいうちに食べましょう

  Atatakai uchi ni tabemashō

  Let's eat them *while they are still warm*

- 大学へ行っているうちに運転免許を取ります

  Daigaku e itte iru uchi ni unten menkyo o torimasu

  I'll take my driving test *when I am (away) at university*

- 雨が降らないうちに片付けた

  Ame ga furanai uchi ni katazuketa

  We tidied up *before it rained*

Particles

What is a particle?

Particles are attached to nouns and other words or phrases to show their grammatical function and role within the sentence or phrase (e.g. topic, subject, direct or indirect object, etc.). They do not occur as independent words. Particles always come after the word, phrase, or clause to which they relate.

The particles ～たら and ～ば, which are sometimes seen as 'forms' of verbs and adjectives, are treated as a separate section in the chapter on conjunctive particles (*see pp. 129–135*).

は

は is used to mark the topic of a sentence, and to express contrast. In this use, は is pronounced the same as わ.

は to mark the topic

The topic is essentially what the sentence is about (*see p. 5*). If the topic is 'Mr Smith', then his name is marked with the particle は, and a comment or question about him can be added:

- スミスさんはアメリカ人ですか
  Sumisu san wa Amerikajin desu ka
  Is **Mr Smith** American?

Once a topic is established, it can be left out of subsequent comments, answers, or questions about that topic:

- いいえ、カナダ人です
  Iie, Kanadajin desu   No, (he's) Canadian

A new topic will be signalled by a new marked word or phrase:

- スミスさんはカナダ人です。ラパポートさんは？
  Sumisu san wa Kanadajin desu. **Rapapōto san wa**?
  Mr Smith is Canadian. How about **Ms Rappaport**?

- ラパポートさんも、レグロンさんもアカナダ人ですよ
  Rapapōto san mo, Reguron san mo Kanadajin desu yo
  Ms Rappaport and Mr Legrand are Canadian too

The part of the sentence following the topic is the predicate. The predicate can identify the topic, or explain it, or comment on it, or enquire about it (*see p. 5*). In the translations in brackets below, the topic particle は can be thought of as the colon, pointing forward to the predicate, i.e. the statement or question following the colon:

- 松原はサラリーマンです
  Matsubara wa **sarariiman desu**
  Matsubara **is a 'salaryman'** (Matsubara: he's a white-collar worker)

- 松原は英語が上手だ
  Matsubara wa **Eigo ga jōzu da**
  Matsubara's **English is good** (Matsubara: his English is good)

- 松原はめがねをかけている人です
  Matsubara wa **megane o kakete iru hito desu**
  Matsubara **is the person wearing glasses** (Matsubara: he's the one wearing glasses)

There is no real equivalent in English for the topic particle. However, translating は with 'as for' can give a sense of how it is used, and show why the following two sentences, which have the same 〜は 〜だ structure, are very different in English. The context of the first is a discussion of people's whereabouts, and the second is ordering food in a restaurant:

- 阿部さんは京都です
  Abe san wa Kyoto desu   **As for Abe,** he's in Kyoto

- 僕はうなぎだ
  Boku wa unagi da   **As for me,** I'll have the eel

In conversational Japanese, a verb in the predicate following は can be replaced by だ・です if the meaning of the verb is implied by the context, as in the example above. The predicate is commonly omitted altogether when it is an obvious question, such as 'What is . . . ?' or 'How about . . . ?':

- お名前は？

  O-namae wa?　　　(What is) your name?

- 明日は？

  Ashita wa?　　(How about) tomorrow?

は cannot be used in a subordinate clause, and is replaced by が:

- 地震は私が結婚した年に起きました

  Jishin wa **watashi ga kekkon shita toshi** ni okimashita

  The earthquake occurred **the year I got married**

- 京野さんが薦めてくれた本は何でしたか

  Kyōno san ga susumete kureta hon wa nan deshita ka

  What was the book **that Mr Kyono recommended?**

は cannot be used with interrogatives such as どこ 'where', だれ 'who', and なに 'what'. Instead, が is used:

- 誰が電話しましたか

  Dare ga denwa shimashita ka

  Who telephoned?

は also marks a previously identified and understood topic about which further information is to be added or a question asked:

- 「は」と「が」の違いか。それは時間がかかるのでまた明日話しましょう

  'Wa' to 'ga' no chigai ka. **Sore wa** jikan ga kakaru node mata ashita hanashimashō

  The difference between 'wa' and 'ga'? **That** will take some time, so let's talk about it tomorrow

は is commonly used in this way with こ・そ・あ・ど words to refer back to previously mentioned topics. For more information, see the section on extended use of こ・そ・あ・ど words (p. 190).

は can also be used to change the focus of a sentence so that it is viewed from a different perspective. Compare the following sentences which show the change of focus on the key element ('photos') as a topic:

- 観光客が写真を撮りました

  Kankōkyaku ga **shashin o** torimashita　　　A tourist took **photos**

- この写真は観光客が撮りました
  Kono shashin wa kankōkyaku ga torimashita
  These photos were taken by a tourist

は to show contrast

は can show a contrast between two elements. In this use, more than one instance of は in a single sentence is possible. The items to be contrasted are both marked with は:

- 今日は行きませんが明日は行きます
  Kyō wa ikimasen ga **ashita wa** ikimasu
  *I am not going **today**, but I am going **tomorrow***

The contrast can be implied, in which case only one element is present and marked:

- 日本語は難しくない
  Nihongo wa muzukashiku nai
  Japanese isn't difficult (but other languages are)

- 込んでいるから図書館では勉強できません
  Konde iru kara **toshokan dewa** benkyō dekimasen
  *Because it's crowded, I can't study **in the library** (but I can study elsewhere)*

は in negative sentences

The use of は in negative sentences is related to the function of contrast. In the following sentence, the implication is that, although the English-kanji dictionary is not available, there are other dictionaries which are:

- 漢英辞典はありません
  Kaneijiten wa arimasen
  I don't have an English-kanji dictionary

This can be explicitly stated using the 〜は〜は of contrast described above:

- 漢英辞典はありません。漢和辞典はあります
  Kaneijiten wa arimasen. **Kanwajiten wa** arimasu
  I don't have an English-kanji dictionary, (but) I do have a Japanese-kanji dictionary

This function of contrast is apparent in the use of は between a
〜て form and a strong negative:

- たばこを吸ってはいけない
  Tabako o sutte wa ikenai   You must not **smoke**

The negative sense of words like だめ and こまる, which indicate
undesirable outcomes, allows the same structure:

- 彼女に仕事について話しては困る。まだ何も決まっていない
  Kanojo ni shigoto ni tsuite hanashite wa komaru. Mada nani
  mo kimatte inai
  It could cause problems **if you were to talk to her about the job.**
  Nothing has been decided yet

は with other particles

は combines with other particles if these are being used with a noun
or phrase which is to be the topic, or to be contrasted. This results
in double particles such as には, では, とは, へは, からは, etc.:

- ここではたばこを吸わないでください
  Koko de wa tabako o suwanaide kudasai
  Please don't smoke **(in) here**

- 庭には、二羽　鶏がいる
  Niwa ni wa niwa niwatori ga iru
  There are two chickens **in the garden**

- 夫とはもう一緒に仕事したくない
  Otto to wa mō issho ni shigoto shitaku nai
  I don't want to work together **with my husband** again!

However, the addition of は to a word or phrase marked with を
or が causes the を or が to be dropped:

- 田中さんがやるというのはどうですか
  Tanaka san ga yaru to iu no wa dō desu ka
  How about **Mr Tanaka** doing it?

- いや。田中はだめだ。山田にやらせよう
  Iya. **Tanaka wa** dame da. Yamada ni yaraseyō
  No. Not **Tanaka**. Let's get Yamada to do it

- こちらに名前を書いてください
  Kochira ni **namae o** kaite kudasai
  Please write **your name** here

- 名前は性・名の順で書いてください
  Namae wa sei-mei no jun de kaite kudasai
  *Please write **your name** with the surname first, then your first name*

When も is added to a word or phrase indicating the topic, it replaces は (see も below):

- 私も　行きます。
  Watashi mo ikimasu   *I'm going, **too***

が

が links the subject with the predicate (*see p. 5*), but as many Japanese predicates describe states in a way that English equivalents do not, the most common uses of が are listed below.

　が can often be replaced by は, either for contrast or to focus on the subject as a topic. This means that the choice of は or が in a particular case can be complicated by questions of context and the speaker's intent.

To introduce a new subject

A new subject is often marked with が, but then with は thereafter, as in the typical むかしばなし 'fairy tale' opening below. Note that the distinction is marked in English by the change from 'a' to 'the':

- 昔々、浜辺に漁師が一人で住んでいました。漁師はぐいと
  釣竿をとても大事にしました
  Mukashi mukashi, hamabe ni **ryōshi ga** hitori de sunde imashita.
  Ryōshi wa gui to tsurizao o totemo daiji ni shimashita
  *Once upon a time there was **a fisherman** living alone by the sea.
  The fisherman took great care of his tackle and rod*

Subsequent references to the fisherman will be a mixture of は and が according to whether he is a subject or topic.

To mark the subject of a sentence

が indicates the subject of a sentence:

- お金がありません
  O-kane ga arimasen   *I have no **money**/There isn't any **money***

- 窓が開いている
  Mado ga aite iru   **The window** is open

- 子どもが三人います
  Kodomo ga san-nin imasu   There are three **children**

With potential verbs and verbs of ability

が is used with the subject of potential verbs (see **potential form**):

- ロシア語ができますか
  Roshiago ga dekimasu ka   Can you speak **Russian**?

- 魚が食べられない
  Sakana ga taberarenai   I can't eat **fish**

が is used in the same way with other verbs showing ability, such as わかる:

- 漢字が少し分かります
  Kanji ga sukoshi wakarimasu   I understand a few **kanji**

With verbs of perception

が is used to mark the subject of verbs of perception, such as those meaning 'see', 'hear', 'taste', and 'smell':

- あの音が聞こえますか
  Ano oto ga kikoemasu ka   Can you hear **that noise**?

- 飛行機から富士山が見えた
  Hikōki kara **Fujisan ga** mieta   I saw **Mt Fuji** from the plane

- 魚の味がする
  Sakana no aji ga suru   It tastes **of fish**

- 醤油の匂いがする
  Shōyu no nioi ga suru   It smells **of soy sauce**

With objects of desire and need

が marks the object of desire with 〜たい and ほしい, and the object of need with いる and ひつよう:

- 庭の広い家が欲しい
  Niwa no hiroi ie ga hoshii   I want **a house with a large garden**

- 南アメリカへ行くなら予防注射が要る
  Minami Amerika e iku nara **yobōchūsha ga** iru
  If you are going to South America you will need **inoculations**

See also the discussion of 〜たい in the chapter on verbs (〜たい).

With adjectives of like/dislike and skill

が marks the object of like or dislike with すき and きらい, and the name of the skill with じょうず and へた:

- 日本の食べ物が好きです
  Nihon no tabemono ga suki desu   I like **Japanese food**

- ポールさん、日本語がとても上手です
  Pōru san, **Nihongo ga** totemo jōzu desu
  Paul, **your Japanese** is very good

With two different subjects

が is used in subordinate clauses in place of は (see は above), or when the subject of the two clauses is different:

- 僕が電話したとき夏美はもういなかった
  Boku ga denwa shita toki **Natsumi wa** mō inakatta
  When I telephoned her, **Natsumi** had already left

- 弟が日本に来たら日光に連れて行きたい
  Otōto ga Nihon ni kitara Nikkō ni tsurete ikitai
  When **my brother** comes to Japan, **I'd** like to take him to Nikko

With question words

が is used with question words such as だれ, いつ, etc. (は cannot be used):

- 誰が来ましたか
  Dare ga kimashita ka   Who came?

- 夏休みに行くでしょう。いつがいい？
  Natsu yasumi ni iku deshō. **Itsu ga** ii?
  We're going in the summer holiday, aren't we? **When** will be good?

There is also a conjunction が (*see pp. 140–141*).

を

To mark a direct object

を marks the direct object of a transitive verb (*see pp. 87–91*):

- 家は毎朝ご飯を食べる
  Uchi wa maiasa **gohan o** taberu   We eat **rice** every morning

- 母は台所でテレビを見ます
  Haha wa daidokoro de **terebi o** mimasu
  Mum watches **TV** in the kitchen

To mark the area in which movement occurs

を marks the point from which movement begins:

- 大学前でバスを降ります
  Daigaku mae de **basu o** orimasu
  Get off **the bus** in front of the university

- 僕は駅を出て、喫茶店の方へ歩いた
  Boku wa **eki o** dete, kissaten no hō e aruita
  I came out of **the station** and walked towards the coffee shop

The point from which movement begins can be abstract:

- 今年の６月大学を卒業しました
  Kotoshi no roku-gatsu **daigaku o** sotsugyō shimashita
  I graduated **from university** in June this year

を also marks the space through which movement occurs:

- 次の信号を右に曲がってください
  Tsugi no shingō o migi ni magatte kudasai
  Please turn right **at the next traffic light**

- 仕事の帰りは下町の狭い道を通る
  Shigoto no kaeri wa **shitamachi no semai michi o** tōru
  On my way home from work I go through **the narrow streets of the downtown area**

With the names of occupations

を is used with the names of occupations and **する** to describe the job someone does:

- 川北さんはニューヨークで弁護士をしている
  Kawakita san wa Nyū Yōku de **bengoshi o shite iru**
  Kawakita **is a lawyer** in New York

See also the sections on passive and causative forms of the verb
(*pp. 70–73 and pp. 74–80*).

で

To show the location of an action

で marks the place where an action occurs:

- 僕は毎日図書館で勉強している
  Boku wa mainichi **toshokan de** benkyō shite iru
  I study every day **at the library**

Note that when the place is where something exists, and not where
there is an action, it is marked with に (see below).

To show the means of doing something

で is also used to mark the means of doing something, or the
instrument used:

- 電車で大学に通っています
  Densha de daigaku ni kayotte imasu
  I commute to university **by train**

- お箸でご飯を食べる
  o-hashi de gohan o taberu   eat **with chopsticks**

- 日本では千円弱で外食ができる
  Nihon dewa **sen-en jaku de** gaishoku ga dekiru
  In Japan you can eat out **for less than 1,000 yen**

With superlatives

で is used with superlatives to show the limit of a group from
which a selection is made:

- このクラスで一番日本語ができる子はリンさんです
  Kono kurasu de ichiban Nihongo ga dekiru ko wa Rin san desu
  The person **in this class** whose Japanese is the best is Lynne

To show the end of a time period

で shows when a period of time finishes:

- 会議は３時で終わる
  Kaigi wa **san-ji de** owaru   The meeting will end **at 3 o'clock**

- おじさんが５０歳で引退しました
  Ojisan ga **go-jus-sai de** intai shimashita
  My uncle retired **at 50**

To show reason

Another use of で is to show cause, although this is actually the conjunctive (〜て) form of だ (*see p. 15*) rather than the particle:

- 智子は風邪で学校を休んだ
  Michiko wa **kaze de** gakkō o yasunda
  Michiko was off school **with a cold**

に

To mark points in time

に marks points in time which can be expressed in numbers, such as time and date, and also days of the week:

- ６時に起きる
  roku-ji ni okiru   get up **at 6 o'clock**

- 火曜日に行きます
  Kayōbi ni ikimasu   I'll go **on Tuesday**

Words of relative time (i.e. those where the time is relative to when the statement is made), such as 'today', 'tomorrow', 'next week', are not marked with に:

- あさってピアノの調律師が来る
  Asatte piano no chōritsushi ga kuru
  The piano tuner is coming **the day after tomorrow**

Use of に is optional with seasons:

- 今年の秋（に）結婚するつもりです
  Kotoshi no aki (ni) kekkon suru tsumori desu
  We intend to get married **this autumn**

に marks the intervals at which something occurs:

- 年に一回実家に帰ります
  Nen ni ik-kai jikka ni kaerimasu
  I go home (to my parents' home) once **a year**

に is used with the verbs いる and ある to mark the place where something exists:

- 駅の前にスーパーがあります
  Eki no mae ni sūpā ga arimasu
  There is a supermarket **in front of the station**

- 子どもは庭にいる
  Kodomo wa **niwa ni** iru   The children are **in the garden**

To mark location

に marks location words:

- テーブルの下にあります
  Tēburu no **shita ni** arimasu   It's **under** the table

- ポケットの中に千円札が二枚ありました
  Poketto no **naka ni** sen-en-satsu ga ni-mai arimashita
  In my pocket there were two thousand-yen notes

に marks the location for verbs describing states (the location of an action is marked with で):

- 彼らはテーブルに座っている
  Karera wa **tēburu ni** suwatte iru
  They are sitting **at the table**

- 兄は大阪に住んでいます
  Ani wa **Ōsaka ni** sunde imasu   My brother lives **in Osaka**

- 浜さんは３０年同じ会社に勤めた
  Hama san wa san-jū-nen **onaji kaisha ni** tsutometa
  Mr Hama worked **for the same company** for 30 years

に marks the place towards which movement occurs (see also へ):

- 横浜に行く
  Yokohama ni iku   go **to Yokohama**

- 家に帰ります
  uchi ni kaerimasu   go **home**

に also marks the place into which movement occurs:

- **犬が部屋に入った**
  Inu ga **heya ni** haitta   A *dog* came **into the room**

- **冷蔵庫に入れてください**
  Reizōko ni irete kudasai   Please put it **in the fridge**

To show purpose

When used with the conjunctive (pre-ます) form of a verb, and certain nouns, に shows purpose:

- **私たちはカナダから勉強に来ました**
  Watashitachi wa Kanada kara **benkyō ni** kimashita
  We came from Canada **(in order) to study**

- **今日の帰りちょっと飲みに行かない？**
  Kyō no kaeri chotto **nomi ni** ikanai?
  Will you come **for a drink** on the way home?

- **ちょっと卵を買いに行ってくる**
  Chotto tamago o **kai ni** itte kuru
  I'm just going out **to buy** eggs

- **私は寿司にします**
  Watashi wa **sushi ni** shimasu
  I'll have the **sushi** (I've decided to order the **sushi**)

To mark an indirect object

に marks the indirect object ('to', 'for') with verbs of giving and receiving, or where an action is performed for someone's benefit:

- **姉に本を上げました**
  Ane ni hon o agemashita   I gave **my sister** a book

- **経緯を先生に話した**
  Ikisatsu o **sensei ni** hanashita
  I explained the background circumstances **to the teacher**

- **高雄は毎週お母さんに手紙を書いています**
  Takao wa maishū **okāsan ni** tegami o kaite imasu
  Takao writes **to his mother** every week

- ジャックはアルバイトで**今井先生の子どもに**英語を教える
  Jakku wa arubaito de **Imai sensei no kodomo ni** eigo o oshieru
  Jack will have a part-time job teaching English **to Imai sensei's children**

- 父は家族のために頑張っている
  Chichi wa **kazoku no tame ni** gambatte iru
  My father is doing his best **for the sake of the family**

With verbs which imply receiving something, the source is marked with に (but see also から below)

- 母にズボンをもらいました
  Haha ni zubon o moraimashita
  I got some trousers **from my mum**

- 皆さんに素敵なお土産をいただいてありがとうございます
  Minasan ni suteki-na omiyage o itadaite arigatō gozaimasu
  I am very grateful for the wonderful present I have received **from you all**

- ショウ先生に習った日本語が役に立ちました
  Shō sensei ni naratta Nihongo ga yaku ni tachimashita
  The Japanese I learned **from Shaw sensei** was very useful

- 宿題ができたら日本人の友達に見てもらった
  Shukudai ga dekitara **Nihonjin no tomodachi ni** mite moratta
  When my homework was finished, I got a **Japanese friend** to look at it

- 日本に留学したとき白石先生に大変お世話になりました
  Nihon ni ryūgaku shita toki **Shiraishi sensei ni** taihen o-sewa ni narimashita
  Professor Shiraishi kindly looked after me when I was studying in Japan

With passive and causative verbs

に shows the agent who performs the action in passive, causative, and causative-passive sentences (*see pp. 70–80*):

- 先生に怒られました
  Sensei ni okoraremashita   **The teacher** was angry with me

- 子供たちに部屋を片づけさせた
  Kodomotachi ni heya o katazukesaseta
  I made **the children** tidy the room

- 父に勉強させられた
  Chichi ni benkyō saserareta
  I was made to study **by my father**

With conjunctive (pre-ます) form and なる to form honorifics

に is used with the conjunctive (pre-ます) form + なる to create an honorific form for certain verbs:

- この証は天皇陛下がお書きニなりました
  Kono shō wa tenno heika ga **o-kaki ni narimashita**
  This certificate **was written** by the emperor himself

For more information and examples, see the section on keigo (*p. 213*).

With なる to indicate change

に with the verb なる 'to become' indicates change:

- 卒業して小学校の先生になりたい
  Sotsugyō shite **shōgakkō no sensei ni** naritai
  After graduating I want to be **a primary teacher**

To make adverbial forms

に is also used with な adjectives to make adverbial forms (*see pp. 106–107, 120*):

- 静かにしなさい
  Shizuka ni shi nasai   Please be **quiet**

- ゆっくり休んだので元気になりました
  Yukkuri yasunda no de **genki ni** narimashita
  I had a good rest, so I feel fully **recovered**

Note also the expression しけんに うかる・試験に受かる 'to pass an exam'.

See also the section on よう（に）in the chapter on conjunctive particles (*pp. 146–147*), and the section on こと（にする and になる）in the chapters on nominalizers (*pp. 206–208, 211–212*) and verbs (*pp. 93–94*).

と

The particle と connects nouns to mean 'and':

* リトルさんは日本語と韓国語とロシア語が話せます
  Ritoru san wa **Nihongo to Kankokugo to Roshiago** ga
  hanasemasu
  Mr Little can speak **Japanese, Korean, and Russian**

* ご飯とみそ汁
  gohan to miso shiru   rice, and miso soup

The use of と means that the list is exhaustive. In a menu, for
example, the above would mean 'rice with miso soup, and nothing
else'. (Compare this with the use of や described below.)
　　The interpretation 'and' can be extended to mark reciprocity.
This can often translate as 'with':

* 友達と行きました
  Tomodachi to ikimashita   I went **with a friend**

* 先週家族と映画を見に行った
  Senshū **kazoku to** eiga o mi ni itta
  Last week I went **with my family** to see a movie

と is used in this sense where there is a mutual or reciprocal
element, such as with the verbs 'to marry', 'to talk (with)',
'to be the same as/different from':

* 私は日本人と結婚しています
  Watashi wa **Nihonjin to** kekkon shite imasu
  I'm married **to a Japanese** (and he is married to me)

* 仕事は前と同じだ
  Shigoto wa **mae to** onaji da
  The job is the same **as before**

* 昨日の晩母と話しました
  Kino no ban **haha to** hanashimashita
  Last night I spoke **with mum** (and she spoke with me)

と is also used to mark a quotation, and with verbs indicating
asking, speaking, and thinking (especially いう 'to say' and
おもう 'to think'):

- 奥さんによろしくと言いました
  Okusan ni yoroshiku **to iimashita**
  She sent her regards to you (**She said** 'Give my regards to your wife')

- 部品は明日届くと聞いた
  Buhin wa ashita todoku **to kiita**
  I heard the parts will arrive tomorrow

- 日本の大学で勉強したいと思います
  Nihon no daigaku de benkyō shitai **to omoimasu**
  I think I'd like to study at a Japanese university

と is used idiomatically in the expression という to identify or give more information about the noun which follows, and is often translated as 'called':

- これは日本語で何と言いますか
  Kore wa Nihongo de nan **to iimasu** ka
  What **do you call** this in Japanese?

- 前橋という市を聞いたことがありますか
  Maebashi to iu shi o kiita koto ga arimasu ka
  Have you heard of a city **called Maebashi**?

- 大郷さんという人から電話がありました
  Osato san to iu hito kara denwa ga arimashita
  There was a phone call from someone **called Osato**

と marks manner with adverbs, especially in sound symbolism (see p. 118):

- 外で突然犬がワンワンとほえはじめました
  Soto de totsuzen inu ga **wanwan to** hoehajimemashita
  Suddenly the dog began to bark **'woof woof'** outside

- 行くか行かないかはっきりと決めなさい
  Iku ka ikanai ka **hakkiri to** kime nasai
  Decide **definitely** whether or not you are going

Note that there is also a conjunction と (see p. 135) which has a different use.

の

The particle の is used to show a relationship between nouns or noun phrases where the first element modifies the second (*see p. 209*). In English translations, the modifying element usually comes first, but in some cases can also be second:

ともだちの　おかあさん
my friend's mother/the mother **of my friend**

The addition of の can have a function similar to that of the apostrophe plus 's' in English:

- これは恵子の辞書です
  Kore wa **Keiko no** jisho desu　　This is **Keiko's** dictionary

- 田中さんのお家は右側にあります
  Tanaka san no o-uchi wa migigawa ni arimasu
  Ms Tanaka's home is on the right

However, the English equivalents will vary and not always have the apostrophe:

- 日本語の辞書
  Nihongo no jisho　　a **Japanese** dictionary

- ３時の授業
  san-ji no jugyō　　the **3 o'clock** class

- 中国からの留学生が増えています
  Chūgoku kara no ryūgakusei ga fuete imasu
  Exchange students **from China** are increasing in number

The addition of の to a word indicating a person shows possession, and is often equivalent to the English 'my', 'her', 'my sister's', etc.:

- 父の友達
  chichi no tomodachi　　a friend **of my father**

- 私の車はあそこです
  Watashi no kuruma wa asoko desu　　**My** car is over there

This usage is wider than the English equivalent:

- マンチェスター大学のバントです
  Manchesutā daigaku no Banto desu
  My name is Bunt, **from Manchester University**

- ６０歳の女の人
  roku-jus-sai no onna no hito   *a woman **of 60***
- リモコンはテレビの上にある
  Rimokon wa **terebi no** ue ni aru
  *The remote control is on top **of the TV***

The noun following の can sometimes be omitted if it is clear from the context, and so is similar to the English 'mine', 'yours', etc.:

- これは僕のです
  Kore wa **boku no** desu   *This is **mine***

At the end of a sentence, の indicates a question (usually to confirm and add detail to known information), and is a stylistic marker for female speech:

- 何時に行くの？
  Nan-ji ni iku no   *What time are you going?*

の can be used instead of が with subjects in modifying clauses:

- アニーの買ってくれたワインはとてもおいしかった
  Anii no katte kureta wain wa totemo oishikatta
  *The wine **that Annie** bought (for us) was really delicious*

の is also a nominalizer (*see p. 206*) and a pronoun (*p. 239*).

∣ へ

へ indicates motion towards a goal or a person. It is generally interchangeable with に:

- いつ日本へ行きますか
  Itsu **Nihon e** ikimasu ka   *When are you going **to Japan**?*
- 弟へ誕生日のカードを送らなかった
  Otōto e tanjōbi no kādo o okuranakatta
  *I didn't send a birthday card **to my brother***

∣ も

も marks equivalence in the sense of 'also', 'both . . . and . . .':

- 彼女はピアノもギターも弾ける
  Kanojo wa **piano mo gitā mo** hikeru
  She can play **both the piano and the guitar**

The equivalent element is often implied from the context:

- 私も行きたい
  Watashi mo ikitai   I want to go **too**

- 日本でも環境汚染がひどかった
  Nihon demo kankyō osen ga hidokatta
  In Japan as well, the environmental pollution was appalling

も also marks emphasis and is added to interrogatives to produce
words such as the following:

いつも	any time, all the time
だれも	nobody
なにも	nothing
どこも	anywhere, nowhere

- あの家のカーテンはいつも閉まっています
  Ano ie no kāten wa **itsumo** shimatte imasu
  The curtains in that house are **always** shut

- 私がうそをついたことを誰も知りません
  Watashi ga uso o tsuita koto o **daremo** shirimasen
  Nobody knows that I lied

- 何回も何回もお願いしたけれどダメでした
  Nan-kai mo nan-kai mo o-negai shita keredo dame da
  I've asked **again and again**, but it's no good

With words indicating extent and amount, も can mean 'even . . .'
or 'not even . . .', depending on whether the predicate is positive
or negative:

- 新聞も読める
  Shinbun mo yomeru   I can **even** read **a newspaper**

- 新聞も読めない
  Shinbun mo yomenai   I can't **even** read **a newspaper**

- 千円もしません
  Sen-en mo shimasen
  It doesn't **even** cost **1,000 yen**/It costs less than 1,000 yen

- 千円もします
  Sen-en mo shimasu   It costs **as much as 1,000** yen

The use of も with the 〜て form is described in the relevant sections on verbs and adjectives. See also でも below.

▎か

か is used at the end of sentences to mark questions (these can be rhetorical questions):

- いつ日本へ行きますか
  Itsu Nihon e ikimasu ka   When are you going to Japan?

- お手洗いはどこですか
  O-tearai wa doko desu ka   Where is the toilet?

- 飯田さんは明日来ないか
  Iida san wa ashita konai ka
  So Iida isn't coming tomorrow then!

か is also used within sentences to indicate uncertainty, or to mark alternatives:

- 来年オランダへ行けるかどうか分かりません
  Rainen Oranda e **ikeru ka dō ka** wakarimasen
  I don't know **if I can go** to Holland (**or not**) next year

- スペイン語かイタリア語かもう一つの科目を選ぶ
  Supeingo ka Itariago ka mō hitotsu no kamoku o erabu
  I am going to choose one more subject, **Spanish or Italian**?

▎だって

This is だ plus a contracted form of という. See below under って.

▎って

This is a contracted form of the particle と and the verb いう. It can indicate either a topic (first example) or report (second example):

- 辞書ってどこ？
  Jisho tte doko?   Where is **the dictionary**?

- さっきの電話は大淵だった。もう着いたって
  Sakki no denwa wa Ōbuchi datta. Mō tsuita **tte**
  That phone call just now was from Obuchi. **He said** he'd arrived

から

The basic meaning of から is 'from':

- 授業は１０時からです
  Jugyō wa **jū-ji kara** desu　　　Classes are **from 10 o'clock**
- 大学は駅から遠いですか
  Daigaku wa **eki kara** tōi desu ka
  Is the university far **from the station**?

から can also mark the source in giving and receiving, in place of に:

- 兄からジャケットをもらいました
  Ani kara jaketto o moraimashita
  I got a jacket **from my brother**
- 母から手紙が届きました
  Haha kara tegami ga todokimashita
  A letter came **from mum**
- 上原さんとの結婚を弟さんから聞いた
  Uehara san to no kekkon o **otōtosan kara** kiita
  I heard about you getting married to Mr Uehara **from your brother**

から is used to mean 'from' with named organizations (where the use of に is ungrammatical):

- 日本の政府から奨学金をもらった
  Nihon no seifu kara shōgakukin o moratta
  I received a scholarship **from the Japanese government**

(There is also a conjunction から whose possible English equivalents include 'because' and 'after'. *See p. 143.*)

まで

まで is used to mark a limit (of time, space, etc.):

- アルバイトは夜６時から１０時までです
  Arubaito wa yoru roku-ji kara **jū-ji made** desu
  *My part-time job is from 6 **to 10** p.m.*

- 駅まで一緒に行きましょう
  Eki made issho ni ikimashō
  *Let's go **as far as the station** together*

- 大学に入るまで毎日３時間ピアノの練習をした
  Daigaku ni hairu made mainichi san-jikan piano no renshū o shita
  Up until I was at university, I practised the piano for 3 hours every day

まで can also be used to show the most extreme extent to which an action might lead:

- 駐車違反だけで強制送還まではしないでしょう
  Chūshaihan dake de **kyōseisōkan made** wa shinai deshō
  Surely they wouldn't go so far as deporting me for a parking offence?

When まで is followed by the particle に, it emphasizes the point at which the time period finishes, e.g. when giving a deadline:

- レポートは来週の木曜日までに提出してください
  Repōto wa **raishū no mokuyōbi made ni** no teishutsu shite kudasai
  *Please hand in the essay **by Thursday next week***

より

より is the particle of comparison, and means 'than' or 'rather than':

- 東京は大阪より寒いです
  Tokyo wa **Ōsaka yori** samui desu
  *Tokyo is colder **than Osaka***

- 日本語はフランス語よりやさしい
  Nihongo wa **Furansugo yori** yasashii
  *Japanese is easier **than French***

- １人で行くより２人で行くのがいい
  Hitori de iku yori futari de iku no ga ii
  *It's better to go together **than (to go) alone***

より is also used to mean 'from' in relation to a point in space or time, similar to から:

- 6番線に電車がまいりますので黄色い線より内側に下がってください
  Roku-ban-sen ni densha ga mairimasu no de **kiiroi sen yori** uchigawa ni sagatte kudasai
  A train is arriving at platform 6, so please step back **behind the yellow line**

- これより先危ないですから気をつけてください
  Kore yori saki abunai desu kara ki o tsukete kudasai
  From this point on it's dangerous, so please be careful

- 僕のアパートは信号より手前にあります
  Boku no apāto wa **shingō yori** temae ni arimasu
  My apartment is just **before the traffic lights**

より can mark the time or place of starting as a formal equivalent of から:

- 只今より演奏が始まります
  Tadaima yori ensō ga hajimarimasu
  The recital will **now** commence

In this usage it is sometimes used to sign off letters:

- 沢井明より
  Sawai Akira yori   from/sincerely, Akira Sawai

でも

でも is an equivalent of the 〜て form of verbs and adjectives, with も (*see p. 54*). It is used to mark emphasis ('even'), or hypothetical situations ('even if . . .'):

- 子供でもできる
  Kodomo demo dekiru   **Even a child** can do it

でも is also used to introduce a disagreement, or add a condition to something previously said:

- でも人によって違うでしょう
  Demo hito ni yotte chigau deshō
  However, it's probably different from person to person

くらい or ぐらい

This indicates an approximate amount or extent:

- 駅はここから歩いて３０分ぐらいです
  Eki wa koko kara aruite **san-jup-pun gurai** desu
  The station is **about 30 minutes** walk from here

- 大学でどのくらい日本語を勉強しましたか
  Daigaku de **dono kurai** Nihongo o benkyō shimashita ka
  How much Japanese did you study in university?

くらい is used in comparisons to mean 'as . . . as . . .':

- 部長のゴルフはプロぐらい上手です
  Buchō no gorufu wa **puro gurai** jōzu desu
  The manager's golf is **as good as that of a professional**

くらい is only used with periods of time, and not with points in time, in which case the noun ごろ is used as a suffix:

- ６時ごろ
  roku-ji **goro**　　　**about** 6 o'clock

- 何時ごろ帰りますか
  Nan-ji goro kaerimasu ka
  About what time will you come home?

See also **numbers and counting** p. 204.

ほど

This particle sets a limit ('to the extent of . . .', 'as far as . . .') or shows an approximate amount:

- ペンが持てないほど手が痛い
  Pen ga motenai hodo te ga itai
  My hand hurts so much **that I can't hold a pen**

- ２００人ほど収容できる講義室がある
  Ni-hyaku-nin hodo shūyō dekiru kōgishitsu ga aru
  There's a lecture theatre that can hold **up to 200 people**

ほど is commonly used in comparisons with the meaning 'not as (much) as . . .' when the predicate is negative:

- 私はスティーブほどビールが飲めません
  Watashi wa **Sutiibu hodo** biiru ga nomemasen
  I can't drink as much beer **as Steve**

- 日本は高い。でも人が言うほどじゃない
  Nihon wa takai. Demo **hito ga iu hodo** ja nai
  Japan is expensive but not as much **as people say**

The idiomatic construction 〜ば〜ほど means 'the more . . . , the more . . .':

- 大きければ大きいほどいい
  Ōkikereba ōkii hodo ii   The bigger, the better

- 漢字は書けば書くほど、よく身につく
  Kanji wa kakeba kaku hodo yoku mi ni tsuku
  The more you write kanji, the more you remember them

ばかり, ばっかり

ばかり shows a limit of amount, and is often translated as 'only', 'just'. It can mean 'not only . . . but also . . .' with a negative:

- 今年はいいことばかりあった
  Kotoshi wa **ii koto bakari** atta
  This year **only good things** happened

- 好きなものばかり食べては行けません
  Suki-na mono bakari tabete wa ikemasen
  It's not good to eat **just the things you like**

- 本ばかり読んでいないで外で遊びなさい
  Hon bakari yonde inaide soto de asobi nasai
  Don't **just** read **books** - play outside!

ばかり is used with the 〜た form to show that something has just happened:

- 日本から帰ったばかりだ
  Nihon kara **kaetta bakari** da
  I have **only just returned** from Japan

It is also used with a negative nuance to mean 'nothing but . . .':

- 天野君は勉強しない。遊んでばかりいる
  Amano kun wa benkyō shinai. **Asonde bakari** iru
  Amano isn't studying. He does **nothing but mess around**

When emphasizing a reason, ばかり is used to mean 'simply because . . .':

- 私は外国人と結婚したばかりに父に勘当された
  Watashi wa **gaikokujin to kekkon shita bakari** ni chichi ni kandō sareta
  My father disowned me **just because I married a foreigner**

だけ

だけ shows a limited quantity ('only', 'just'):

- 彼女だけ弁当を持ってきました
  Kanojo dake bentō o motte kimashita
  Only she brought a packed lunch

- このCDは5百円だけでした
  Kono shiidii wa **go-hyaku-en dake** deshita
  This CD was **only 500 yen**

だけ is used with ではなく to express 'not only . . . but also . . .':

- ティーブは日本語だけではなく韓国語もロシア語も話せるよ
  Sutiibu wa **Nihongo dake dewa naku** Kankokugo mo Roshiago mo hanaseru yo
  Steve speaks **not only Japanese** but also Korean and Russian

It is also used in the expressions おすきなだけ 'as much as you like', and できるだけ 'as much as possible':

- お寿司をお好きなだけ食べてください
  O sushi o **o-suki-na dake** tabete kudasai
  Please eat as much sushi **as you like**

- できるだけ早く来てください
  Dekiru dake hayaku kite kudasai
  Please come as early **as possible**

さえ

さえ is used for emphasis to mean '(not) even':

- 上野先生さえ知らない字でした
  Ueno sensei sae shiranai ji deshita
  It was a kanji character that **not even Professor Ueno** knew

- 千円さえあったらあの本が買えたんだ
  Sen-en sae attara ano hon ga kaeta n da
  If I'd had **even just 1,000 yen** I could have bought the book

しか

This particle is always used with a negative predicate, and shows limit in the sense of 'merely', 'no more than':

- ニューヨークには　２日しか　いませんでした
  Nyū Yōku niwa **futsuka shika** imasen deshita
  We were **only** in New York for **two days**

- １０００円しかない
  Sen-en shika nai   I have **only** got **1,000 yen**

Used with verbs, しか is used to mean 'there is nothing to do except . . .':

- 彼女はもう来ないから帰るしかない
  Kanojo wa mō konai kara **kaeru shika nai**
  She's not coming so **there's nothing to do but go home**

こそ

This adds emphasis, but English translations will vary considerably:

- 来年こそ合格したい
  Rainen **koso** gōkaku shitai
  NEXT year I want to pass (the exam)!

- だからこそ怒っている
  Dakara **koso** okotte iru   **THAT's** why I am angry!

こそ is used in the expression こちらこそ meaning 'Not at all' when responding to thanks:

- どうも　ありがとう　ございました
  Dōmo arigatō gozaimashita   Thank you very much

- こちらこそ
  Kochira koso   Not at all!

など

など indicates that the given example is only one item from a list, and so has a meaning similar to 'and so on', 'etc.':

- **日本語はロシア語などスラブ言語族とは違います**
  Nihongo wa **Roshiago nado** Surabu gengozoku towa chigaimasu
  Japanese is different from Slavonic languages such as **Russian etc.**

- **お茶など一杯どうですか**
  O-cha nado ip-pai dō desu ka
  Would you like **tea or something**?

ね

ね is used to express emphasis or agreement with someone, and is also used to seek confirmation. This is in some ways similar to tag questions in English (e.g. 'isn't it?', 'aren't you?', 'don't they?', etc.). The function of ね is to mark information as already known to the listener. In written dialogue, ね is also found written as ねえ and ねぇ:

- **暑いですね**
  Atsui desu **ne**   It's hot, **isn't it**

- **そうですね**
  Sō desu **ne**   Yes, **you're right**!

- **日本語は上手だね**
  Nihongo wa jōzu da **ne**   Your Japanese is very good!

- **高かったね**
  Takakatta **ne**   It was expensive, **wasn't it**?

- **いいですね**
  Ii desu **ne**   That's good/I'm pleased to hear it

- **日曜の試合は２時からですね**
  Nichiyō no shiai wa ni-ji kara desu **ne**
  The match on Sunday is from 2 o'clock, **right**?

- **吉田さんは明日来るでしょうかね**
  Yoshida san wa ashita kuru **deshō ka ne**
  I suppose Yoshida's coming tomorrow?

The use of ね can also add emphasis, or soften the tone of requests and commands:

- ちょっと待ってね
  Chotto matte **ne**　　Just a moment

- 忘れないでね
  Wasurenaide **ne**　　Don't forget, **eh**!

な

This is a more masculine version of ね, and should not to be confused with the negative imperative (*see p. 84*):

- 面倒なことになったな
  Mendō-na koto ni natta **na**　　That's a pain!

- そうだよな
  Sō da **na**　　That's right (**isn't it**?)

さ

さ is used to soften statements in male speech:

- 僕は出来るだけやるさ
  Boku wa dekiru dake yaru **sa**　　I'll do as much as I can

よ

よ is a sentence-ending particle used to mark information new to the listener (familiar information is marked with ね). This draws attention to whatever is marked:

- 早く起きなさい。　8時過ぎですよ
  Hayaku oki nasai. Hachi-ji sugi desu **yo**
  Get up quickly. It's after 8 o'clock

- ジョージさんは　アメリカ人ですね
  Jōji san wa Amerikajin desu ne
  George is an American, isn't he?

  違います。ブラジル人ですよ
  Chigaimasu. Burajirujin desu **yo**
  No, he isn't, he's Brazilian

よ also softens commands and rebukes:

* だめですよ
  Dame desu **yo**　　Don't do that!/Stop it!/No!

* もうちょっと気をつけてよ
  Mō chotto ki o tsukete **yo**　　Be more careful!

ぞ

This is a more emphatic and male version of よ:

* あまり池に近づくと落ちるぞ
  Amari ike ni chikazuku to ochiru **zo**
  If you get too close to the pond, you'll fall in

かなあ

This is used to show uncertainty, and is often translated as 'I wonder if . . .':

* 木村君は彼女にもう一度電話したかなあ
  Kimura kun wa kanojo ni mō ichido denwa shita **kanā**
  I **wonder if** Kimura called his girlfriend again

It is also written かなぁ:

* 今日の夕飯はなにかなぁ
  Kyō no yū han wa nani **kana**
  I **wonder** what's for dinner tonight

かしら

かしら is a distinctly female-speaker version of かなあ:

* 亜紀ちゃんは彼にもう一度電話したかしら
  Aki chan wa kare ni mō ichido denwa shita **kashira**
  I **wonder if** Aki called her boyfriend again

わ

わ is used by women to express emotion and soften the tone:

* **難しいわ**
  Muzukashii **wa**   It's difficult

* **また行きたいですわ**
  Mata ikitai desu **wa**   I'd like to go again

かい

This is a masculine version of the question particle か:

* **もうお終いかい**
  Mō o-shimai **kai**   Finished already?

Auxiliary suffixes

What is an auxiliary?

In English, auxiliaries are verbs such as 'be', 'do', and 'will',
which are used with other verbs to show changes in function
or meaning. For example, 'do' can be used to express questions
('Do you understand?'), and 'will' can be used to express a future
time ('She will understand when she's older').

Japanese auxiliaries, or **jodōshi** (助動詞), cannot exist as
independent words, but instead are used as endings attached
to certain stems of verbs or adjectives. They often have modal
meanings expressing likelihood or obligation, comparable to
English 'may', 'must', etc.

Types of auxiliary

Many Japanese auxiliaries are used in ways that are often thought
of as 'forms' of verbs and adjectives. These include ます, たい,
ない, させる, and （ら）れる. For more information on these,
see the chapters on style, verbs, and adjectives. There are,
however, other auxiliaries which are usually treated as suffixes.
The most important of these is だ, which is given a chapter of
its own because of its importance (see p. 15).

らしい
らしい is added to the plain forms of verbs and adjectives,
and conjugates like an い adjective, with the meaning 'seems'.
(There are other structures with similar meanings – see よう（だ）
and そう（だ）below.) It is generally used to show that
information the speaker has heard or seen leads him to believe
that something is (or is not) the case with a very high degree
of certainty. In this use, らしい follows plain forms:

- 日本の国立大学の入学試験は難しいらしいです
  Nihon no kokuritsu daigaku no nyūgaku shiken wa **muzukashii rashii** desu
  Apparently Japanese national university entrance examinations are **difficult**

- 豊田先生は明日来ないらしい
  Toyoda sensei wa ashita **konai rashii**
  It seems that Mrs Toyoda **isn't coming** tomorrow

- 道路工事が珍しく予定通り終るらしい
  Dōrokōji ga mezurashiku yotei-dōri **owaru rashii**
  The roadworks are **apparently going to finish** on time, for a change

- 早く帰ったほうがいいよ。奥さんが怒っているらしい
  Hayaku kaetta hō ga ii yo. Okusan ga **okotte iru rashii**
  You'd better go home quick. Your wife **seems to be angry**!

The use of らしい with a noun indicates the conformity of someone or something to a type, as in the English 'teacher-like' or 'typical teacher':

- そんなばかなことをするのは先生らしくない
  Sonna baka-na koto o suru no wa **sensei rashiku nai**
  Doing something that stupid is **not fitting for a teacher**

- ナンシーさんの日本語は上手だが日本人らしい日本語じゃない
  Nanshii san no Nihongo wa jōzu da ga, **Nihonjin rashii** Nihongo ja nai
  Nancy's Japanese is good, but it is not **like a native speaker's** Japanese

そう（だ）

そう（だ）is used in two ways. With the plain forms of verbs and adjectives, and だ, it indicates information based on hearsay:

- 彼は再婚するそうです
  Kare wa **saikon suru** sō desu   **I've heard** that he's **remarrying**

- 来年度の試験には面接試験もあるそうだ
  Rainendo no shiken ni wa mensetsu shiken mo **aru sō da**
  I hear that there is going to be an oral test in next year's examination

- 入院する直前まで元気だったそうです
  Nyūin suru chokuzen made **genki datta sō desu**
  They say that he was well until just before he was admitted to hospital

- 明日雨だそうです
  Ashita ame **da sō desu**
  Apparently it's going to rain tomorrow

The second use of そう (だ) is to indicate a judgement based on what is seen, with the meaning 'it looks like'. In this case it is used with the pre-ます forms of verbs and with adjective stems. い adjectives drop the final い and な adjectives lose the final な:

- 雨が降りそうだ。早く布団をしまったほうがいい
  Ame ga **furi-sō da**. Hayaku futon o shimatta hō ga ii
  It looks like it's going to rain. You'd better bring the futon inside quick

- 自分で作ったか。おいしそうだ
  Jibun de tsukutta ka. **Oishi-sō da**
  You made them yourself? **They look delicious**

- 彼は落ちそうだから見てはいられない
  Kare wa **ochi-sō dakara** mite wa irarenai
  He **looks like he's going to fall** – I can't bear to watch

- 子供は元気そうでよかった
  Kodomo wa **genki-sō** de yokatta
  I'm glad the children are **looking well**

- 部品の質が悪そうだ
  Buhin no shitsu ga **waru-sō da**
  The quality of the parts **looks poor**

The adjective いい 'good' has the form よさそう (だ):

- 明日の天気がよさそうです
  Ashita no tenki ga **yosa-sō desu**
  The weather tomorrow **looks good**

みたい (だ)

This is added to the plain forms of verbs and adjectives to mean 'seems', 'apparently':

- 川村さんは明日来るみたいです
  Kawamura san wa ashita **kuru mitai desu**
  It looks like Ms Kawamura **will come** tomorrow

- 日本の物価は高いみたいだ
  Nihon no bukka wa **takai mitai da**
  Prices in Japan **seem high**

- 違うバンドが同じタイトールを使ったみたいだ
  Chigau bando ga onaji taitōru o **tsukatta mitai da**
  Apparently a different band **has used** the same song title

In informal speech the final だ is sometimes omitted:

- 彼がもう読み終わったみたい
  Kare ga mō **yomi-owatta mitai**
  It looks like he's **finished reading** already

まい

まい is added to the plain forms of verbs and adjectives to give the negative meaning 'ought not'. It is a negative equivalent of the volitional form of the verb (e.g. いこう、しよう). It is relatively uncommon except in formal writing:

- このテロリズムが第3次世界大戦に発展することはあるまい
  Kono terorizumu ga dai-san-ji sekai taisen ni hatten suru koto wa **aru mai**
  This act of terrorism **ought not** (**to be** allowed) to develop into a third world war

It is also used to show that the speaker doesn't want to do something:

- 2度と行くまい
  Ni-dō to **iku mai**   I **have no intention of going** again

だろう・でしょう

だろう is used after the plain forms of verbs and adjectives to give the meanings 'probably', 'ought to', 'should'. (Note that だろう is a part of だ similar to the volitional form of verbs, but is not an exact equivalent as it is not used for the meaning 'Let's . . .')
(*see p. 33 and p. 15*):

- 所長は明日たぶん来ないだろう
  Shōchō wa ashita tabun **konai darō**
  The director is **probably not coming** tomorrow

- 義明はお兄さんと一緒ですから大丈夫だろう
  Yoshiaki wa oniisan to isshō desu kara **daijōbu darō**
  Yoshiaki is with his big brother, so they **should be OK**

The polite form of だろう is でしょう:

- 今夜雨が降るでしょう
  Konya ame ga **furu deshō**   It will **probably rain** tonight

- もうこの人は助からないでしょう
  Mō kono hito o **tasukaranai** deshō
  He **probably can't be saved** now

でしょう can be used for seeking agreement in ways similar to the particle ね *(see pp. 177–178)*:

- 日本は高いでしょう？
  Nihon wa **takai** deshō   Japan's **expensive, isn't it!**

べき（だ）

This follows the dictionary form of a verb to add the meaning 'must', 'should', or 'ought to':

- 明日行くべきです
  Ashita **iku beki desu**   I **must go** tomorrow

- 職場では男女が平等に扱われるべきだ
  Shokuba de wa danjo ga byōdō ni **azukawareru beki da**
  In the workplace men and women **should be treated** equally

The こ・そ・あ・ど group of words

This chapter deals with words indicating location and their corresponding question words. When referring to location, English distinguishes between the two categories of the area near the speaker ('this', 'here'), and any area not near the speaker ('that', 'there'). In Japanese there are three categories: words beginning with こ〜 indicate the area near the speaker, そ〜 words indicate the area near the listener, and あ〜 words refer to the area which is distant from both the speaker and the listener. As English does not distinguish the three ways, translations into English of words in the そ〜 and あ〜 groups are often the same.

Question words equivalent to the English 'wh-?' (e.g. 'which?', 'where?') begin with ど〜.

The words forming this group belong to various parts of speech, but they are best treated together as they form a distinct group. Some words of this type with following particles are used as conjunctions (*see p. 129*).

'This', 'that', and 'which?'

In English, the words 'this' and 'that' can act both as pronouns (standing alone) and as determiners (indicating a particular noun):

This is expensive
This car is expensive

In Japanese, there are different forms. When used without a following noun, the forms are これ 'this/these', それ 'that/those', and あれ 'that/those over there':

- これは何ですか
  Kore wa nan desu ka   What is **this**?

- **いい靴だよね。それは新しいですか**
  Ii kutsu da yo ne. **Sore** wa atarashii desu ka
  Nice shoes. Are **they** new?

- **あれは富士山だ**
  Are wa Fujisan da   That's Mt Fuji **over there**

When used with a following noun, the forms are この〜,
その〜, あの〜:

- **この言葉の意味が分かりません**
  Kono kotoba no imi ga wakarimasen
  I don't understand the meaning of **this word**

- **あの高いビルは何ですか**
  Ano takai **biru** wa nan desu ka
  What is **that** tall **building over there**?

The question word どちら (or in conversation どっち) meaning
'which?' is used to distinguish between two choices. (See below
for other meanings of どちら.) If there are more than two choices,
どれ is used:

- **テニスかバレーボールか、どっちが好き？**
  Tenisu ka barēbōru ka, **dotchi** ga suki?
  Which do you prefer, tennis or volleyball?

- **このチョコレートの中でどれが好きですか**
  Kono chokorēto no naka de **dore** ga suki desu ka
  Which of these chocolates do you like?

With a following noun, the word for 'which?' is どの:

- **どの本ですか**
  Dono hon desu ka   Which book is it?

- **事務局長さんはどの人ですか**
  Jimukyoku-san wa **dono hito** desu ka
  Which one is the personnel manager?

'Here', 'there', and 'where?'

The words for 'here', 'there', and 'over there' are ここ, そこ, and
あそこ:

- **車の鍵はここにありますよ**
  Kuruma no kagi wa **koko** ni arimasu yo   The car keys are **here**!

- **駅はあそこですか**
  Eki wa **asoko** desu ka   *Is the station **over there**?*

The word for 'where?' is どこ, or the more polite どちら:

- **すみませんが地下鉄の入り口はどこですか**
  Sumimasen ga chikatetsu no iriguchi wa **doko** desu ka
  *Excuse me! **Where** is the entrance to the subway?*

- **お国はどちらですか**
  O-kuni wa **dochira** desu ka
  ***Where** (**which** country) are you from?*

こちら, そちら, あちら, どちら

This is another set of こ・そ・あ・ど words, meaning 'this direction', 'that direction', 'which direction?':

- **こちらへ来てください**
  Kochira e kite kudasai   *Please come **this way/here***

These words are also used as polite equivalents of ここ, そこ, あそこ, and どこ:

- **お客様の部屋はこちらです**
  O-kyaku sama no heya wa **kochira** desu
  ***Here** is your room, Sir/Madam*

These forms can be used to refer politely to people, for example on the phone:

- **すみません。佐藤ですが、そちらに息子がお邪魔していますでしょうか**
  Sumimasen. Satō desu ga **sochira** ni musuko ga o-jama shite imasu deshō ka
  *Excuse me. It's Satō. Is my son **with you** at the moment?*

- **どちら様ですか**
  Dochira sama desu ka   *Who is it, please?*

The abbreviated forms こっち, そっち, あっち, どっち are used in informal speech:

- **彼女は来週こっちへ来る**
  Kanojo wa raishū **kotchi** e kuru   *She is coming **here** next week*

- **どっちがいい？**
  Dotchi ga ii?   *Which (of the two) is better/do you want?*

'This kind', 'that kind', and 'what kind?'

The phrases このような～, そのような～, etc. are commonly contracted to こんな, そんな, あんな, どんな to mean 'this/that/what kind of?':

- 彼はどんな人ですか
  Kare wa **donna hito** desu ka   **What kind of person** is he?

- 日本語はそんなに難しくない
  Nihongo wa **sonna ni muzukashiku nai**
  Japanese is **not that difficult**

- こんな暑い夏はもう耐えられない
  Konna atsui natsu wa mō taerarenai
  I can't bear **this kind of hot summer** any more

'In this way', 'in that way', and 'in which way?'

The words こう・そう・ああ・どう 'this/that/which way?' are used with verbs (notably する) to show the manner in which something is done:

- そう食べてはいけない
  Sō tabete wa ikenai   You shouldn't eat **like that/that way**

- こうすれば少し楽になる
  Kō sureba sukoshi raku ni naru
  If you do it **this way** it will be slightly easier

- そうしよう
  Sō shiyō!   Let's do **that**!

- どうしたんですか
  Dō shita n' desu ka
  What's happened?/Is anything the matter?

- どうでしたか
  Dō deshita ka   Well?/**How** was it?

- どうでもいい
  Dō demo ii   Whatever/I don't care **which**

- どうにか　なるよ
  Dō ni ka naru yo
  It will be all right/**Somehow or other** it will be OK

The forms こういう, そういう, ああいう, どういう are commonly used to modify nouns and noun phrases, meaning 'this/that/what kind of?' (see **modifiers**):

- これはどういう意味ですか
  Kore wa **dō iu imi** desu ka   What does this **mean**?

- 毎週６０時間以上働いている。こういう生活はもうだめだ
  Maishū roku-jū jikan ijō hataraite iru. **Kō iu seikatsu** wa mō dame da
  I am working more than 60 hours every week. I can't take **this kind of lifestyle!**

For use of どうして, see the chapter on interrogatives (p. 224).

Use of そ and あ to refer back

Words beginning with そ and あ (and occasionally こ) are used to refer back to previously mentioned topics and phrases:

- ３０歳で大阪の実家に戻った。そのとき初めて政田さんに出会った
  San-jū-sai de Ōsaka no jikka ni modotta. **Sono toki** hajimete Masada san ni deatta
  At the age of thirty I went back to the family home in Osaka. It was **at that time** that I first met Masuda

- お祖父さんがかぶを買いました。それはあまくておいしいかぶでした
  Ojiisan ga kabu o kaimashita. **Sore wa** amakute oishii kabu deshita
  Grandfather bought a turnip. **It was** a sweet, delicious turnip

Words in the あ group tend to refer to some information shared between speaker and listener:

- 一緒に浅間山に登ったときのことが覚えている？あれは面白かったね
  Issho ni Asamayama ni nobotta toki no koto ga oboete iru? **Are** wa omoshirokatta ne
  You remember when we climbed Mt Asama together? **That** was fun!

Numbers, counters, time, dates

Japanese numerals are generally written in kanji in vertical text, and in numerals (1, 2, 3, etc.) in horizontal text.

Cardinal numbers

Cardinal numbers are those which are used when counting ('one', 'two', 'three'):

number	pronunciation and kanji
0	ゼロ or れい・零
1	いち・一
2	に・二
3	さん・三
4	し or よん・四
5	ご・五
6	ろく・六
7	しち or なな・七
8	はち・八
9	きゅう or く・九
10	じゅう・十
11	じゅういち・十一
12	じゅうに・十二
13	じゅうさん・十三
14	じゅうし or じゅうよん・十四
15	じゅうご・十五
16	じゅうろく・十六
17	じゅうしち or じゅうなな・十七

number	pronunciation and kanji
18	じゅうはち・十八
19	じゅうきゅう or じゅうく・十九
20	にじゅう・二十 or 二〇
21	にじゅういち・二十一
22	にじゅうに・二十二
23	にじゅうさん・二十三
24	にじゅうよん or にじゅうし・二十四
25	にじゅうご・二十五
26	にじゅうろく・二十六
27	にじゅうしち or にじゅうなな・二十七
28	にじゅうはち・二十八
29	にじゅうきゅう or にじゅうく・二十九
30	さんじゅう・三十 or 三〇
31	さんじゅういち・三一
40	よんじゅう・四十 or 四〇
50	ごじゅう・五十 or 五〇
60	ろくじゅう・六十 or 六〇
70	ななじゅう・七十 or 七〇
80	はちじゅう・八十 or 八〇
90	きゅうじゅう・九十 or 九〇
100	ひゃく・百
200	にひゃく・二百 or 2百
300	さんびゃく・三百 or 3百
400	よんひゃく・四百 or 4百
500	ごひゃく・五百 or 5百
600	ろっぴゃく・六百 or 6百
700	ななひゃく・七百 or 7百
800	はっぴゃく・八百 or 8百
900	きゅうひゃく・九百 or 9百
1,000	せん・千
2,000	にせん・二千 or 2千

number	pronunciation and kanji
3,000	さんぜん・三千 or 3千
4,000	よんせん・四千 or 4千
5,000	ごせん・五千 or 5千
6,000	ろくせん・六千 or 6千
7,000	ななせん・七千 or 7千
8,000	はっせん・八千 or 8千
9,000	きゅうせん・九千 or 9千
10,000	いちまん・一万 or 1万
11,000	いちまんせん or いちまんいっせん
20,000	にまん・二万 or 2万
40,000	よんまん・四万 or 4万
70,000	ななまん・七万 or 7万
90,000	きゅうまん・九万 or 9万
100,000	じゅうまん・十万 or 10万
1,000,000	ひゃくまん・百万 or 100万
10,000,000	いっせんまん・一千万 or 1千万
100,000,000	いちおく・一億 or 1億
1,000,000,000,000	いっちょう・一兆 or 1兆

Note that there are two ways of saying the number 4 (し and よん) and two ways of saying the number 7 (しち and なな). Their use is shown in the charts relating to time, dates, and counting people and objects below. In general, the number 4 is pronounced し when counting on the fingers, but otherwise よ(ん) is preferred.

Numbers are expressed from greatest to least:

603	ろっぴゃくさん
1,800	せんはっぴゃく
12,813	いちまんにせんはっぴゃくじゅうさん

- この車は639万円です
  Kono kuruma wa **rop-pyaku san-jū-kyū-man** en desu
  This car is **six million, three hundred and ninety thousand** yen

Counting objects, people, animals

Counting objects

When counting inanimate objects, there is a different set
of numbers from 1 to 9 which incorporate the counter つ.
(Although there is an alternative number 10, it is not used for
counting items and so appears in brackets below.) After 10, the
system of じゅういち, じゅうに is used. The よん alternative is
used for numbers over 10 which include 4, e.g. じゅうよん, 14:

number of items	Kanji and pronunciation
1	ひとつ・一つ・1つ
2	ふたつ・二つ・2つ
3	みっつ・三つ・3つ
4	よっつ・四つ・4つ
5	いつつ・五つ・5つ
6	むっつ・六つ・6つ
7	ななつ・七つ・7つ
8	やっつ・八つ・8つ
9	ここのつ・九つ・9つ
10	(とお・十)
11, etc.	じゅういち, etc.

- これを1つください
  Kore o **hitotsu** kudasai   *Can I have **one** of these, please?*

- りんごがななつあります
  Ringo ga **nanatsu** arimasu   *There are **seven** apples*

Counters

Various words can be used in English to attach to a number when
counting things ('one **slice** of bread', 'two **bars** of soap', 'three
bunches of flowers'). In Japanese, the system is even more
developed, with a system of suffixes or 'counters' added to the
numbers. (Where there is no special counter for a given object,
the system of **hitotsu**, **futatsu**, etc. is used.) Counters are mostly

used with the いち, に, さん set of numbers. The more common ones are given below.

Chart of common counters

Irregular formations are shown with an underline.

counter	pronunciation and other information
まい・枚 for flat objects, e.g. sheets of paper, postage stamps, plates	いちまい, にまい, さんまい, よんまい, ごまい, ろくまい, ななまい, はちまい, きゅうまい, じゅうまい, なんまい?
こ・個 for small items, e.g. pieces of fruit, eggs, sweets	<u>いっこ</u>, にこ, さんこ, よんこ, ごこ, <u>ろっこ</u>, ななこ, <u>はっこ</u>, きゅうこ, じゅうこ, なんこ?
ひき・匹 for animals, birds, fish	<u>いっぴき</u>, にひき, さんびき, よんひき, ごひき, <u>ろっぴき</u>, ななひき, きゅうひき, じゅっぴき, なんびき?
さつ・冊 for books, magazines, published matter	<u>いっさつ</u>, にさつ, さんさつ, よんさつ, ごさつ, ろくさつ, なんさつ, <u>はっさつ</u>, きゅうさつ, じゅうさつ, なんさつ?
だい・台 for cars, TVs, machinery	いちだい, にだい, さんだい, よんだい, ごだい, ろくだい, ななだい, はちだい, きゅうだい, じゅだい, なんだい?
ほん・本 for long, thin items, e.g. bottles, pens, cigarettes	<u>いっぽん</u>, にほん, <u>さんぼん</u>, よんほん, ごほん, <u>ろっぽん</u>, ななほん, <u>はっぽん</u>, きゅうほん, <u>じゅっぽん</u>, なんぼん?
かげつ・ヵ月 for months	<u>いっかげつ</u>, にかげつ, さんかげつ, よんかげつ, ごかげつ, <u>ろっかげつ</u>, ななかげつ, <u>はっかげつ</u>, きゅうかげつ, <u>じゅっかげつ</u>, なんかげつ

counter	pronunciation and other information
さい・才・歳 for age (of people and animals)	<u>いっさい</u>, にさい, さんさい, よさい, ごさい, ろくさい, ななさい, <u>はっさい</u>, きゅうさい, <u>じゅっさい</u>, NB 20 years old = <u>はたち</u>, なんさい?
けん・軒 for buildings	<u>いっけん</u>, にけん, さんけん, よんけん, ごけん, <u>ろっけん</u>, ななけん, <u>はっけん</u>, きゅうけん, じゅうけん なんけん?
はい・杯 for cups or glasses full, e.g. of water, beer, juice	<u>いっぱい</u>, にはい, さんばい, よんはい, ごはい, <u>ろっぱい</u>, ななはい, きゅうはい, <u>じゅっぱい</u>, なんばい?
かい・回 for number of times (once, twice, etc.)	<u>いっかい</u>, にかい, さんかい, よんかい, ごかい, <u>ろっかい</u>, ななかい, <u>はっかい</u>, きゅうかい, <u>じゅっかい</u>, なんかい?
かい・階 for floors of a building	<u>いっかい</u>, にかい, <u>さんがい</u>, よんかい, ごかい, <u>ろっかい</u>, ななかい, <u>はっかい</u>, きゅうかい, <u>じゅっかい</u>, <u>なんがい</u>?
じ・時 for hours (clock time)	いちじ, にじ, さんじ, <u>よじ</u>, ごじ, ろくじ, しちじ, はちじ, <u>くじ</u>, じゅうじ, なんじ?
ふん・分 for minutes	<u>いっぷん</u>, にふん, <u>さんぷん</u>, <u>よんぷん</u>, ごふん, <u>ろっぷん</u>, ななふん, <u>はっぷん</u>, きゅうふん, <u>じゅっぷん</u> or <u>じっぷん</u>, なんぷん?
びょう・秒 for seconds	いちびょう, にびょう, さんびょう, よんびょう, ごびょう, ろくびょう, ななびょう, はちびょう, きゅうびょう, なんびょう?
にん・人 for people	<u>ひとり</u>, <u>ふたり</u>, さんにん, <u>よにん</u>, ごにん, ろくにん, しちにん or ななにん, はちにん, きゅうにん, じゅうにん, なんにん?

counter	pronunciation and other information
つう・通 for letters, items of mail	いちつう, につう, さんつう, よん つう, ごつう, ろくつう, ななつう, はちつう, きゅうつう, じゅうつう, なんつう?

- 車2台
  kuruma ni-dai   *two cars*
- 馬6匹
  uma rop-piki   *six horses*
- ハンバーガー三個とコーヒー二杯おねがいします
  Hanbāgā **san-ko** to kōhii **ni-hai** onegai shimasu
  Three hamburgers and two coffees, please

The number and counter are usually placed after the noun (and its particle) if one is present:

- 私がりんごを3個買いました
  Watashi ga **ringo o san-ko** kaimashita
  I bought three apples

The number and counter can also be joined to the noun with の:

- 引き出しに7枚の切手がある
  Hikidashi ni **nana-mai no kitte** ga aru
  There are seven stamps in the drawer

Other counters in common use include those used for measurement such as センチ 'centimetre', メートル 'metre', キロ 'kilogram' or 'kilometre', and リットル 'litre', and foreign currency such as ドル, 'dollar', ポンド, 'pound', etc. Japan uses the metric system of measurement, although some traditional measures are still in use. Floor area in Japanese homes is measured in 'mats' with the counter じょう・畳.

Sometimes single items are counted with the ひと〜 alternative for 'one':

- 1パックいくつ入りですか
  Hito-pakku ikutsu iri desu ka
  How many are there in one pack?

Ordinal numbers and 'number 1'

Ordinal numbers are used to talk about the order of things (e.g. 'first', 'second', 'tenth' in English). In Japanese, the suffix め・目 is added to the number and counter combination ひとつ, ふたつ, etc. to mean 'the first (one)', 'the second (one)', etc.:

- 郵便局は一つ目の信号を右に曲がります
  Yūbinkyoku wa **hitotsu-me no shingō** o migi ni magarimasu
  For the post office, you turn right at the **first (set of) lights**

- 二つ目の事件についてさきに話しましょう
  Futatsu-me no jiken ni tsuite hanashimashō
  Let's discuss the **second incident**

め is also added to cardinal number + counter combinations:

いっかいめ・一回目	the first time
いちばんめ・一番目	the first (for number and ばん, see below)
にはいめ・二杯目	the second cup
さんぼんめ・三本目	the third bottle
ひとりめ・一人目	the first person
ふたりめ・二人目	the second person

- 一回目の出張は大変だった。交通事故に巻き込まれた
  Ik-kai-me no shutchō wa taihen datta. Kōtsūjiko ni makikomareta
  My **first business trip** was terrible. I was involved in a car accident

- また靴が取られた。田中君が３人目の被害者だ
  Mata kutsu ga torareta. Tanaka kun ga **san-nin-me no higaisha** da
  Shoes have been stolen again! Tanaka is the **third victim**!

- 僕がアルコールに慣れていないから二杯目を飲んで気持ち悪くなった
  Boku ga arukōru ni narete inai kara **ni-hai-me** o nonde kimochi waruku natta
  Because I am unused to alcohol, I felt ill after drinking the **second glass**

The prefix だい・第 is sometimes added:

- 山田さんを推薦します。第一に責任感がありますから
  Yamada san o suisen shimasu. **Dai-ichi ni** sekininkan ga arimasu kara
  I recommend Mrs Yamada. **Firstly,** because she is very responsible

- 第3番目の理由は気温が高すぎるということです
  Dai-san-ban-me no riyū wa kion ga takasugiru koto desu
  The third reason is that the air temperature is too high

- 第6回目の BATJ 会議はロンドンで行われます
  Dai-rok-kai-me no BATJ kaigi wa Rondon de okonawaremasu
  The 6th BATJ conference will be held in London

To say 'in third place' etc., the counter い・位 is added to the number. This is often prefixed with だい・第, e.g. when announcing results of a competition, without any change in meaning:

- 第6位に佐伯雄太君
  Dai-roku-i ni Saeki Yūta kun   In **sixth place**, Yūta Saeki

The suffix ばん・番 is added to a numeral to give the meaning 'number one', 'number two', etc.:

- 次の大阪行きは三番線からです
  Tsugi no Ōsaka-yuki wa **san-ban-sen** kara desu
  The next train for Osaka is from **platform number three**

- 6番窓口へ行ってください
  Roku-ban madoguchi e itte kudasai
  Please go to **window/counter number six**

This can be prefixed by だい without any difference in meaning:

- 今年の抱負は第一番に遅刻しないこと。第二番に、宿題をきちんとやること
  Kotoshi no hōfu wa **dai-ichi-ban ni** chikoku shinai koto, **dai-ni-ban ni** shukudai o kichinto yaru koto
  My resolutions for this year are: **first,** to not be late; **second,** to do my homework properly

Time

Time is given from the largest to the smallest unit:

- 7時28分
  shichi-ji ni-jū-hap-pun   *twenty-eight minutes past seven*

- 2分13秒
  ni-fun jū-san-byō   *two minutes and thirteen seconds*

The half hour can be represented with **はん・半** 'half' added after the counter for 'o'clock':

- 11時半
  jū-ichi-ji han   *half past eleven*

Minutes between half past the hour and just before the next hour can be expressed by adding **まえ・前** 'before' to the number of minutes:

- 6時10分前
  roku-ji jūp-pun mae (= 5.50)   *ten to six*

Approximate points in time are represented by the suffix **ごろ**:

- 10時ごろ
  jū-ji goro   *about ten o'clock*

The words **ごぜん（午前）** 'a.m.' and **ごご（午後）** 'p.m.' are placed in front of the time:

- 午前6時10分
  gozen roku-ji jūp-pun mae (= 5.50 a.m.)
  ten to six in the morning

- 午後4時
  gogo yoji (= 4.00 p.m.)   *four o'clock in the afternoon*

Railway timetables etc. use the 24-hour clock:

- この電車は15時36分発東京行きです
  Kono densha wa **jū-go-ji san-jū-rop-pun** hatsu Tokyo yuki desu
  *This train is the **15:36** (departure) for Tokyo*

Points in time are marked with particle **に**:

- 6時に会いましょう
  Roku-ji ni aimashō   *Let's meet **at** 6 o'clock*

For more on the particle **に** with points in time, see the chapter on particles (*p. 159*).

Periods of time

The suffix かん・間 is added to hours, days, and weeks to indicate a period of time. It is sometimes added to months and years, although it is not always used, as 10年 itself, for example, can mean 'a 10-year period':

- 2時間
  ni-ji-kan   two hours

- 3日間
  mikka-kan   three days

- 10年 (間)
  jū-nen-kan   ten years

Periods of months are given with the number followed by かげつ・ヵ月. This suffix is often written as ヶ月, but note that the character ヶ is an abbreviation of the kanji 箇 (pronounced か), and not the katakana ケ:

- 3ヶ月
  san-ka-getsu   three months

- 私は東京大学に6ヶ月留学しました
  Watashi wa Tōkyō Daigaku ni **rok-ka-getsu** ryūgaku shimashita
  I was an exchange student at Tokyo University for **six months**

Dates

Years

Years are expressed with the number followed by the counter ねん・年 'year':

- 1965年
  sen kyū-hyaku roku-jū-go-nen   1965

- 2000年
  ni-sen-nen   2000

BC is expressed with 西暦紀元前・せいれきききげんぜん + number + 年・ねん:

- 西暦紀元前453年
  seireki kigenzen yon-hyaku go-jū-san-nen   453 BC

Japanese era system

Japan has its own system of counting years, based on the number of years of the current emperor's reign. The correspondence to Western calendar dates is shown below. Two era names in a single year show that the imperial succession changed during that year:

Japanese era	Western calendar
めいじいちねん・明治１年	1868
めいじよんじゅうごねん・明治４５年 and たいしょういちねん・大正１年	1912
たいしょうごねん・大正１５年 and しょうわいちねん・昭和１年	1926
しょうわにねん・昭和２年	1927
しょうわろくじゅうさんねん・昭和６３年	1988
へいせいいちねん・平成１年	1989
へいせいじゅうにねん・平成１２年	2000

- 昭和３９年
  Shōwa san-jū-kyū-nen　　　year 39 of Showa (＝1964)

Dates of birth and other significant events are usually given with the name of the era, especially in official documents:

- 生年月日は昭和５８年３月２日です
  Seinengappi wa **Shōwa go-jū-hachi-nen san-gatsu futsuka** desu
  My date of birth is **March 2nd, Showa 58** (＝1983)

- 家の長男は平成７年生まれです
  Uchi no chōnan wa **Heisei nana-nen** umare desu
  My older son was born in **Heisei 7** (＝1995)

- 昭和２０年に世界で始めて原子爆弾が広島に落とされました
  Shōwa ni-jū-nen ni sekai de hajimete genshibakudan ga Hiroshima ni otosaremashita
  The first atomic bomb was dropped **in Shōwa 20** (＝1945) on Hiroshima

Months

The names of months of the year consist of the number followed by the counter がつ・月. The し and しち alternatives are used for April and July:

3月・さんがつ	March
4月・しがつ	April
7月・しちがつ	July
11月・じゅういちがつ	November

For describing duration i.e. 'for 6 months', see the section on periods of time above.

Dates of the month

The dates of the month are shown below:

1	ついたち・1日
2	ふつか・2日
3	みっか・3日
4	よっか・4日
5	いつか・5日
6	むいか・6日
7	なのか・7日
8	ようか・8日
9	ここのか・9日
10	とおか・10日

After 10, the pronunciation follows that of the cardinal numbers with the suffix にち・日. The しち and く alternatives are used for 7 and 9:

17日・じゅうしちにち	
29日・にじゅうくにち	
31日・さんじゅういちにち	

There are three exceptions:

14日・じゅうよっか
20日・はつか
24日・にじゅうよっか

Dates are given from the largest to the smallest unit:

- 11月26日
  jū-ichi-gatsu ni-jū-roku-nichi   November 26th

- 1983年2月4日
  sen kyū-hyaku hachi-jū-san-nen ni-gatsu yok-ka
  February 4th 1983

Fractions, decimals, and percentages

Fractions are expressed with 分 'part' as follows:

はんぶん・半分	half
さんぶんのいち・三分の一	one-third
ごぶんのに・五分のに	two-fifths

Decimals are expressed with てん・点:

| 3.6 | san ten go |
| 5.75 | go ten nana-go |

Percentages are expressed with パセント:

| 60% | roku-jū pasento |

Approximate numbers

くらい or ぐらい is added to an amount to mean 'approximately':

- 30分ぐらい
  san-jūp-pun gurai   about thirty minutes

- 何人ぐらい来ると思いますか
  Nan-nin gurai kuru to omoimasu ka
  About how many people do you think are coming?

It is common to use the adverb だいたい 'more or less' with
ぐらい:

- だいたい６人ぐらい
  daitai roku-nin gurai   *about six people*

Alternatively, the quantity is prefixed with やく・約 or およそ:

- 約３０人
  yaku san-jū-nin   *approximately thirty people*

- およそ３個
  oyoso san-ko   *about three (pieces)*

'One each' and 'each one'

The addition of ずつ to a number of items means '. . . each':

- 数学と英語のテストは１時間ずつです
  Sūgaku to Eigo no tesuto wa **ichi-jikan zutsu** desu
  *The maths and English tests are **one hour each***

- 机の上に紙６枚ずつ置いてください
  Tsukue no ue ni kami **roku-mai zutsu** oite kudasai
  *Please put **six pieces of paper each** on the desks*

The prefix element かく・各 'each', 'every' can be added to some nouns, e.g. かくクラス・各クラス 'every class', かっこく・各国 'each country', etc. An English translation with 'all' or 'every' may be appropriate:

- 各国の首相が環境サミットに参加しました
  Kak-koku no shushō ga kankyō samitto ni sanka shimashita
  The prime ministers of each of the countries took part in the environment summit

Nominalization: the nominalizer の and the noun こと

The addition of the noun こと or the nominalizer の to a sentence or clause transforms the whole of that sentence or clause into a noun phrase. (Other nouns can also be used to form noun phrases: see below in the section 'Modifiers and relative clauses'.) This resulting noun phrase can then be used as a subject, direct object, etc. in the same way as other noun phrases. In the following example, the nominalizer の added to the verb phrase さかなをつる 'catch fish' produces a noun phrase:

- 魚を釣るのが好きです
  Sakana o tsuru no ga suki desu   I like **fishing**

The addition of the noun こと, literally '(abstract) thing', to the phrase えいがをみる 'watch films' produces a noun phrase 'watching films':

- 私の趣味は映画を見ることです
  Watashi no shumi wa **eiga o miru koto** desu
  My hobby is **watching films**

The noun こと used in this way and the nominalizer の both follow the plain forms of verbs and adjectives. When a nominalized phrase is based on a noun or a な adjective, it is linked to the nominalizer の (or the noun performing a similar function) with な:

- １６歳なのを隠して、成人映画を見に行った
  Jū-roku-sai na no o kakushite, seijin eiga o mi ni itta
  Hiding **(the fact) that I was 16**, I went to see an adult film

The noun phrase can then be marked as the subject, object, topic, etc. with the appropriate particle. In the sentence above, the noun phrase 1 6歳なの 'being sixteen' is the direct object of かくす 'to hide (something)', and so is marked with the particle を. In the next example, the noun phrase 'the first time Mike met a Japanese person' is marked as the topic with は:

● マイクが始めて日本人に出会ったのは高校の 2 年だった
  Maiku ga hajimete Nihonjin ni deatta no wa kōkō no ni-nen datta
  The first time Mike met a Japanese person was in the second year of high school

Differences between the use of の and こと

The nominalizer の and the noun こと are largely interchangeable, except when the nominalized phrase is the predicate in a ~は ~だ sentence (ending with だ・です). In this case, only こと is correct. In the sentence below, the first use of こと can be replaced with の but the second cannot:

● 難しいこと / のはその違いを簡単に説明することだ
  Muzukashii koto/no wa sono chigai o kantan ni **setsumei suru koto** da
  The difficulty is to explain this difference simply

Perceptions that are immediate and concrete, or emotionally and empathetically involving, tend to be marked with の, and abstract or less empathetic elements are marked with こと. の is rather more informal. In the following example, only こと is acceptable:

● 見ることは信じること
  Miru koto wa **shinjiru koto**   Seeing is believing

Of the next two examples, the second sentence is more formal and less emotionally involving than the first, although the translation has to show this by changing the vocabulary, where the Japanese changes the style:

● いくら読んでも経験するのはやっぱり違う
  Ikura yonde mo **keiken suru no** wa yappari chigau
  No matter how much you've read about it, it's obviously different when you **experience it** yourself!

- いくら読んでも経験することはやはり違いますよね
  Ikura yonde mo **keiken suru koto** wa yahari chigaimasu yo ne
  No matter how much you may have read about it, it's somewhat
  different when you **experience it** personally!

のだ・のです・んだ・んです

The のだ sentence ending (and the polite style equivalent のです)
is a nominalized sentence plus だ. The contracted form is んだ,
or the polite style んです. のだ is used for explanations and
connects a statement with a situation in a way that implies
'the fact is that . . .' or 'the explanation is that . . .':

- 遅くなってすみません。電車が遅れたんです
  Osoku natte sumimasen. **Densha ga okureta n desu**
  Sorry to be late! The train was delayed

- クリスマスの前デパートは込んでいるんです
  Kurisumasu no mae **depāto wa konde iru n desu**
  Before Christmas the stores are crowded

- きのうは仕事を休みました。風邪を引いたんです
  Kinō wa shigoto o yasumimashita. **Kaze o hiita n desu**
  Yesterday I took the day off work as I had a cold

のだ can be used to mark a realization or assumption:

- 今日は患者に言わないほうがいいんだ
  Kyō wa kanja ni **iwanai hō ga ii n da**
  (So) it's best not to tell the patient today

のだ adds an emotive or emphatic element where the speaker is
attempting to emphasize shared knowledge or an assumption from
the context. This can sometimes be translated with tag questions
('isn't it?', 'don't you?', etc.). In the next example, the speaker is
perhaps looking at Mrs Kawamura's bookshelf and noting all the
French books:

- 川村さんはフランス語が分かるんですか
  Kawamura san wa **Furansugo ga wakaru n desu ka**
  So you understand French, do you, Mrs Kawamura?

A response would be likely to use an explanatory んです:

- はい、大学でフランス語を勉強したんです
  Hai, daigaku de **Furansugo o benkyō shita n desu**
  Yes, (that's because) I studied French at university

のだ is common in questions to confirm assumptions based on visible evidence:

- どうしてまだここにいるんですか。何かあったんですか
  Dōshite **mada koko ni iru n desu ka**. Nan ka **atta n desu ka**
  Why **are you still here**? Has something **happened**?/Is something **wrong**?

- どうしたんですか
  Dō shita n desu ka   What's the matter?/What's happened?

Use of this structure can sometimes imply doubt:

- 本当にいいんですか
  Hontō ni **ii n desu ka**   Is it really OK?/Are you sure **it's OK**?

- 学生なんですか
  Gakusei na **n desu ka**   Are you really a student?

The phrase んですが is used to signal a request:

- 日本語で手紙を書いたんですが、ちょっと見てくれませんか
  Nihongo de tegami o **kaita n desu ga**, chotto mite kuremasen ka
  I've written a letter in Japanese – would you check it for me?

A following phrase can be omitted when the context makes the intended request clear:

- もしもし。ちょっと伺いたいんですが
  Moshi moshi. Chotto **ukagaitai n desu ga**
  Hello. **I'd like** some information, please (Literally **I'd like to ask**, but . . .)

Modifiers and relative clauses

A modifier is a word, sentence, or clause that describes or 'modifies' a following noun or pronoun, as in the English '**yesterday's** newspaper', '**the most difficult** one', or '**pretty** student'. Japanese adjectives and nouns with の can be modifiers:

- おもしろい人
  omoshiroi hito   a **funny** person

- きれいな学生
  kirei-na gakusei   a **pretty** student

- きのうの新聞
  kinō no shinbun   **yesterday's** newspaper

Japanese does not have relative pronouns ('that', 'which', 'who', etc.), and so English relative clauses such as 'the woman **who is standing over there**' or 'the textbooks **that I used in university**' are conveyed in Japanese by taking the nouns 'woman' and 'book' and modifying them with a descriptive phrase. This modifying phrase always precedes the modified element and is in the plain style. Verbs and adjectives in the plain style (*see p. 10*) or clauses with plain style forms (such as 〜ない, 〜た, the dictionary form, etc.) can be used as modifiers. Literal translations of such phrases would be, for example, 'the over-there-standing woman' and 'the in-university-used book':

- あそこに立っている女の人は金田さんです
  Asoko ni tatte iru onna no hito wa Kaneda san desu
  The woman who is standing over there is Ms Kaneda

- 大学で使った教科書はそのあと全然使わない
  Daigaku de tsukatta kyōkasho wa sono ato zenzen tsukawanai
  The textbooks that I used in university I never used afterwards

More than one modifier may be used in a complex sentence, and it is necessary to relate them to the correct noun phrase or 'head' to understand the overall meaning. In the following sentence, the head おとこのこたち 'boys' is modified by both the adjective わかい 'young' and the verb phrase meaning 'have previously shown no interest in languages':

- このマンガがおもしろいという理由で、今まで言語になにも興味を示さなかった若い男の子達が日本語を勉強し始めたという話しもあるそうだ
  Kono manga ga omoshiroi to iu riyū de, ima made **gengo ni nani mo kyōmi o shimesanakatta wakai otoko no ko tachi** ga Nihongo o benkyō shihajimeta to iu hanashi mo aru sō da
  Apparently, **young boys who've previously shown no interest in languages** have started to study Japanese because they find this comic strip fun

The topic particle は cannot be used in a relative clause, and is replaced by が, or の (see **particles**).

こと **in idiomatic structures**

There are a number of idiomatic structures using the noun こと. A dictionary form of a verb followed by ことができる is an alternative way of expressing the potential 'can . . .', 'be able to . . .'

* 日本語を話すことができますか
  Nihongo o **hanasu koto ga dekimasu ka**
  Can you speak Japanese?

For more on this, see the chapter on verbs (*p. 126*).

A verb in the 〜た form and followed by ことがある is a way of talking about past experience, as in 'Have you ever . . . ?' and 'I have never . . .':

* 日本へ行ったことがありますか
  Nihon e **itta koto ga arimasu ka**
  Have you ever been to Japan?

* 一回だけ馬に乗ったことがある
  Ik-kai dake **uma ni notta koto ga aru**
  I have ridden a horse just once

* 教室以外で日本人と話したことがない
  Kyōshitsu igai de Nihonjin to **hanashita koto ga nai**
  Outside the classroom I've never spoken to anyone Japanese

The dictionary form followed by ことがある means that something may happen on occasion:

* この仕事は電話で日本人のお客さんと話すことがあります
  Kono shigoto wa **denwa de Nihonjin no okyaku san to hanasu koto ga arimasu**
  In this job you will speak to Japanese customers on the telephone

The use of ことにする following plain forms means 'to decide on':

* あの会社に入ることにしました
  Ano kaisha ni **hairu koto ni shimashita**
  I decided to join the company/take the job

- 毎日３０分勉強することにした
  Mainichi san-jup-pun **benkyō suru koto ni shita**
  I *decided to study/I studied* for 30 minutes a day

The use of ことになる following plain forms means that
something has come about, or been decided on:

- オーストラリアへ行くことになりました
  Osutoraria e **iku koto ni narimashita**
  It was decided/has been decided that I go to Australia

- 妻が入院したので炊事することになった
  Tsuma ga nyūin shita no de **suiji suru koto ni natta**
  Because my wife went into hospital I *did the cooking*

Another use of こと is close to its original meaning of 'an abstract
thing', as in the following example where it translates as 'things
about . . .' or simply 'about':

- 日本の歴史のことはよく知っていますか
  Nihon no rekishi no koto wa yoku shitte imasu ka
  Do you know lots **about Japanese history**?

こと can also be used where the normal word order is reversed for
emphasis:

- そのとき心配したのは娘が一人になることだ
  Sono toki shinpai shita no wa **musume ga hitori ni naru koto** da
  What I worried about at the time was **my daughter ending up
  alone**

こと is also used to highlight parts of lists of orders, points, and
rules, etc.:

- 新年抱負。第一、たばこを吸わないこと
  Shinnenhōfu. Dai-ichi, tabako o suwanai koto
  New Year's resolutions: 1. not smoking

Keigo

What is keigo?

Speakers of all languages tend to adapt the level of politeness and formality of their speech to their audience. For example, an English speaker might say 'I'm sorry to bother you, but would you mind telling me the time, please?' to a complete stranger, but 'What's the time?' to a close friend. In Japanese, respectful language, or 'honorific and humble language', is known as **keigo** (敬語), and is a major feature of the language. Keigo reflects distinctions in social position or roles (*see p. 7*) by changes in language, especially verbs.

Types of keigo

One way to show respect is to use special forms of verbs or special alternative verbs when speaking to or about a person to whom politeness should be shown. Use of these verbs, known as **sonkeigo** (尊敬語), meaning 'respectful words', gives elevated status to the person. In the first sentence below, the speaker uses いきます for 'go' to refer to himself, but in the second he uses the respectful いらっしゃいます, also meaning 'go', as the subject is the teacher:

- 僕はよく東京へ行きます
  Boku wa yoku Tōkyō e **ikimasu**　　*I often go to Tokyo*

- 先生はよく東京へいらっしゃいます
  Sensei wa yoku Tōkyō e **irasshaimasu**
  The teacher often goes to Tokyo

Another way to show respect is to use alternative 'humble' verbs or special forms of verbs to refer to oneself, thereby elevating the status of the other person by contrast. These verbs are known as **kenjōgo** (謙譲語), meaning 'humble words'.

In the following sentence, the speaker uses まいります for 'go' to refer to himself:

- ご招待をいただいてありがとうございます。明日参ります
  Go-shōtai o itadaite arigatō gozaimasu. Ashita **mairimasu**
  Thank you very much for the invitation. I will go tomorrow

Both respectful and humble verbs can be used not only when referring to a person directly but also when talking about matters connected with that person:

- 先生のご家族も神戸にいらっしゃいますか
  Sensei no **go-kazoku** mo Kōbe ni **irasshaimasu** ka
  Are your family in Kobe as well?

- 佐伯様のお家にはご本がたくさんございます
  Saeki san no o-uchi ni wa **go-hon** ga takusan **gozaimasu**
  There are lots of books in your house, Mr Saeki

The third subdivision of keigo is **teineigo** (丁寧語), meaning 'polite words'. This refers to respect or politeness shown through the use of 〜ます verb endings (〜ます, 〜ません, 〜ました, etc.), the use of です rather than だ, and the prefixing of nouns or adjectives with お or ご. Most uses of special verbs occur with 〜ます verb endings (see **verbs**). Although plain forms of keigo verbs exist and can be used in the middle of complex sentences, they are otherwise only rarely encountered. For more on this, see the chapter on style (*p. 10*).

Formation of honorific and humble verbs

Some verbs have completely separate honorific or humble equivalents, but the majority of verbs change their form.

Regular honorific verb form

The honorific form is created by adding the prefix お to the conjunctive (pre-ます) stem of the verb, followed by になる:

～ます *form*	pre ～ます *form*	honorific form
よみます・読みます to read	よみ・読み	およみになる・ お読みになる
かえります・帰ります to return, go home	かえり・帰り	おかえりになる・ お帰りになる

- ここにおかけになりませんか
  Koko ni **o-kake ni narimasen** ka   Won't **you sit down** here?

- 「こころ」をお読みになりましたか
  'Kokoro' o **o-yomi ni narimashita** ka   Have **you read** 'Kokoro'?

In the case of verbs made up of a noun and する, the prefix お or ご is added to the noun, e.g. ごあんないする 'to show (someone) the way', and おべんきょうする 'to study'. (For information on the choice of お or ご, see **Use of prefix お and ご with nouns** below.)

Sometimes なさる, the honorific alternative for する, may be used:

- 先生はどちらでお勉強なさいましたか
  Sensei wa dochira de **o-benkyō nasaimashita** ka
  Where **did you study?**

Regular humble verb form

The regular humble form of verbs, used when the speaker or a member of his or her in-group is the subject, is formed with the prefix お and the conjunctive (pre-ます) stem of the verb, followed by する, e.g. おあいする 'to meet', and おまちする 'to wait':

- お願いします
  O-negai shimasu
  Please/If you'd be so kind (literally 'I ask a favour')

  Householder • どうぞお上がりくださ
  Dōzo o-agari kudasai
  Please come in

  Visitor • お邪魔します
  O-jama shimasu
  Thank you (literally '**I will interrupt**')

Where a verb is made up of a noun plus する, the prefix お or ご is added to the noun, followed by いたす, which is the humble alternative for する. (For the use of お and ご prefixes with nouns, see **Use of prefix お and ご with nouns** below.)

- ご案内いたします
  Go-annai itashimasu   I will show you the way

- 後ほどお電話いたします
  Nochi hodo o-denwa itashimasu   I will telephone later

Alternative honorific and humble verbs

There are a number of common verbs that have completely different **keigo** alternatives, rather than adding a prefix.

ordinary verb	honorific alternative verb	humble alternative verb
あげる to give	くださる・下さる	さしあげる・ 差し上げる
ある to exist, to be, to have	ござる or おありです	ござる
あう・会う to meet	おめにかかる・ お目にかかる	–
いく・行く to go	いらっしゃる or おいでになる・ お出でになる	まいる・参る
いる to exist, to be	いらっしゃる or おいでになる	おる
いう・言う to say	おっしゃる・仰る	もうす・申す or もうしあげる・ 申し上げる
かりる・借りる to borrow	–	はいしゃくする・ 拝借する
きく・聞く to ask	おききになる・ お聞きになる	うかがう・伺う

ordinary verb	honorific alternative verb	humble alternative verb
きる・着る to wear	おめしになる・ お召しになる	–
くる・来る to come	いらっしゃる or おいでになる or おこしになる or おみえになる	まいる・参る or おじゃまする・ お邪魔する
しる・知る to know	ごぞんじです・ ご存知です	ぞんじる・存じる
する to do	なさる	いたす
たべる・食べる to eat	めしあがる・ 召し上がる	いただく
たずねる・訪ねる to visit	–	おじゃまする・ お邪魔する
たずねる・尋ねる to ask	–	うかがう・伺う
のむ・飲む to drink	めしあがる・ 召し上がる	いただく
みる・見る to see	ごらんになる・ ご覧になる	はいけんする・ 拝見する
みせる・見せる to show	–	おめにかける・ お目にかける
もらう to receive	–	いただく

The following examples provide illustrations of the use of these special verbs.

Respectful:

- 原田様のことをご存知ですか
  Haruda sama no koto o **go-zonji desu** ka
  Do **you know** Mr Haruda?

- 先生はもう召し上がりましたか
  Sensei wa mō **meshiagarimashita** ka
  Have you already **eaten**, Professor?

- 娘さんは毎日ピアノの練習をなさいますか
  Musumesan wa mainichi piano no renshū o **nasaimasu ka**
  Does **your daughter practise** the piano every day?

- クラス代表が市長に花束を差し上げます
  Kurasu daihyō ga shichō ni hanataba o **sashiagemasu**
  The class representative **will give** the mayor the bouquet

- 小池雅夫様、小池雅夫様。いらっしゃいましたらフロント
  までお越しになってください
  Koike Masao sama, Koike Masao sama. **Irasshaimashitara**
  furonto made **o-koshi ni natte** kudasai
  Mr Masao Koike. If Mr Masao Koike **is here**, please could he **come**
  to the reception desk

Humble:

- 高橋伸と申します
  Takahashi Shin to **mōshimasu**　　　**My name is** Shin Takahashi

- すみませんちょっと伺いたいんですが
  Sumimasen, chotto **ukagaitai** n desu ga
  Excuse me, but **I'd like to enquire** (about something)

- 切符を拝見いたします
  Kippu o **haiken itashimasu**
  Tickets, please! (literally **I'll look** at your tickets)

- 田中さんは存じておりますが、山田さんはお目にかかって
  おりません
  Tanaka san wa **zonjite orimasu** ga, Yamada san wa **o-me ni
  kakatte orimasen**
  I know Mr Tanaka but **I haven't met** Mr Yamada

Irregular forms of keigo verbs

The following verbs have some irregularities in the 〜ます form
and imperative. Forms other than those given here are made
regularly from the dictionary form:

dictionary form	～ます form	imperative form
いらっしゃる to come	いらっしゃいます	いらっしゃい
くださる・下さる to give	くださいます	ください
なさる to do	なさいます	なさい
ござる to be, to have	ございます	(not used)
おっしゃる・仰る to say	おっしゃいます	おっしゃい

The ～て form plus いる in keigo

When the verb いる follows a ～て form, it can be replaced with its keigo alternatives, the respectful いらっしゃいます or the humble おります:

- 栗原様は東大で勉強していらっしゃいますか

  Kurihara sama wa Tōdai de **benkyō shite irasshaimasu** ka

  Are you **studying** at Tokyo University, Mrs Kurihara?

- すみません　ただいま　奥村はちょっと席をはずしております

  Sumimasen, tadaima Okumura wa chotto seki o **hazushite orimasu**

  I'm sorry but Ms Okumura **is away** from her desk at the moment

For the formation and uses of the ～て form, see the chapter on verbs (p. 38).

Use of plain forms, ～ます forms, respectful forms, and humble forms

Plain forms

Plain forms (e.g. いく, いかない, いった) are used to refer to oneself and others in conversations with family and peers. Typical situations are:

- between classmates
- between work colleagues of similar age and status
- senior to junior staff
- older to younger people

～ます forms

～ます forms (e.g. いきます, いきません, いきました) are used to refer to oneself and others in slightly more formal interaction with people who are not close friends or family. Typical situations are:

- a class presentation
- a letter to a pen pal
- a chat between casual acquaintances

Respectful forms

Respectful forms (e.g. いらっしゃいます, めしあがります) are used to refer to someone of a high social status in highly formal or professional situations, e.g.:

- a student to lecturer or teacher in formal situations (e.g. when asking for something)
- a formal letter
- talking to an older person
- staff to senior management
- staff in shops and restaurants to customers

Humble forms

Humble forms (e.g. まいります, はいけんします, おもちいたします) are used to refer to oneself and one's in-group in highly formal or professional situations, e.g.:

- student to lecturer or teacher in formal situations
- a formal letter
- talking to an older person at a formal event
- staff in shops and restaurants to customers

For more on these issues see the chapter on style (*p. 10*).

Use of the passive form to show respect

Passive verb forms can be used to show formality and respect:

- 専務さんはよく東京の本部へ行かれますか
  Senmu san wa yoku Tōkyō no honbu e **ikaremasu** ka
  Do you (the Managing Director) often **go** to the Tokyo head office?

- きょう名古屋大学のハリソン先生が講演をされました
  Kyō Nagoya Daigaku no Harison sensei ga kōen o **saremashita**
  Today a lecture **was given** by Professor Harrison of Nagoya
  University

- 二年 B 組を担当してくださった藤井先生が、先週日曜、無事
  に女のお子さんを出産されました
  Ni-nen B-gumi o tantō shite kudasatta Fujii sensei ga senshū
  nichiyōbi buji ni onna no o-ko-san o **shussan saremashita**
  Ms Fujii, who was in charge of class 2B, **gave birth** safely to a baby
  girl last Sunday

- お父様はよく出張でアメリカへ行かれるのですか
  Otōsama wa yoku shutchō de Amerika e **ikareru** no deshō ka
  Does your father often **go** to America on business?

For more information on the passive, see the chapter on verbs
(*p. 70*).

Nouns and adjectives in keigo

Use of prefixes お and ご with nouns

Nouns can be prefixed with お or ご to indicate the speaker's
respect for the person addressed. This pattern is also used to sound
generally polite or elegant. The choice of prefix depends mainly on
the origin of the word. The prefix ご is used with kanji compounds
of Sino-Japanese origin, and お with words of native Japanese
origin:

おうち・お家	(your) house, (your) home
おこさん・お子さん	(your) child
おてがみ・お手紙	(your) letter
ごしゅじん・ご主人	(your) husband
ごきょうりょく・ご協力	(your) cooperation
ごかぞく・ご家族	(your) family

There are a few common Sino-Japanese words which are prefixed with お instead of ご:

おでんわ・お電話	telephone, telephone call
おへんじ・お返事	reply (to a letter), response
おせわ・お世話	care, looking after
おべんきょう・お勉強	study, studying

In some cases the polite forms have become so common as to have largely replaced the basic word in everyday conversation, especially in women's speech. Some examples are given below:

basic noun	meaning	everyday polite noun
ちゃ・茶	tea	おちゃ
みず・水	drinking water	おみず
いわい・祝い	celebration	おいわい・お祝い
てあらい・手洗い	toilet	おてあらい・お手洗い
かね・金	money	おかね・お金
まつり・祭り	festival	おまつり・お祭り
こめ・米	uncooked rice	おこめ・お米
きゃく・客	customer	おきゃくさん・お客さん

Some words have only the polite forms:

おみやげ（お土産）	'a gift souvenir'
ごちそう（ご馳走）	'a treat', 'a feast'
ごはん（ご飯）	'cooked rice', 'a meal'

Note that the plain word for a meal めし (飯) is distinctly male usage.

Use of お and ご with adjectives

Keigo forms of adjectives, used to indicate respect for the person addressed, or to sound generally polite or elegant, are mostly confined to the addition of a prefix お or ご and, very formally, the replacement of だ・です with でござる:

* お元気ですか
  O-genki desu ka   How are you? (literally Are you **well**?)

- お忙しい時にお願いして申し訳ありませんでした
  O-isogashii toki ni o-negai shite mōshiwake arimasen deshita
  I am sorry to trouble you with this when you are so **busy**

- お早いですね
  O-hayai desu ne   You're early!

Other **keigo** forms of adjectives are used in certain set expressions:

ありがたい 'grateful'
  ありがとうございます   thank you
はやい 'early'
  おはようございます   good morning, hello
めでたい 'auspicious'
  おめでとうございます   congratulations

Alternative vocabulary choice in keigo

Some words have polite alternatives, rather than adding a prefix:

basic word	meaning	polite version
ひと・人	person	かた・方
どっ	how?	いかが
どこ	where?	どちら
だれ	who?	どなた
～さん	Mr, Mrs, Ms	～さま・～様
トイレ	toilet	おてあらい・お手洗い

- あの方はどなたですか
  Ano **kata** wa **donata** desu ka   Who is that **person**?

- お茶はいかがですか
  O-cha wa **ikaga** desu ka   How about some tea?

Interrogatives

Question words such as どこ, どちら, なに, だれ, いつ, and いくつ behave grammatically as nouns, but they must always take the particle が when they are the subject of a sentence, and never は. (See the discussion of は and が in the chapter on particles.)

Question words are sometimes omitted when the question is only implied, with the sentence left incomplete:

- **お名前は？**
  O-namae wa?   (What is) your name?

Question words can also be omitted when there are several questions with the same pattern:

- **これはいくらですか。2000円ですか。じゃ、それは？**
  Kore wa ikura desu ka. Ni-sen-en? Ja, sore wa?
  How much is this one? ¥2,000? And that one?

Word order

The word order for a simple question in Japanese is exactly the same as for a statement, but with the addition of the question particle か at the end (*see p. 169*). Note that it is not necessary to have a question mark when か is present:

- **池田さんは学生です**
  Ikeda san wa gakusei desu   Ms Ikeda is a student

- **池田さんは学生ですか**
  Ikeda san wa gakusei desu ka   Is Ms Ikeda is a student?

- **リンさんは日本語が話せます**
  Rin san wa Nihongo ga hanasemasu
  Ms Lin can speak Japanese

- **リンさんは日本語が話せますか**
  Rin san wa Nihongo ga hanasemasu ka
  Can Ms Lin speak Japanese?

In the plain style, the particle か is omitted and the intonation rises. This is often shown in writing by the use of a question mark:

- リンさんは日本語が話せる？
  Rin san wa Nihongo ga hanaseru?
  Can Ms Lin speak Japanese?

There are other particles, such as の, which can form questions (see **particles**).

Tag questions

Tag questions in English are in the form of a statement, with a tag such as 'doesn't it?', 'isn't she?', 'didn't they?' at the end. In Japanese, ね and だろう・でしょう can be used at the end of statements with a similar effect:

- 今日は暑いですね
  Kyō wa atsui desu **ne**   *It's hot today, **isn't it?***

- 若葉さんはも来週来るでしょう
  Wakaba san wa raishū mo kuru **deshō**
  *You are coming next week as well, **aren't you**, Ms Wakaba?*

For more information on ね, see the chapter on particles (*pp. 177–178*). For more on だろう・でしょう, see the chapters on だ・です (*p. 15*) and auxiliaries (*p. 181*).

Asking about things

The word for 'what?' is なに:

- 明日何をしますか
  Ashita **nani** o shimasu ka
  ***What** are you going to do tomorrow?*

- 鞄に何がありますか
  Kaban ni **nani** ga arimasu ka   ***What's** in the bag?*

However, this often becomes なん in compounds, e.g. なんじ 'what time?', なんばん 'what number?' In some compounds with counters, it can be translated as 'how many?' or 'which?' (see **numbers and counting**):

なんさつ・何冊	how many books/magazines?
なんにん・何人	how many people?
なんがい・何階	which floor?

なん is also used in front of sounds from the た, だ, and な rows of the kana chart:

- それは何ですか
  Sore wa **nan** desu ka   **What** is that?

- 何の本ですか
  Nan no hon desu ka   **What** kind of book is it?

Asking about people

To ask about a person's identity ('who?'), use だれ:

- あそこにたっている人は誰ですか
  Asoko ni tatte iru hito wa **dare** desu ka
  Who is that person standing over there?

To ask who something belongs to, use だれの:

- これは誰の辞書ですか
  Kore wa **dare no** jisho desu ka   **Whose** dictionary is this?

どなた is used as a polite equivalent of だれ:

- 失礼ですが、どなたですか
  Shitsurei desu ga, **donata** desu ka
  Excuse me, but **who** are you?

The suffix 〜さま is often attached when speaking politely on the telephone:

- もしもし。どなた様ですか
  Moshi moshi. **Donata sama** desu ka
  Hello? **Who** is this, please?

Asking about quantity and number

To ask 'how many?', use いくつ:

- 卵がいくつありますか
  Tamago ga **ikutsu** arimasu ka   **How many** eggs are there?

To ask about the approximate number, the suffix くらい or ぐらい is added:

- 卵がいくつぐらいありますか
  Tamago ga **ikutsu gurai** arimasu ka
  About how many eggs are there?

Note that いくつ is also used as a polite alternative to the usual なんさい, meaning 'how old?' with reference to people's age, in which case it is usually prefixed with お:

- おいくつですか
  O-ikutsu desu ka   How old are you?

To ask 'how much?' with regard to time and quantity, use どのくらい or どのぐらい:

- 時間は後どのくらいですか
  Jikan wa ato **dono kurai** desu ka   How much time is left?

- どのくらい　かかりますか
  Dono kurai kakarimasu ka
  How long will it take?/**How much** will it cost?

Asking about price

To ask 'how much (money)?', use いくら:

- この茶碗はいくらですか
  Kono chawan wa **ikura** desu ka   How much is this bowl?

To ask the approximate price, the suffix ぐらい or くらい is added:

- 日本への往復の切符はいくらぐらいかかりますか
  Nihon e no ōfuku no kippu wa **ikura gurai** kakarimasu ka
  About how much does a return ticket to Japan cost?

Asking about reason

To ask the reason for something ('why?'), use なぜ:

- なぜ日本語を勉強していますか
  Naze Nihongo o benkyō shite imasu ka
  Why are you studying Japanese?

A less formal equivalent of なぜ is どうして:

- 川場さんはどうして来ませんでしたか
  Kawaba san wa **dōshite** kimasen deshita ka
  Why didn't Mr Kawaba come?

As どうして can be translated as both 'why?' and 'how?',
the meaning is sometimes ambiguous:

- どうして日本語を勉強していますか
  Dōshite Nihongo o benkyō shite imasu ka
  How/why are you studying Japanese?

なんで can also mean both 'why?' and 'how?':

- 何で日本語を勉強していますか
  Nande Nihongo o benkyō shite imasu ka
  How/why are you studying Japanese?

- 何で日本へ行きますか
  Nande Nihon e ikimasu ka   **How/why** are you going to Japan?

If the meaning intended is 'how?', then the unambiguous
どうやって can be used (see below).

Asking about manner or means

どうやって is used to mean 'how?', 'in what manner?':

- どうやって日本へ行きますか
  Dō yatte Nihon e ikimasu ka   **How** are you going to Japan?

Other ways of asking 'in what way?', 'how?' are with どのように
and どういうふうに:

- 学生の生活はこの十年間どのようにかわりましたか
  Gakusei no seikatsu wa kono jū-nen-kan **dono yō ni**
  kawarimashita ka
  In what way has student life changed in the last ten years?

- どういう風に返事すればいいか分からなかった
  Dō iu fū ni henji sureba ii ka wakaranakatta
  I just didn't know **how** to respond

どう can also be used by itself to mean 'how':

- どうでしたか
  Dō deshita ka   How was it?

For more information on どう, *see p. 186 and following pages.*

Asking about time

いつ is used to ask 'when?' about the time of an action or event:

- いつ買い物に行きますか
  Itsu kaimono ni ikimasu ka   When are you going shopping?

To ask about approximate time, the suffix ごろ is added:

- いつごろ東京に帰りますか
  Itsu goro Tōkyō ni kaerimasu ka
  About when are you returning to Tokyo?

Asking about location

どこ is used to ask where something is, or where someone is
going:

- どこへ行きますか
  Doko e ikimasu ka   Where are you going?

どちら can also be used as a polite alternative to どこ:

- どちらへいらっしゃいますか
  Dochira e irasshaimasu ka   Where are you going?

For more information, *see p. 186 and following pages.*

Asking 'Which?'

どちら, or the more informal contraction どっち, is used to ask
'which' when there are two alternatives:

- テニスかバレーボールか、どっちが好き？
  Tenisu ka barēbōru ka **dotchi** ga suki?
  Which do you prefer, tennis or volleyball?

If there are more than two choices, then どれ is used, or どの if
there is a following noun:

- このチョコレートの中でどれが好きですか
  Kono chokorēto no naka de **dore** ga suki desu ka
  Which of these chocolates do you like?

- どの本ですか
  Dono hon desu ka   **Which book** is it?

The word **どんな** can be used to mean both 'which' and 'what kind of':

- 熊谷さんはどんな人ですか
  Kumagaya san wa **donna hito** desu ka
  Which person is Kumagaya?/**What kind of person** is Kumagaya?

For more information, *see p. 186 and following pages.*

Asking 'How . . . ?'

To say 'how tall?', 'how hot?', etc., the adjective can be preceded by どのくらい or どのぐらい:

- どのくらい高いでしょうか
  Dono kurai takai deshō ka   **How expensive** is it?

Perspective and pronouns

What is a pronoun?

A pronoun is a word that is used instead of the name of the person or thing concerned, i.e. in place of a noun or noun phrase. In the following examples, the pronouns 'she', 'it', and 'them' are used instead of 'Keiko', 'the camera shop', and 'the keys', as well as the possessive pronoun 'her' (instead of 'Keiko's'):

Keiko said **she** doesn't like **her** new teacher
You know the camera shop on the corner by the station? **It's** closed
The keys weren't where I left **them**

Absence of pronouns in Japanese

In Japanese, the information conveyed in English by pronouns (both personal and possessive) can often be conveyed by other means, and it is generally unnecessary to use the equivalents of 'I', 'you', 'she', etc. For example, here is a message left on a telephone answering machine:

* もしもし、木村です。昨日駅でご主人に会いました。新しい電話番号を教えてくれました。非常に疲れている様子ですよ。仕事は大変でしょう。ところで新しいアパートはどうですか

Moshi moshi, Kimura desu. Kinō eki de **go-shujin** ni aimashita. Atarashii denwa bangō o **oshiete kuremashita**. Hijō ni tsukarete iru yōsu desu yo. Shigoto wa taihen deshō. Tokorode atarashii apāto wa dō desu ka

Hello, it's Kimura. I met **your husband** yesterday at the station. **He told me** your new phone number. **He** seemed really tired. **His** work must be tough! Anyway, how is **your** new apartment?

The vocabulary item しゅじん・主人 'husband' has the polite prefix ご, and so means 'your husband' (*see pp. 221–222*). The use of the verb くれる 'give (me)' as an addition to おしえる 'tell' adds the meaning 'to me', and so gives an overall meaning of 'told me' (*see pp. 94–95*). It is therefore clear from these pointers and the context who is being referred to, but where the English translation requires the use of the pronouns 'your', 'me', 'he', and 'his', these are not present in the Japanese as separate words.

Equivalents to many English pronouns do exist in Japanese, but pronouns are not a separate part of speech (*see p. 1*). English pronouns such as 'I', 'you', and 'her' are often not represented at all in Japanese:

- 新しい車があります
  Atarashii kuruma ga arimasu   I have a new car

- とても高かったです
  Totemo takakatta desu   It was very expensive

- すみません。ペンはありますか
  Sumimasen. Pen wa arimasu ka
  Excuse me. Have **you** got a pen?

Family words do not require pronouns:

- お母さんはお元気ですか
  Okāsan wa o-genki desu ka
  Is **your** mother well?/How's **your** mother?

- 兄は大学生です
  Ani wa daigakusei desu
  My older brother is a university student

Context is very important for deciding which English pronoun to use when translating a Japanese verb. For example, the following Japanese sentence can mean 'I am going to London on Saturday', 'We are going to London on Saturday', and 'She is going to London on Saturday', depending on the context:

どようび　ロンドンへ　いきます・土曜日ロンドンへ行きます

The speaker is assumed to be referring to himself or herself unless the context indicates otherwise. If the statement is part of a discussion about family holidays, for example, then the English translation of いきます would be 'we will go'. If the conversation is about Mary's whereabouts next weekend, then the English translation would more likely be 'she is going'.

The next two sentences are identical in form and have no pronouns, so only the context indicates the intended meaning:

- 大阪に行くことになっているんですか
  Ōsaka ni iku koto ni natte iru n desu ka
  Are **you** going to be posted to Osaka?

- 大阪に行くことになっているんですか
  Ōsaka ni iku koto ni natte iru n desu ka
  Am **I** going to be going to be posted to Osaka?

Once a noun or noun phrase has been established as the topic under discussion, shown by a particle such as は, it remains the topic until a new one is introduced, and so does not need to be mentioned specifically each time something is said about that topic:

- 兄は大学生です。電子工学を勉強しています
  Ani wa daigakusei desu. Denshi kōgaku o benkyō shite imasu
  My (older) brother is a university student. He is studying electrical engineering

This can happen in English in exchanges such as 'What's Jim doing tonight?' 'Going to the theatre', where it is understood that 'Jim' is the one going to the theatre, as he is the topic under discussion (see the section on は in the chapter on particles, *pp. 149–154*).

Japanese people prefer to use names, family relationship words, or job titles rather than words for 'you', 'he', 'she', and 'they'. Within the family, it is common for people to refer to themselves with words meaning 'mum', 'dad', 'big sister', etc., and to address older siblings (but not younger) with the equivalent of 'big brother' and 'big sister' (*see pp. 7–8*).

Japanese equivalents of English personal pronouns

The most common Japanese nouns with meanings similar to English personal pronouns are listed below.

I – わたし・私

There are various equivalents of 'I'. The most common is わたし, but other words include ぼく・僕 (used by young male speakers in informal situations), おれ・俺 (used by male speakers in informal situations), あたし (used by female speakers in informal situations), and わたくし・私 (used in very formal situations). Within the family, people often refer to themselves by using their family role or other relationship words. For example, a father might say to his children おとうさん　いきます・お父さん行きます 'Father is going' where the English translation would be 'I am going'. There is a similar usage in English (e.g. 'Stop crying now, mummy's here'), but it is much more widespread in Japanese and is not restricted to use with small children (*see pp. 7–8*).

you – あなた

Although the word あなた can be translated as 'you' (singular), it is not used in the same way as the English, and can sound rude if used incorrectly as it is overfamiliar. It is often used by women to address their husbands, and in this context is similar to 'darling' or 'dear' in English. Its use is therefore best avoided. Instead, the person's name or job title can be used where the context does not allow 'you' to be omitted altogether.

- 池田さんも行きますか
  Ikeda san mo ikimasu ka　　Are **you** going too, **Mr Ikeda**?

- 課長、このレポートに目を通してください
  Kachō, kono repōto ni me o tōshite kudasai
  Please could **you** look over this report (**section manager**)?

- 運転手、何時に着くと思いますか
  Untenshu san, nan-ji ni tsuku to omoimasu ka
  What time do **you** think we'll arrive (**driver**)?

Other words for 'you' include きみ・君 (used by a male to a junior, close friend, girlfriend, or wife), おまえ (used by senior males to juniors), and あんた (used informally, mostly by senior males to juniors).

These words for 'you' can be given a plural meaning by adding the plural suffix たち・達. The expression みなさん・皆さん (or みんなさん in informal speech) meaning 'everybody' is often used to address a group (for an example of usage, see じぶん below).

he – かれ・彼

This is less commonly used than in English. かれ can also mean 'boyfriend'.

she – かのじょ・彼女

This is less commonly used than in English. かのじょ can also mean 'girlfriend'.

it

There is no real equivalent of 'it'. If the topic is clearly understood, then there is no need to use a pronoun:

- 新しい車があります。とても高かったです
  Atarashii kuruma ga arimasu. Totemo takakatta desu
  I have a new car. It was very expensive

Japanese may also use one of the words for 'this/that' such as それ (see こ・そ・あ・ど for details). There is no equivalent of the English use of 'it' with adjectives ('It is difficult') or when referring to the weather ('It is raining'):

- 明日までにこの仕事を終えるのは無理です
  Ashita made ni kono shigoto o oeru no wa muri desu
  It is impossible to finish this job by tomorrow

- 雨が降っています
  Ame ga futte imasu   It is raining

- 寒いです
  Samui desu   It's cold

we – わたしたち・私たち

The most common equivalent of 'we' is わたしたち, but other words include われわれ・我々 (formal) and わたくしども・私ども (very formal).

they

The word かれ 'he' can be followed by the plural suffix ら to
mean 'they'. When referring to things rather than people, the
appropriate noun is generally used if the context does not make the
topic clear, as Japanese nouns do not have separate singular and
plural forms (いえ・家, for example, can mean 'house' or 'houses').

A few nouns referring to people can have the plural suffix
たち・達 added to specifically mark them as plural, although
this is not obligatory, and a plural meaning is also possible without
the suffix. Words with the suffix 〜たち are often used to refer
to specific groups under discussion where there is a degree of
empathy or politeness, e.g. 'the children' rather than a general
category 'children':

* 子供達はどこにいますか
  Kodomotachi wa doko ni imasu ka   Where are **the children**?

The following words are commonly used with 〜たち:

こどもたち・子供達	the children
せんせいたち・先生達	the teachers
せいとたち・生徒達	the (school) students
がくせいたち・学生達	the (university) students
しゃいんたち・社員達	the staff (of a company)

Possessive pronouns

English possessive pronouns are words such as 'my', 'mine',
'your', and 'his' (see **glossary**). Japanese uses an appropriate noun
(including those discussed above such as わたし and かれ)
followed by the particle の (*see pp. 166–167*). However, the noun
with の is often not used if the context is clear or can be inferred.
For example, 'my car' could be translated as わたしのくるま,
but is more likely just to be くるま unless there is a need for explicit
contrast with another car:

* 車が盗まれた
  Kuruma ga nusumareta   **My** car was stolen

Where a noun with の is used to indicate possession, the following noun can sometimes be omitted if it is clear from the context, and so is similar to the English 'mine', 'yours', etc.:

● これは僕のです

Kore wa **boku no** desu   This is **mine**

As discussed above, family words and certain verbs of giving and receiving have restrictions on their use, and so the possessive marker is not needed as much as in English as it is obvious from the family word or verb used (see the sections on verbs of giving and receiving in the chapter on verbs, *pp. 94–95 and 47–49*, and the section on family words in the chapter on in-group and out-group):

● 兄は大学生です

Ani wa daigakusei desu

My older brother is a university student

Demonstrative pronouns

The Japanese equivalent of 'this' is これ, and 'that' is represented by either それ or あれ. Something close to the speaker is これ, something close to the listener is それ, and something distant from both listener and speaker is あれ (see こ・そ・あ・ど).

If a noun follows the demonstrative word (e.g. 'this book', 'that pen', 'which pen?', etc.), then the Japanese equivalents are この, その, あの, and どの (see the section on 'this' and 'that' in the chapter on demonstrative words (こ・そ・あ・ど)).

Relative pronouns

Relative pronouns such as 'which', 'that', and 'who' (as in 'the exam **that** I took yesterday', 'the man **who** is standing over there', etc.) do not exist in Japanese, and relative clauses are created by other means (see the section on modifiers, *p. 209*).

Interrogative pronouns

For information on the interrogative pronouns 'who?', 'what?', and 'which?', see the chapter on interrogatives, *p. 224*.

Reflexive pronouns

The word じしん・自身 'self' can be attached to words such as わたし and かれ, and also to names, as in the following examples. Note the addition of the polite prefix ご in the second example (*see p. 221*):

- 私自身知らなかった
  Watashi jishin shiranakatta   I myself didn't know

- タンさんご自身はお金で苦労されましたか
  Tan san go-jishin wa okane de kurō saremashita ka
  Did **you yourself** suffer financially, Mr Tan?

The noun じぶん・自分 is similar to the 'self' in such words as 'myself' and 'herself'. It can also be used with the particle の to mean 'his own', 'their own', etc. The English translation depends on the context:

- 皆さん自分の荷物を持っていってください
  Minasan **jibun no** nimotsu o motte itte kudasai
  Could everybody take **their own** luggage, please

- サムは自分がたばこを吸うのに子供に「タバコを吸うな」
  といつも言います
  Samu wa **jibun** ga tabako o sū no ni kodomo ni 'tabako o sū na'
  to itsumo iimasu
  Even though he smokes **himself**, Sam always says 'Don't smoke!'
  to the children

- 宝くじに当たったのが自分だとは信じられなかった
  Takarakuji ni atatta no ga **jibun** da towa shinjirarenakatta
  I couldn't believe that **I was the person who** won the lottery!

- 私はテープを3回聞いても自分の声だと分からなかった
  Watashi wa tēpu o san-kai kiite mo **jibun no** koe da to
  wakaranakatta
  Even though I heard the tape three times, I didn't realize it was **my
  own** voice!

The pronoun 'one'

The pronoun の can be used in a way similar to the English 'one' in phrases such as 'the big one', 'the other one', etc. (*see p. 206*):

- **青いかばんは高いです。赤いのは安いです**
  Aoi kaban wa takai desu. **Akai no** wa yasui desu
  *The blue bag is expensive. **The red one** is cheap.*

There is no equivalent for the English pronoun 'one' as in 'one often feels that . . .'

Punctuation and script terms

Some of the most commonly used Japanese punctuation marks and terms used about the script are listed below. The names given are commonly used in the classroom.

まる　　　　。
This is the Japanese full stop to end a sentence.

てん　　　　、
This is a mark to show a pause and is commonly used when sentences are joined with a conjunction or conjunctive particle:

かっこ　　　「」
These square brackets are used to mark quotations and direct speech. For examples see under と in the section on particles.

ぎもんてん　？
The question mark is common when representing speech to show a question marked by intonation:

- 明日暇？
  Ashita hima
  Are you free tomorrow?

The use of the small つ to show the doubling of the following consonant as in がっこう 'school' is commonly referred to as ちいさい つ and the effect produced as そくおん (促音). Words with this feature are listed in a dictionary as if spelled with a full size つ.

Small kana characters written above or beside kanji to show the pronunciation are called ふりがな or ルビ:

- 各漢字に振り仮名を振ってください
  Kaku-kanji ni **furigana o futte** kudasai
  Please **write furigana** for each kanji

When a kanji character is used to write the stem of a word there is often a 'tail' of hiragana characters (especially with verbs and adjectives where there are inflectional endings such as 〜かった in あたらしかった・新しかった or 〜ます in いきます・行きます etc.). Kana which follow a kanji character are called okurigana (送り仮名) and their correct use is very important in writing well.

Glossary of grammatical terms

This section explains the grammatical terms used in this book. The list includes Japanese terms but examples are mostly given with reference to English. An analysis of Japanese parts of speech appears as a separate chapter and sometimes the glossary refers to a particular chapter or chapters of the grammar.

Words in **bold** letters have their own entries in the glossary.

Active: In a sentence with an active verb, the **subject** of the verb performs the action, e.g. *Sam* (subject) *identified* (verb) *the suspect* (as opposed to the passive construction *The suspect was identified by Sam*, where the suspect is the subject but is not doing the identifying). Cf. **Passive**.

Adjective: A word used to describe or add extra information to a noun or noun phrase, e.g. *difficult* in 'a *difficult* job', *beautiful* in 'she is *beautiful*' and 'a *beautiful* way to cook salmon'.

Adverb: A word used to describe or add extra information to a verb, an adjective, or another adverb, e.g. *slowly*, *extremely*, and *quickly* in 'to walk *slowly*', '*extremely* difficult', 'come *quickly*'. Some Japanese adverbs introduce particular types of sentences. See the chapter on adverbs.

Adverbial: Used or functioning as an **adverb**.

Agent: The person who or thing which carries out an action, e.g.

Mike in 'The letter was written by *Mike*'.

Animate: Denoting something that is alive, such as a person or animal. Cf. **Inanimate**.

Arabic numerals: The symbols 1, 2, 3, etc. used for writing numbers.

Article: The words *the* (**definite article**) and *a* or *an* (**indefinite article**) used before a **noun**. Japanese does not have articles.

Aspect: A grammatical category of the verb that expresses the nature of an action or process, viewing it either as continuous or habitual (imperfective aspect), or as completed (perfective aspect). Cf. **Tense**.

Aspectual relationship: A relationship between things in terms of **aspect**.

Attributive: An attributive adjective is one used in front of the noun it describes, e.g. *expensive* in 'an *expensive* meal'. One type of adjective in Japanese (**na-adjective**) has a distinctive form when used in this way. Cf. **Predicative**.

Auxiliary: In Japanese, there are conjugating suffixes called **jodōshi** (助動詞) and the word 'auxiliary' is used in this book as an equivalent of that term. See the chapter on parts of speech. Cf. **Jodōshi**.

Auxiliary suffix: = **Auxiliary**.

Auxiliary verb: A verb used in forming compound structures from other verbs, e.g. *do* in 'Do you know Michael?' and *have* in 'I *have* been there before'.

Cardinal Number: The sequence of numbers 1, 2, 3, etc. Cf. **Ordinal number**.

Case: The function of a noun within the clause or sentence (e.g. whether it is the **subject** or **object** etc.), or the form of the noun expressing this. Japanese nouns express case by adding **particles** rather than by changing form.

Causative: see **Causative form**, **Causative-passive**.

Causative form: An English term for the Japanese 'shiekikei' (使役形). This is where the **auxiliary** (さ) せる is added to a verb to give meanings relating to compulsion or permission.

Causative-passive: The addition of the **auxiliary** (さ) れる to a verb already having the causative auxiliary (さ) せる, to give the idea of being made to do something.

Chinese characters: An English translation of the Japanese word **kanji**. Cf. **Kana**.

Clause: A sentence, or part of a sentence, consisting of a subject and a verb, e.g. *Mike snores*, or a structure containing some verbal forms, participles, or infinitives, but no subject, e.g. '*While waiting for a bus* I fell asleep' or 'I asked her *to call a taxi*'. Japanese clauses do not have to contain verbs as other parts of speech can also form predicates.

Colloquial: Informal spoken or written language.

Comment: The part of a **sentence** that gives information about the **topic**. Cf. **Topic**.

Comparative: The form of the adjective or adverb used when comparing two or more nouns or pronouns. In English, this is usually done by putting *more* or *less* before the adjective or adverb, or by adding *-er* to the base form. Japanese adjectives and adverbs do not have different comparative forms. See the chapters on adjectives and adverbs.

Complex sentence: A sentence made up of more than one **clause**.

Compound: A word or phrase made by putting two or more existing forms together.

Compound noun: A noun made up of two or more distinct parts, e.g. *windscreen-wipers, watermelon*.

Compound verb: A Japanese verb made up of two or more parts e.g. のりかえる 'change trains' from the verbs のる 'to ride' and かえる 'to change'. The first verb is a **conjunctive stem**.

Conditional: A conditional sentence is one in which the statement contained in the **main clause** can only be fulfilled if the condition stated in the **subordinate clause** is also fulfilled, e.g. *If it is fine* tomorrow, *we'll go to the seaside* or *I would go to Japan if I had lots of money*. This condition is usually introduced by *if* in English. Japanese has a variety of structures with similar functions. See the chapters on verbs, particles, and conjuctions and conjunctive particles, and see **Conditional form**.

Conditional form: A form of a word that indicates it is a condition in a sentence or clause and expresses what would happen (or would have happened) under certain conditions. English normally uses *if* with a form of *would* to express this notion. Japanese can use several structures to make equivalents. The most common are ～たら, ～ば, なら, and と.

Conjugate: Change the **form** of a verb according to its **subject**, e.g. 'I *go*' but 'She *goes*', or to indicate, for example, a **negative** or a **past** meaning, e.g. 'He *didn't go*', 'He *went*'. Japanese verbs and adjectives conjugate, as do some auxiliaries. See the chapters on verbs, adjectives, and parts of speech.

Conjugation: The process of conjugating a verb (and some other parts of speech in Japanese). Also, = **Conjugation group**.

Conjugation group: Each of the patterns of conjugation changes in verbs. Cf. **Godan** and **Ichidan**.

Conjunction: Either (i) a word like *and* or *but* which is used to join words or simple sentences together, or (ii) a word like *when*, *although*, *if*, *where*, which is used to join clauses or sentences, thus forming a **complex sentence**.

Conjunctive particle: A **particle** whose function is to join two clauses or sentences together.

Conjunctive (pre-masu) form: = **Conjunctive (pre-masu) stem**.

Conjunctive (pre-masu) stem: An English equivalent for the Japanese term **renyōkei (連用形)** = the **stem** of a **verb** that precedes the **jodōshi** ～ます (among others), e.g. いき from いきます.

Consonant stem verb: An English term for **godan** verbs. Cf. **Vowel stem verb**.

Continuous: Referring to the fact that an action or state is/was currently happening or existing. English often uses the verb *be* with the present participle ending *-ing* to express this notion, e.g. 'He *is/was waiting*'.

Contracted form: A form which is a shorter alternative, e.g. *haven't* is a contracted form of *have not*.

Counter: An English term for the Japanese part of speech called sūshi (数詞) = a suffix added to numbers in Japanese when counting objects, people, or animals according to the category of thing being counted, e.g. *nin* (人) for people, *satsu* (冊) for books and magazines. See the chapter on numbers and counting.

'Da' style: = **Plain style**.

'De-aru' style: = **Written style**.

Declension: The process of declining a noun. Also, each of the patterns of declension changes in nouns.

Decline: In some languages, change in the **form** (usually the ending) of nouns to show **case** relationships.

Definite article: The word *the* in English. Japanese does not have articles. Cf. **Indefinite article**.

Demonstrative: A word indicating the person or thing referred to, e.g. *this*, *that*, *these*, *those*.

'Desu-masu' style: The polite style of writing and speaking which uses the auxiliaries ～ます (on verbs) and ～です (with nouns and adjectives). Cf. **Plain style** and **Written style**.

Dictionary form: The basic form of a Japanese verb (or adjective).

Direct object: See **Object**.

Ending: The concluding part of a word or sentence, especially one conveying grammatical information such as tense, case, or number (singular or plural), e.g. wish*ed*, book*s*.

Exclamation: A word or phrase conveying a reaction such as surprise, shock, disapproval, indignation, or amusement. In English it is usually followed by an exclamation mark: *Excellent!*; *What nice weather!* Cf. **Interjection**.

Finite verb: A verb which has a specific tense (present, past, etc.), number (singular or plural), and person (I, you, etc.), e.g. *rings* in 'She *rings* the doctor'.

Form: One of the possible ways in which a word may appear, e.g. *go*, *goes*, *went*, *gone*.

Gender: The sex of a person or animal (male or female) or, (in some languages) a classification of nouns (masculine, feminine, etc.). This latter sense is not found in Japanese.

Godan: Verbs whose vowel changes when endings are added. Examples include はなす, いく, まつ. See the chapter on verbs.

Group one verb: a **godan** verb.

Group two verb: an **ichidan** verb.

Hiragana: The Japanese script used to write many everyday words and the endings of verbs and adjectives whose **stem** is written in **kanji**. The hiragana chart is given at the back of the book. Cf. **Katakana**, **Kanji**, and **Rōmaji**.

Honorific: (Of a word form or verb) elevating the listener/reader relative to the speaker/writer. See the chapter on keigo.

Honorifics: Certain words and forms which elevate the listener/reader relative to the speaker/writer. This term is sometimes used for **sonkeigo**.

Humble (Of a word form, verb, or language) elevating the listner/reader relative to the speaker/writer by its nuance of humility, e.g. まいる and いたす. See the chapter on keigo.

I-adjective: An English term for the Japanese **part of speech** called a **keiyōshi** (形容詞).

Ichidan: Verbs whose vowel does not change when endings are added. **Dictionary forms** of these verbs always end in an え line kana + る (-eru), or an い line kana + る, (-iru). Examples include たべる, でる, おきる, みる. See the chapter on verbs.

Idiom: A conventionally accepted way of expressing an idea, especially one where the meaning cannot be predicted from the meanings of the separate words, e.g. *Raining cats and dogs*.

Imperative: A form or structure used to express an order, command, prohibition, or exhortation, e.g. *Come here!*, *Don't smoke!*, *Have fun!*

Inanimate: Not alive. Cf. **Animate**.

Indefinite article: The words *a* and *an* in English. Japanese does not have articles. Cf. **Definite article**.

Indirect object: See **Object**.

Indirect passive: A passive verb used in a Japanese sentence to indicate the speaker's negative perception of an experience. See the section on the passive in the chapter on verbs.

In-group: The speaker's own family or colleagues. Cf. **Out-group**.

Interjection: A word used usually in isolation to express sudden emotion, e.g. *alas*, *oops*, and *no*. Cf. **Exclamation**.

Interrogative: A question or a word used to make a question, e.g. *who*, *what*, *where*, *why*, *when*, etc.

Interrogative pronoun: A pronoun used to form a question, e.g. *which* in '*Which* do you want?'

Intonation: The sound shape of a word or phrase that can convey meaning, e.g. the rise in pitch at the end of an English question such as *Shall we go?*

Intransitive verb: A verb not taking a direct object, e.g. *slept* in 'He *slept* well'. See the section on transitive and intransitive verbs in the chapter on verbs. Cf. **Transitive verb**.

Irregular: A word or form of a word that does not fit a standard pattern of changes to its forms.

Jōdōshi: An **auxiliary** which is attached to a word or sentence and alters or augments its meaning. Most endings on verbs and adjectives in Japanese are jōdōshi. See the chapters on parts of speech and auxiliary suffixes.

Kana: The Japanese syllabic scripts **hiragana** and **katakana**. Cf. **Kanji** and **Rōmaji**.

Kana chart: The script chart that provides Japanese with its 'alphabetical' order and which plays a part in the conjugation patterns of some words. The kana charts are given at the back of the book.

Kanji: The romanized form of the Japanese word 漢字. Kanji are Chinese characters used in writing Japanese. Cf. **Hiragana**, **Katakana**, and **Rōmaji**.

Katakana: The Japanese script used primarily for writing foreign names and places and words of foreign (Western) origin. The katakana chart is given at the back of the book. Cf. **Hiragana**, **Kanji**, and **Rōmaji**.

Keigo: The romanized form of the Japanese word 敬語. Keigo is a system of showing differences in status between individuals, and of being polite by changing the **form** of words.

Keiyōdōshi: The Japanese **part of speech** called 形容動詞 is usually referred to in English as a **na-adjective**.

Keiyōshi: The Japanese **part of speech** called 形容詞 is usually referred to in English as an **i-adjective**.

Kenjōgo: A subdivision of **keigo** which shows the speaker's humility and thus exalts the listener by contrast. Cf. **Sonkeigo**.

Literary style: A style of writing that features である in place of だ・です. See the chapters on style and だ・です.

Main clause: In a **sentence** with more than one **clause**, the clause which is not subordinate to any of the others, e.g. *Peter stopped* in 'When it got too dark to see where he was going, *Peter stopped*'. A main clause can stand alone as a sentence.

Main verb: The verb contained in a **main clause** as opposed to one in a **relative clause**.

Modifier: A word or clause placed in front of a **noun** or **noun phrase** to describe it, e.g. '*Cave-dwelling* animals such as these are commonly blind'. Modification is very important in Japanese as this is how **relative clauses** are constructed. See the section on modifiers in the chapter on nominalization.

Modify: Describe a following noun or noun phrase.

Na-adjective: An English term for the Japanese part of speech called a **keiyōdōshi** (形容動詞). See the chapters on adjectives and parts of speech.

Negation: Making something **negative**.

Negative: A sentence or a form of a word that asserts that something is not the case, for example by using *not* in English.

Negative condition: A condition which is negative, e.g. '*If there is not enough* we will have to go to the shop'.

Negative imperative: An order to not do something, or a form/structure with that meaning, e.g. '*Don't open* the door!'

Negative predicate: A **predicate** with a **negative** form or meaning, e.g. *was not very good* in 'The party *was not very good*'.

Nominalization: Converting a **clause** into a **noun phrase** by adding a noun or の. See the chapter on nominalization.

Nominalizer: A word the addition of which changes a **clause** into a **noun phrase**. See the chapter on nominalization.

Noun: A word used to identify a person, an animal, an object, an idea, or an emotion (e.g. *girl*, *horse*, *book*, *beauty*, *sadness*). It can also be the name of a specific individual, place, or institution (e.g. *John*, *London*, *Inland Revenue*).

Noun phrase: A word or group of words functioning as a noun, e.g. *my mother's little dog* in 'My mother's little dog is quite delightful'.

Object: The word or group of words which is immediately affected by the action indicated by the verb. In the English sentence 'The child broke the toy', the word *child* is the subject, *broke* is the verb, and *the* *toy* is the object. There may be two kinds of object in a sentence, a direct object and an indirect object. In the example above, *the toy* is a direct object. However, in the sentence 'He gave the child a toy', *he* is the subject, *gave* is the verb, *the child* is the indirect object, and *a toy* is the direct object. Unlike English, the objects and subject in Japanese sentences are marked with **particles** and word order is less important. See the chapter on particles, especially the sections on が and に. Cf. **Subject**.

Ordinal number: The sequence of numbers 1st, 2nd, 3rd, etc. Cf. **Cardinal number**.

Out-group: People who are not close to the speaker, e.g. not family members or colleagues. Cf. **In-group**.

Particle: A marker placed after an element in a Japanese sentence, principally to show a grammatical relationship. It can be thought of as similar in function to English prepositions such as *to*, *from*, *at*, *by*, etc. There is also a group of particles which come at the end of sentences and whose function is to give expressive nuances of meaning and distinguish male and female speech. Some particles can also join clauses or sentences together and are thus 'conjunctive' particles.

Part of speech: The grammatical type of a word, e.g. noun, verb, adjective, etc. For Japanese parts of speech (which are slightly different from those in English), see the chapter on parts of speech.

Passive: In English, the form of the verb used when the **subject** undergoes (rather than performs) the action, e.g. 'The student *was nominated* for an award'. In Japanese, the passive has additional uses. See the section on the passive in the chapter on verbs.

Passive form: In Japanese, a verb which has the auxiliary (ら) れる added to it to express the passive.

Past: A form which indicates that an event or state has already occurred, e.g. *went* in 'Mike *went* to London'.

Personal pronoun: A word that stands in for a name of a person or thing, often to avoid repetition, e.g. *He* in 'That's Mike. *He* is a student'. Japanese does not use pronouns in the same way as English and people's names are preferred to words like *he* and *she*. See the chapter on perspective and pronouns.

Perspective: A person's viewpoint. This is important in Japanese as words and sentences can be different from different viewpoints, e.g. give is either くれる (gives me) or あげる (I give). See the chapter on perspective and pronouns, and the section on verbs of giving and receiving in the chapter on verbs.

Phrase: A group of words which function together in a clause. See **Noun phrase** and **Verb phrase**.

Plain style: The style of Japanese used informally which does not feature the use of the polite auxiliaries 〜です and 〜ます.

Plain (style) form: A form of a conjugating word such as a verb or an adjective which does not feature the polite auxiliaries 〜です and 〜ます. This means in particular the **dictionary form**, ない form, and た form.

Plural: A word or form referring to more than one person or object, e.g. *children*, *books*, *we*, *are*. Japanese words do not generally have different singular and plural forms. See the chapter on nouns. Cf. **Singular**.

Polite language: Words and structures appropriate for use between adults who are not familiar with one another, or who are in formal situations.

Polite prefix: An element added to the beginning of a word to make it more polite when it refers to someone other than the speaker, e.g. *go* in the word *go*-shujin (ご主人) 'your husband'.

Polite style: The style of speech (or writing) that uses the auxiliaries 〜ます and 〜です.

Polite (style) form: A form of a word that is used when speaking or writing in the **polite style**.

Positive predicate: A **predicate** with a positive form or meaning, e.g. *was very good* in 'The party *was very good*'. Cf. **Negative predicate**.

Possessive pronoun: A pronoun expressing ownership, e.g. *my*, *mine*, *your(s)*, *her(s)*, etc. Those preceding a noun (*my*, *your*, *her*, etc.) are sometimes termed possessive determiners or (in more traditional grammars) possessive adjectives (e.g. '*my* book').

Potential form: The form of Japanese verbs having to do with possibility and ability.

Potential verb: A verb in the potential form or a verb whose meaning is dominantly potential such as できる or わかる.

Predicate: The part of a clause that contains a verb and states something about the **subject**, e.g. *closed the door softly* in 'Mary *closed the door softly*', or *went home* in 'We *went home*'. In Japanese, parts of speech other than verbs can form predicates. See the chapter on topic, comment, and predicate.

Predicative: A predicative adjective is one used after the noun it describes, e.g. *expensive* in 'The meal was *expensive*'. Cf. **Attributive**.

Prefix: An element added to the beginning of a word, usually to change its meaning, e.g. *mis*understood, *re*consider. Cf. **Suffix**.

Pre-masu form: The stem of a verb that precedes the **auxiliary** ます. This is also referred to as the **conjunctive stem**.

Preposition: A word such as *under*, *beside*, *across*, *in*, which is usually followed by a noun or pronoun in English. There is no equivalent part of speech in Japanese, but Japanese has **particles** (placed after the noun) which often act in a similar way. See the chapter on particles.

Pronoun: (i) = **Personal pronoun**; (ii) any of the other types of pronoun, e.g. demonstrative, interrogative, possessive, reflexive, and relative pronoun.

Question particle: A **particle** used to mark a question. The most common Japanese question particle is か.

Reflexive pronoun: A pronoun that is the **object** of the verb but that refers back to the **subject** of the clause and denotes the same individual, e.g. *herself* in: 'She blamed *herself* for the misunderstanding'. Japanese does not have reflexive pronouns as such. See the chapter on perspective and pronouns.

Relative clause: In English, a clause introduced by a **relative pronoun**. Japanese forms relative clauses by modification and does not use relative pronouns. See the section on modifiers in the chapter on nominalization.

Relative pronoun: In English, a pronoun (*who*, *whose*, *which*, or *that*) used to introduce a subordinate clause and referring back to a person or thing in the preceding clause, e.g. 'Tanaka lost the camera *that/which* he bought', 'That is the man *whose* daughter I was telling you about'.

Renyōkei: The Japanese term for the **conjunctive (pre-masu) form**.

Report: The reporting of what someone has said, using an introductory reporting verb and a subordinate clause, e.g. *He said that he was hungry*.

Respectful form: A changed form of a word to make it appropriate for use in **sonkeigo**. Cf. **Keigo**.

Respectful verb: A verb used in **sonkeigo**, e.g. いらっしゃる, めしあがる. Cf. **Keigo**.

Respect language: An English translation of the Japanese term **sonkeigo**. Cf. **Keigo**.

Rōmaji: The Japanese word ローマ字 meaning roman alphabet (a, b, c, etc.). Cf. **Kanji**, **Hiragana**, and **Katakana**.

Romanization: The process or system of writing Japanese in the roman alphabet, or the resulting text.

Sentence: In English, a structure with at least one **finite verb**, and consisting of one or more **clauses**, e.g. 'John laughed', 'John sat down and waited', 'While waiting for the bus, John saw an accident'. Japanese can have sentences without verbs.

Singular: A word or form referring to just one person or object, e.g. *child*, *I*, *is*, *laughs*. Japanese nouns do not generally have different singular and plural forms – see the chapter on nouns. Cf. **Plural**.

Sonkeigo: A style of **keigo** which elevates the person referred to and is thus polite, e.g. irasshaimasu in 先生はよく東京へいらっしゃいます. Cf. **Kenjōgo**.

Sound symbolism: The representation of actions, states, and moods by particular combinations of sounds. English has onomatopoeia, e.g. *crash*, *bang*, and *thud*, but Japanese has a much richer system which has no English equivalent.

Stem: The unchanging part of a word to which **endings** are added.

Style: The conventions governing ways in which language is used in particular situations, e.g. formal and informal, or written and spoken.

Subject: The word or group of words which causes the action indicated by the verb. In the sentence 'John fed the cat', *John* is the subject of the verb *fed*. Unlike English,

Japanese does not need to have a subject expressed in a sentence when the context makes it clear. Cf. **Object**.

Subject particle: In Japanese, the particle used to mark the **subject** is が, although a grammatical subject can also be marked as a **topic**. See the chapter on particles.

Subordinate clause: A clause that cannot normally stand alone without a **main clause** and is often introduced by a conjunction, e.g. *when it rang* in 'She answered the phone *when it rang*'. Cf. **Main clause**.

Suffix: An element that is added to the end of a word or **stem** to change its meaning or grammatical form, e.g. understand*able*, kind*ness*, wish*ed*, fast*er*. Cf. **Prefix**.

Superlative: The form of the adjective or adverb used to express the highest or lowest degree. In English, this is usually done by putting *most* or *least* before the adjective or adverb, or by adding *-est* to the base form. Japanese adjectives and adverbs do not have different superlative forms. See the chapters on adjectives and adverbs.

Syllable: A word or part of a word that contains one vowel sound, often with one or more vowels before or after it. In Japanese, each **kana** symbol represents one syllable, so しんぶん (newspaper) has four syllables.

Tag question: A question ending with a verb followed by a pronoun, e.g. *didn't you?*, *haven't we?*

Teineigo: The romanized form of the Japanese word 丁寧語 which means a polite style of speaking and writing and features the 〜ます auxiliary and verbs and です. See the chapter on keigo.

Tense: The tense of a verb expresses whether the action takes place in the past, present, or future. Japanese verbs have only a past and a non-past, and the tense of a sentence is determined by the final verb. Continuing states or activities are shown with the 〜て form of a verb and います. However, this is not a tense but an **aspect** marker. See the chapter on verbs, especially the section on the 〜て form. Japanese adjectives also show tense; see the chapter on adjectives.

Tentative expression: An expression indicating uncertainty, such as one ending in かもしれな い or でしょう.

Tentative form: A form such as でしょう or だろう which indicates uncertainty or provisional judgement.

Topic: The part of the sentence which shows what is to be discussed or commented on. See the chapter on topic, comment, and predicate.

Topic marker: A word such as the topic particle は, marking a topic.

Topic particle: The particle は.

Transitive verb: A verb taking a **direct object**, e.g. *read* in 'She *was reading* a book'. See the section on transitive and intransitive verbs in the chapter on verbs. Cf. **Intransitive verb**.

Verb: A word that describes an action, a process, or a state of affairs (e.g. *run, buy, freeze, exist*). The verb is at the end of a basic Japanese sentence, but some Japanese sentences can be made without verbs because **predicates** can be made with other types of words. Japanese verbs do not change form for *I, you, he,* etc.

Verb of motion: A verb which describes movement, e.g. *come, go, return.*

Verb phrase: Either (i) a phrase consisting of a single-word verb, or of a group of verb forms functioning in the same way as a single-word verb, e.g. *went, has been going, was forgotten, ran off,* or (ii) = **Predicate**.

Volitional: Referring to someone's intention, or to actions which are within their subject's control.

Volitional form: The form of a Japanese verb that expresses intention, e.g. いこう from いく, and たべよう from たべる.

Vowel stem verb: An English term for **ichidan** verbs. Cf. **Consonant stem verb**.

Written style: The style of Japanese used for prose where **plain forms** of verbs are used and the **auxiliary** だ・です becomes である. See the chapter on style.

Appendices

Hiragana chart

'a' line		'i' line		'u' line		'e' line		'o' line	
あ	a	い	i	う	u	え	e	お	o
か	ka	き	ki	く	ku	け	ke	こ	ko
が	ga	ぎ	gi	ぐ	gu	げ	ge	ご	go
さ	sa	し	shi	す	su	せ	se	そ	so
ざ	za	じ	ji	ず	zu	ぜ	ze	ぞ	zo
た	ta	ち	chi	つ	tsu	て	te	と	to
だ	da	ぢ	ji	づ	zu	で	de	ど	do
な	na	に	ni	ぬ	nu	ね	ne	の	no
は	ha	ひ	hi	ふ	fu	へ	he	ほ	ho
ば	ba	び	bi	ぶ	bu	べ	be	ぼ	bo
ぱ	pa	ぴ	pi	ぷ	pu	ぺ	pe	ぽ	po
ま	ma	み	mi	む	mu	め	me	も	mo
や	ya			ゆ	yu			よ	yo
ら	ra	り	ri	る	ru	れ	re	ろ	ro
わ	wa							を	o
ん	n								

Consonant plus small や, ゆ, or よ

きゃ	kya	きゅ	kyu	きょ	kyo
ぎゃ	gya	ぎゅ	gyu	ぎょ	gyo
しゃ	sha	しゅ	shu	しょ	sho
じゃ	ja	じゅ	ju	じょ	jo
ちゃ	cha	ちゅ	chu	ちょ	cho
にゃ	nya	にゅ	nyu	にょ	nyo
ひゃ	hya	ひゅ	hyu	ひょ	hyo
びゃ	bya	びゅ	byu	びょ	byo
ぴゃ	pya	ぴゅ	pyu	ぴょ	pyo
りゃ	rya	りゅ	ryu	りょ	ryo

Small つ

A small つ has an effect similar to doubling the following consonant. For example in the word ちょっと, the と following the small つ is pronounced in a similar manner to the double t in 'hot toddy'.

は, へ, and を

は is read 'ha' when it is part of a word, but when used as the subject marker particle it is pronounced 'wa'. Similarly, へ is pronounced 'he' when it is part of a word but 'e' when it is used as a particle showing the direction of travel. Note that を (ヲ) is only used to write the particle.

Katakana chart

'a' line		'i' line		'u' line		'e' line		'o' line	
ア	a	イ	i	ウ	u	エ	e	オ	o
カ	ka	キ	ki	ク	ku	ケ	ke	コ	ko
ガ	ga	ギ	gi	グ	gu	ゲ	ge	ゴ	go
サ	sa	シ	shi	ス	su	セ	se	ソ	so
ザ	za	ジ	ji	ズ	zu	ゼ	ze	ゾ	zo
タ	ta	チ	chi	ツ	tsu	テ	te	ト	to
ダ	da	ヂ	ji	ヅ	zu	デ	de	ド	do
ナ	na	ニ	ni	ヌ	nu	ネ	ne	ノ	no
ハ	ha	ヒ	hi	フ	fu	ヘ	he	ホ	ho
バ	ba	ビ	bi	ブ	bu	ベ	be	ボ	bo
パ	pa	ピ	pi	プ	pu	ペ	pe	ポ	po
マ	ma	ミ	mi	ム	mu	メ	me	モ	mo
ヤ	ya			ユ	yu			ヨ	yo
ラ	ra	リ	ri	ル	ru	レ	re	ロ	ro
ワ	wa							ヲ	o
ン	n								

┃ Consonant plus small ヤ, ユ, or ヨ

キャ	kya	キュ	kyu	キョ	kyo
ギャ	gya	ギュ	gyu	ギョ	gyo
シャ	sha	シュ	shu	ショ	sho
ジャ	ja	ジュ	ju	ジョ	jo
チャ	cha	チュ	chu	チョ	cho
ニャ	nya	ニュ	nyu	ニョ	nyo
ヒャ	hya	ヒュ	hyu	ヒョ	hyo
ビャ	bya	ビュ	byu	ビョ	byo
ピャ	pya	ピュ	pyu	ピョ	pyo
リャ	rya	リュ	ryu	リョ	ryo

In katakana, long vowels are usually written by putting a ー (ぼう) after the sound as in the case of コーヒー (coffee) or ヒーター (heater).

There are other possible katakana combinations (such as ティ in パーティ 'party') not shown in the charts, which are used to represent foreign (non-Japanese) words and names.

Finding the dictionary form

Japanese verbs and adjectives conjugate and can sometimes end up in long chains of auxiliaries (see **parts of speech**). The resulting 'words' may seem very unfamiliar. This problem is compounded by the fact that Japanese is normally written with the words not separated. Where words are separated (as in textbooks for foreigners), the auxiliaries may still be attached to the stem, する and particles may be attached to nouns, and verbs may directly follow a ～て form. For these reasons you need to look carefully at the word you are trying to untangle. The following chart should provide basic help with finding a dictionary form (i.e. something that you can look up in a dictionary) by changing some commonly found endings.

ending	how to change it back to a form you can look up	Example from	Example to
～かった	remove ending and add い	さむかった	さむい
～くない	remove ending and add い	おおきくない	おおきい
～くなかった	remove ending and add い	おいしくなかった	おいしい
～た ～て	remove ending and add る	たべた たべて	たべる
～った ～った	remove ending and add る or う	あった あって	ある・あう
～んだ ～んで	remove ending and add む or ぶ or ぬ there is only one verb with the latter ending	よんだ あそんだ あそんで しんで	よむ あそぶ しあ
～いた ～いて	remove ending and add く	きいた きいて	きく
～いだ ～いだ	remove ending and add ぐ	およいだ およいで	およぐ
～した ～して	remove ending and add す	はなした はなして	はなす

ending	how to change it back to a form you can look up	Example from	Example to
～たい	remove ending and add る or change the last syllable before the ending from '-i' to '-u' i.e. り to る or き to く etc.	みたい やりたい あいたい ききたい	みる やる あう きく
～たくない	as above	みたくない	みる
～ます	remove ending and add る or change the last syllable before the ending from '-i' to '-u' i.e. り to る or き to く etc.	たべます おきます とります ききます	たべる おきる とる きく
～ません	as above	とりません	とる
～ました	as above	ききました	きく
～ましょう	as above	いきましょう	いく
～ない	remove ending and add る or change the last syllable before the ending from '-a' to '-u' i.e. ら to る or か to く etc.	たべない おわらない いかない	たべる おわる いく
～なかった	as above	とらなかった みなかった	とる みる
～ら	always follows either ～た or ～だ so find the appropriate form of that ending in the chart	きいたら	きく
initial word followed by する, しない, した, したい, します, しません, しましょう, したら, すれば	look up the initial word and then the relevant part of する in the section on する in the chapter on verbs. Note that the elements in front of these forms are usually nouns written with Chinese characters	べんきょうすれば けんきゅうした	べんきょう けんきゅう

ending	how to change it back to a form you can look up	Example from	Example to
〜なければ なりません	as for 〜ない or 〜くない	かかなければ なりません	かく
〜なければな らなかった	as for 〜ない or 〜くない	いかなければ ならなかった	いく
〜ければ	remove ending and add い	たかければ	たかい
〜えば or other endings with -eba such as 〜せば or 〜てば	remove the ば and add る or remove the ば and change the preceding '-e' to '-u' i.e. せ to す	とれれば みせれば はなせば	とる みせる はなす
〜くて	remove ending and add い	あたらしくて	あたらしい

English index

Japanese index